# THE PHILOSOPHY OF THE MARQUIS DE SADE

The Marquis de Sade is famous for his forbidden novels, like *Justine, Juliette*, and the *120 Days of Sodom*. Yet, despite Sade's immense influence on philosophy and literature, his work remains relatively unknown. His novels are too long, repetitive, and violent. At last in *The Philosophy of the Marquis de Sade*, a distinguished philosopher provides a theoretical reading of Sade.

Airaksinen examines Sade's claim that in order to be happy and free we must do evil things. He discusses the motivations of the typical Sadean hero, who leads a life filled with perverted and extreme pleasures, such as stealing, murder, rape, and blasphemy. Secondary sources on Sade, such as Hobbes, Erasmus, and Brillat-Savarin are analyzed, and modern studies are evaluated. *The Philosophy of the Marquis de Sade* greatly enhances our understanding of Sade and his philosophy of pain and perversion.

**Timo Airaksinen** is Professor of Philosophy at the University of Helsinki, Finland. He has written extensively on ethics, epistemology, and the history of philosophy.

# THE PHILOSOPHY OF THE MARQUIS DE SADE

*Timo Airaksinen*

London and New York

Cover image: every effort has been made to contact the copyright holders of this image. In the event of any queries, please contact Victoria Peters at Routledge, London.

First published in the USA in 1991
by Longwood Inc.
as *Of Glamor, Sex and de Sade*

First published in the UK in 1995
by Routledge
11 New Fetter Lane, London EC4P 4EE

Simultaneously published in the USA and Canada
by Routledge
29 West 35th Street, New York, NY 10001

© 1991, 1995 Timo Airaksinen

Typeset in Garamond by
Michael Mepham, Frome, Somerset

Printed and bound in Great Britain by
Mackays of Chatham PLC, Chatham, Kent

All rights reserved. No part of this book may be reprinted or reproduced or utilized in any form or by any electronic, mechanical, or other means, now known or hereafter invented, including photocopying and recording, or in any information storage or retrieval system, without permission in writing from the publishers.

*British Library Cataloguing in Publication Data*
Airaksinen, Timo
Philosophy of the Marquis de Sade
I. Title
843.6

*Library of Congress Cataloguing in Publication Data*
A catalogue record for this book has been requested

ISBN 0–415–11228–1 (hbk)
ISBN 0–415–11229–x (pbk)

# CONTENTS

|   |   |   |
|---|---|---|
| | *Preface* | vii |
| | INTRODUCTION | 1 |
| 1 | SADE: PHILOSOPHY AND ITS BACKGROUND | 5 |
| | *Facts* | 5 |
| | *Topics* | 11 |
| | *The refutation of optimism* | 17 |
| | *The definition of perversity* | 21 |
| 2 | THE MEANING OF PERVERSION | 26 |
| | *Harm to moral self* | 27 |
| | *Imprudent preference-formation* | 35 |
| | *Weakness and core-perversity* | 39 |
| | *Facts or fictions?* | 42 |
| 3 | NATURE AND THE VOID | 45 |
| | *The two notions of nature* | 46 |
| | *Nature and value* | 50 |
| | *The scavenger* | 54 |
| | *Luck and transgression* | 62 |
| 4 | HEDONISM IN PSYCHOLOGY | 67 |
| | *Personal identity* | 68 |
| | *Women* | 74 |
| | *Pleasure or brain* | 78 |
| | *The avenger* | 87 |
| 5 | THE ETHIC OF VICE | 94 |
| | *Plans of life* | 95 |
| | *The parody of inversion* | 101 |
| | *Educating vice* | 103 |
| | *Love* | 109 |

## CONTENTS

| | | |
|---|---|---|
| 6 | THE PARODY OF THE CIVIL CONTRACT | 117 |
| | *Social criticism* | 118 |
| | *Utopia and beyond* | 122 |
| | *The theater of pain and pleasure* | 127 |
| | *The falsification of phallocracy* | 133 |
| | *The mature and free predator* | 136 |
| 7 | STYLE AND THE AMBIGUITY OF VICE | 140 |
| | *Repetition* | 141 |
| | *The grammar of violence* | 146 |
| | *The reader* | 148 |
| | *Ambiguity* | 149 |
| | *Metaphors* | 157 |
| 8 | THE PRIMACY OF THE GOOD | 161 |
| | *The good on surface* | 161 |
| | *The depth of goodness* | 167 |
| | *On a life-boat* | 169 |
| 9 | SADE THROUGH THE LOOKING-GLASS | 175 |
| | *Dealing with filthy things* | 175 |
| | *Virtue and control* | 180 |
| | *The failure of narcissism* | 184 |
| | *Notes* | 189 |
| | *Bibliography* | 194 |
| | *Index* | 199 |

# PREFACE

I gratefully acknowledge the following persons who have provided valuable help during the various stages of this project: Gerald Doherty, Pamela Doherty, Maija-Riitta Ollila, Ilkka Patoluoto (†), George Berger, Juha Airola, Paul J. Johnson, Heta and Matti Häyry, Jarkko Savolainen, Manfred Holler, Aristides Baltas, and Timothy Stroup. Financial support was provided by the Humanities Council of the Academy of Finland. The Department of Philosophy, University of North Carolina at Chapel Hill, offered a congenial environment to develop the first ideas which led towards the book, although I do not know whether they knew what they were spawning. My thanks are due to Professors Jay Rosenberg and Geoffrey Sayre McCord. I have presented material borrowed from this book in Helsinki, Nottingham, Dominguez Hills, Athens, Jerusalem, and Atlanta. I have profited from all of these discussions, regardless of the degree of dismay the audiences might have felt and expressed.

Sade is not an easy topic. The subject matter is that which is evil, and perhaps one cannot quite want to know what evil is like. Sade is a revolutionary thinker who has much to offer any student of ethics, literary criticism, and cultural history. The characterization of virtue as a vice, the deliberate repetitiveness of his style, and the enlightened choice of what is worthless, are all paradoxical themes which Sade introduces and analyzes with great care and skill. My basic motive in writing this book has been the conviction that there is much in this world which is neither directly visible nor readily thinkable. One is a victim of shame, which makes one assume that something does not exist because it should not. Sade deals efficiently with this problem by forcing his reader to recognize what is dirty, disgusting, and forbidden. A liberating effect follows when the reader overcomes his shame.

# PREFACE

He is then able to take a look behind without becoming a pillar of salt, as happened once outside Sodom and Gomorrah.

The book is divided into nine chapters. The second, on the meaning of perversion, is perhaps more difficult and certainly more analytical than the rest. It presents a review of human action and weakness as a technical theory to be deconstructed in the chapters that follow. It cannot be skipped without losing much of the main thesis; however, the chapter can be read cursorily so that one will at least get an impression of the notions of perversity and moral harm to self. The final chapters deal with more general issues, like censorship and the primacy of values in human life. Sade himself is the real hero of the book.

# INTRODUCTION

D. A. F. Sade is a challenge to anyone who reads his black, or clandestine and censored novels. This book is a systematic study of the kind of challenge that is involved. At the same time it is a treatise on evil in the private world, where there is a mirror reflection of the social world of coercion, persecution, punishment, and war. I have said something about the aspects of cruelty in the public world in my book *Ethics of Coercion and Authority*.[1] In the present book we shall encounter the enigmatic aspects of privacy when it is accompanied by actual plans to be wicked – which is a stronger sense of wickedness than weakness of the will, to say nothing of mere error and self-deception.

Sade's novels invite a mixed mode of reading which combines literary criticism and moral philosophy. Sade is indeed a kind of moralist, but because he deals with a subject matter which is buried deep in the Id, it would be silly to think that he could provide a neutral description of the facts. Instead of science or ontology, one finds a rich assemblage of metaphors and other rhetorical devices, used in a narrative which works like no other text. The reader of Sade must learn a method of coping in the jungle of nausea and terror Sade creates.

Four terms provide the skeleton of my study. The first, *inversion*, refers to Sade's habit of turning his topic inside out. He deals with a topic as if it were a rubber ball that is cut open, and the inside pulled out with firm hands; the result is a deformed hemispherical object, its shape forever destroyed and half its insides obscenely visible. Such inverted objects are what Sade's world is all about; they are far from any neat mirror image of familiar objects like virtue, sex, and love. The deformation involved is itself a complex procedure and interpreted in terms of the rituals of debauchery. It starts from *transgression* – the crossing of a limit – but in the Sadean world the first step is merely destruction, because it leads nowhere. Man is confronted by nature, an enemy which is as majestic as it is incomprehensible and unconquerable. Therefore, the first step across the borders of decency and shame promises only fear and trembling. It shatters the borders. *Subversion*, the essence of perversion, is to undermine all the known rules and principles, in order to derive pleasure from what is inside, underneath, out of sight. Here one leaves behind all that is transgressed and violated. The ultimate result is *transcendence* inside, not beyond, the shattered limits.

Sade provides a whole new world for his illuminated heroes, who can now celebrate their cruel friendship under the gaze of the audience – the readers, the victims, who are themselves unable to reach transcendence and are instead buried under the ruins of their values. The Sadean friends produce waste, excrement, upon which they live in their inverted world of nightmares. They like pain, worship all that cannot be respected, and enjoy what is disgusting. They aim at pleasure, now understood in terms of suffering.

The finished Sadean world, as it emerges from his novels, is like a Möbius strip. The Möbius strip that results from joining the two ends of a strip of twisted surface is unexpected and ambiguous. It is a surface with only one side, which may be called either the top or the bottom. The surface itself leaves everything visible to anyone who travels along it; nothing can be hidden or found on such a surface, because it has only one side. It sounds like an impossibility, but like the ultimate Sadean transcendence, it follows simple mechanical laws. Like Sade's anti-humanism, it is one-sided and unique.

One cannot work only from the inside out in analyzing an author like Sade, and I have tried to provide an outside to my discussion by referring to a number of other authors. For the same reason I have provided some standard philosophical material borrowed from ethics and more extensively from the theory of action. Admittedly, it can seem almost foolish to use standard moral philosophy as a frame of reference, because from that perspective Sade can look like merely an inconsistent pedant, or at most a second-rate philosopher. The kind of philosophical frame which supports both virtue and akrasia must be deconstructed here. In reality, the object of study here is a source with a mixed nature in at least two different ways. First, Sade's project is a concatenation of philosophy and literature put together in such a way that the result is neither the one nor the other. Murder and sex are both described and recommended with solid reasons. Second, the source is tainted by the profane language and the obscenity of the situations he describes. Sade deals with shit and fucking, but if the reader cannot handle this he is lost.

I have already said something about the first problem, that is, mixed sources. As for the problem of pornography in Sade's work, it has often been treated by means of a method which may be called "the celebration of embarrassment." This term refers to a set of rhetorical methods of coping. For instance, take the problem of war from a soldier's point of view. He may glorify the participation in institutionalized cruelty, mask his sense of terror, and forget war crimes by means of stories of patriotism, legends of duty, assumptions of a good cause, dreams of friendship between comrades in arms, and so on. War is recalled as something that it cannot be in order to help the soldier live with memories and consequences. Something similar can be said of studies on Sade. In dealing with the perverted subject matter, the less interesting of them either condemn and correct Sade, or camouflage him behind a biography.[2] This does not seem to produce good results, although some of their conclusions may be stimulating. Another strategy is to make a linguistic study of Sade. Roberta Hackel has produced a superb little book along these lines.[3]

The third strategy is to celebrate one's own embarrassment before Sade's language and style as well as the content – all the discharges, orgasms, the meals of shit, and scenes of torture and blood. This is the right strategy, as shown for instance by Jane Gallop and Angela Carter. Jane Gallop offers a critical summary and discussion of some French language work on Sade, and her development of these themes is admirable. A fascinating picture of Sade's world is created by Roland Barthes, whose imagination and keen eye for structural details are unsurpassed. Barthes's Sade speaks to the reader with all of his combined power and wealth of imagination. Simone de Beauvoir offers a more conventional, liberal reading in its own cultural context, while Philip Hallie is a moralist who wants to understand Sade's wicked will in order to create a better world.[4]

My own intention in this book is different. What I shall try to do is to provide a philosophical theory both of Sade and of the wicked will. Unlike most studies on Sade, my project serves some rather direct philosophical interests, but at a more descriptive level than, for instance, Hallie's treatise. I want to understand wickedness as such without evaluating or condemning the mind which emerges. It is, after all, a wicked mind whose own nature dictates the proper attitude towards it. At the same time I would like to reflect on the main features of the Sadean world of fiction, and how it can be used as a new philosophical tool. Fiction may tell us a most truthlike story about evil and madness, simply because the field is so strange. It is the realm of the forbidden, the banned, and the repressed. In fact it does not exist, because its world is so full of irony, ambiguity, and paradox. Therefore, we must read fiction as philosophy, use metaphor as argument, rely on rhetoric, and believe in the plots of the stories. We shall learn what we are not or – which is the same – what we are afraid of. Certainly this fear is so real that its causes harass us more cruelly than any representation of facts.

For my own part I will try to follow that lead of the festival of style. The modification I shall make to it is the inclusion of philosophical elements which create an artificial exterior enclosing the mystery of Sade's inner vision. Therefore perversion deconstructs moral philosophy, which is seen as lacking the potential to penetrate. Philosophy is one of the original metaphors of the void, or castration, that is, of Wittgenstein's flybottle or of Hobbes's house in which "birds that entring by the chimney, and finding themselves inclosed in a chamber flutter at the false light of a glasse window, for want of wit to consider which way they came in."[5]

# 1

# SADE: PHILOSOPHY AND ITS BACKGROUND

The Marquis de Sade creates a comprehensive literary project in order to examine the wickedness of the will in all its forms. His aims are at least half philosophical as he tackles some paradoxical issues and attempts to relate their meaning to his reader. Such a project, which combines narrative form and theoretical speculation, may be too complicated to be perspicuous. Indeed, if the subject matter tends to be paradoxical, Sade's texts themselves are enigmatic. They appear to be novels, yet one cannot really read them as such without concluding that they are failures. As is often said – mistakenly, of course – they cannot be read. We can read Sade, but only with a key. I shall argue that this key is the realization that Sade is actually a philosopher in disguise. Although we cannot read Sade as a conventional philosopher for some obvious reasons, his fiction (including its style) serves counter-ethical and metaphysical goals. Once we read Sade as a philosopher, we can then go on to appreciate his more literary achievements, which may otherwise escape the reader. My overall strategy, then, will be to start with an account of Sade's work and career, to look at his philosophy, and then return to matters concerning his style and narrative technique.

## FACTS

It is evident that the books and other writings of Sade are not well known except in the form of rumors and legends which say, correctly enough, that they are bizarre, demanding, and very long. They also have the reputation of being unpleasant to read. Although they contain a wealth of pornographic and sadistic detail, they are not sexually arousing in any familiar way; and many readers see the texts as too rambling and boring to warrant careful study. The reader who does wish to give careful study to Sade is confronted by the obstacle that often his books are available only in truncated versions; and it is usually Sade's philosophical speculations that are eliminated. Unfortunately, it is the speculative parts which are supremely important for a real understanding of Sade.

Sade wrote many plays, but his main ambition of becoming a successful playwright was never satisfied. Even today the plays remain largely unpublished and unproduced. As Lely says, "By the evidence we now possess, the Marquis de Sade was the author of seventeen plays. It seems unlikely that he wrote more, for the truth is that all that he wrote in this form was so humdrum that neither his family nor the authorities thought it worth consigning to judicial flames."[1] Yet he took this aspect of his work quite seriously, and his secondary career as a novelist reflects his theatrical background – an interpretive clue which should not be forgotten by those studying his novels. Besides being a dramatist, Sade was also a libertine, and his biography reveals a unique personality, amazing in its adventurousness, originality, irritable violence, and literary productivity. After spending over twenty years in prison, Sade was confined at the end of his life to the Charenton mental asylum in Paris. Napoleon himself refused to set Sade free, partly because of his destabilizing cultural and moral influence. The Comte de Montalivet, Minister of the Interior, issued the following order on October 18, 1810: "The greatest care [must] be taken to prevent any use by him [Sade] of pencils, pens, ink, or paper. The director of the asylum is made personally responsible for the execution of this order." Sade's ink is fertile, and the attempt to deny him the use of the pen may be taken as a kind of castration. Nevertheless, Sade wrote and produced his plays at the asylum, where the inmates were said to have become uncontrollable because of this entertainment. The performances seem to have been public. Doctor Royer Collard complained about Sade and Charenton in 1808, saying:

> They were so improvident at the asylum that they had a theater erected for the performance of comedies and did not think of the harmful effects of such a tumultuous proceeding upon the mind. De Sade is the director of this theater. He presents the plays, hands out the roles and directs them. He is also the asylum poet. . . . How can such things be in an insane asylum? Such crimes and immorality![2]

The production of morally disgusting stage performances for madmen was one of Sade's minor crimes, and it provides a clue to the interpretation of Sade's philosophy. The fictional account of outrageous and unexplainable behavior is his ultimate vice, and the theatrical displays of imaginary cruelty is the topic in which he is interested.

It is indeed typical of Sade's fate that he was placed in a mental asylum despite being certainly sane, as the five paragraphs of his last will show.[3] It is a small masterpiece. He also provided some antipsychiatric treatment for the patients – as we now understand it after reading Thomas Szasz. Nevertheless, Sade was not interested in caring for people, as he makes clear in his novels. Was he trying to create chaos inside the asylum? The final enigma of his life centers on what he was doing with the insane in the hospital, but the picture is as fragmented as it is fascinating.

As we have said, during his life Sade was not only an asylum inmate but also a prisoner. Although he was always saved through cunning and luck, he even received death sentences for some of his alleged crimes, as the following entry indicates:

> 1772 September – The public prosecutor's sentence at Marseille: Sade and Latour are condemned to make due apology in front of the cathedral door before being taken to the Place Saint-Luis where "the said Sr. de Sade is to be beheaded on a scaffold and the said Latour hung and strangled on a gibbet ... then the body of the said Sr. de Sade and that of the said Latour shall be burned and their ashes thrown to the wind." The crime is stated to be poisoning and sodomy. . . . Sade and Latour are executed and burnt in effigy at Aix.[4]

They in fact violated the prostitutes who accused them, but in general the evidence for their crimes remains questionable. Such an example shows more about how the law worked then and how serious sex-related crimes were considered during that period. Sodomy led to capital punishment, and blasphemy was just as bad. Sade was considered guilty of both, and to increase his troubles, he was later mistakenly thought to be the author of the notorious pamphlet *Zoloe* (1800), which attacked Bonaparte and other important people. This mistake in literary attribution explains some of the persecution Sade experienced later in his life. He was not freed by Napoleon in spite of his pleas, even after his son was killed in action. His reputation was already tainted to the extent that he was no longer in control of his own fate. He was even harassed by his mother-in-law, Lady de Montreuil, who had him arrested and seemed to want to get rid of her kin for good. This fact has prompted speculations as to whether Sade's representations of women are biased in some typical way because of his problematic relation to Lady de Montreuil.

Sade quite early became nationally famous for his debauchery and scandals, later for his books, and finally for his republican political activities during the French Revolution. Although he was himself a revolutionary, typically enough the revolutionaries also came very close to executing him as an aristocrat. He avoided the guillotine only because, in the confusion resulting from so many executions, he could not be definitely identified:

> 1794 – Sade's name appears eleventh on a list of twenty-eight prisoners to be brought to trial. For some reason not wholly explained, the court bailiff fails to take Sade and returns with only twenty-three of the twenty-eight. All but two are guillotined the same day on a square.[5]

Knowledge of Sade's life is of some importance to the understanding of his philosophical doctrine, as I shall show, but it is also worth noting that his life was not always congruent with his fiction. First, he was an unhappy libertine, a fact which refutes his own pet theory of the beneficial effect of vice. Second, many of his recent biographers seem to have exaggerated the degree of Sade's personal debauchery, trying to see it as the image of the debauchery in his fiction. Certainly, he was a wicked and violent person who enthusiastically recommended crime, yet life is not fiction. One may ask the question, for example: did Sade ever kill anyone for the pure enjoyment of it all, as is prescribed by his own doctrines? The answer, evidently, is "no." He may have been used to drawing blood with a whip and a dagger, but he does not seem to have killed anyone, except perhaps in the war in which he had participated as a young man. He may have wanted to kill, but in the context of the legal and social order of the period it was prudent for him to repress any such motive. The constraints on one's personal life and career are severe compared to the liberty of the novel, where abstraction rules. Sade's cruelty is ultimately fictional.

In this book I shall concentrate on four of Sade's principal works, the ones called his black novels. They made him famous, and not without reason. His more conventional larger works and groups of shorter writings are less known than the clandestine black novels, but they are also less interesting. One exception, of course, is Sade's essay on the art of fiction, "Reflections on the Novel," which deserves to be read carefully. It claims to be an explication of the main features of

Sade's grand literary project; however, even this essay is perverted, because in it Sade gives the calculated impression of being a conventional novelist whose aims are neither surprising nor revolutionary. His strategy here resembles his attempts to deny the authorship of his most important clandestine works; he produces elaborate proofs that he could not possibly be the author of a book like *Justine*. (Sometimes he was not, as the case of *Zoloe* shows.) Sade writes in a typically deceptive manner:

> Never, I say it again, never shall I portray crime other than clothed in the colors of hell. I wish people to see crime laid bare, I want them to fear it and detest it, and I know no other way to achieve this end than to paint it in all its horror.... Given which, let no one any longer ascribe to me the authorship of J [*Justine*], I have never written any such works, and surely I never shall.[6]

In his "A Note on My Detention," he uses two arguments to show that he is not the author of *Justine*. First, he argues, to write such a book at the Bastille would mean the risk of returning to prison, and such a self-destructive act cannot be expected of anyone. Second, to show that the obvious presupposition concerning his prudence is justified, he argues that his other books and stories, like *Aline et Valcour*, are indeed moral.[7] This may even be true. If one reads them without presupposing the knowledge of the black novels and their system of anti-ethics, one may agree. In the more conventional works, virtue emerges victorious over vice. Why, he asks, should he write something as disturbing and dangerous as *Justine*? It is a good question.

There is one additional aspect of this bluffing which we must recognize, namely, Sade's declaration of his psychological goals in his books. In the "Reflections on the Novel," he says that the novel is a faithful mirror of the mind, so that "the most essential requirement for the novelist's art is most certainly the knowledge of the human heart."[8] One may understand this as a blatant lie and say that Sade was merely a subversive writer whose novels are devoid of verisimilitude. However, one can equally well argue that Sade is being honest here. Perhaps he really tries to depict realistic characters and to show us what human nature is like in its vacillation between virtue and vice. My own opinion is that although Sade is a subversive writer, he does fictionally depict the subconscious mind and its repressions in a manner which is convincing. It does not resemble anything we know or have previously thought of. This region is a bizarre conglomeration of all the waste and filth of the subconscious Id, kept intact as long as the processes of decay will allow before it vanishes into nothingness. In spite of such a mystery, Sade allows his audience to see the inner aspect of human life in all of its forbidden glamor. When the gaze is turned inwards, one sees what should not be seen.

It is impossible to say whether Sade denies the authorship of his books because he is prudently aware of the danger of legal prosecution, or whether he wants to play the game as it is prescribed – either by vice as an instinct or by the theory of perverse behavior. Perhaps both of these factors are relevant, for such standards are typical of the negativity and the ambiguity of vice.

According to the principles of perverse action, an attempt to turn people away from evil is more apt to attract them towards its acceptance than any direct recommendation. It is therefore not so strange that Sade, who insists on his indecency, denies authorship of his clandestine books like *Justine*. He first boasts about his wickedness and then denies it. By so doing, he is faithful to his own theoretical principles, difficult as they are to understand. The duplicity and ambiguity involved can also be explained, of course, on the grounds of his fear of punishment. This fear was well founded. He was arrested once again in 1801 in his publisher's office and duly imprisoned because of his books. The texts are still censored in many countries; indeed, the legal history of paternalism surrounding Sade and his books can be used with profit in any study of cultural oppression and censorship.

The black novels I shall discuss are the shorter *Justine*, *Juliette*, *Philosophy in the Bedroom*, and the long, great *120 Days of Sodom*. The first two novels represent the two sides of one story; they respectively follow the rather similar careers of two different women – one good, the other bad; one unsuccessful and unhappy, the other not. *Juliette* alone is 1200 pages long and consists of six volumes. *Justine* adds several volumes to the double story. The other books are smaller, but even the shortest, *Philosophy in the Bedroom*, is more than 200 pages long. The sheer mass of text, then, is enormous, especially considering that Sade began his writing when he was 42 years old, when he was starting his career as a prisoner. Moreover, Sade's son, "that dismal, greedy creature," burned all his father's notebooks and manuscripts, assisted by the police, after the death of the old man.[9] The Divine Marquis was clearly a hard-working person. Sade's fictional heroes are also hard-working. Their vice forces on them a busy life-style which resembles that of a modern businessman more than that of a classic aristocrat, in that they acquire raw materials, shape them into a new and more pleasing form, and sell products to their fellow citizens; the main difference is that the material with which his libertines work is the human body and soul.

Sade's project also assumes that the reader is a hard-working individual – determined, independent, even virtuous. Certainly, only those who are least vulnerable to his rhetoric can read Sade all the way through; but for everyone he presents an enormous challenge by the special nature of his text. Perhaps the moral danger comes from reading only part of the whole.

## TOPICS

In Sade's doctrine, I shall distinguish between five levels. *First*, we find in his work a parody of the social contract theory, together with the idea of the state of nature and the utopian social order. We can also appreciate the discussions of elitism and anarchism, focusing on social inequality and exploitation. According to Sade's syllogism, the civilized life is part of the state of nature, because of its inherent violence; our social world is already evil and society unjust; one should therefore make all this explicit and learn how to enjoy its possibilities. To form a social context fit for the cruel exploitation of the weaker by the stronger is the ultimate role of civilization. The social contract crystallizes a medium, explicating a *chronique scandaleuse*, or a good story of the wicked order of things.

*Second*, we are provided with a psychology of the person who is seeking for pleasure, or rather stimulation, and whose motivation is explained by this search. The illuminated Sadean hero is one who is longing for extreme pleasure, even if it is only for the short run. Pleasure is understood in an anti-Epicurean manner, so that the resulting hedonism is a caricature of the utilitarian calculus of benefits. Sade rejects the ideology of maximizing expectations, according to which the agent is a prudent egoist who abhors unreasonable risks. On the contrary, the Sadean person wants everything at once, regardless of consequences. Such pleasure is related to deliberate cruelty, perverse sex, and the climax of sexual excitement which is crazy pleasure, that is orgasm – understood as the simple act and fact of discharging. Obviously, a serious effort must be made to explicate such a strange pseudo-psychological theory whose key metaphor refers to military life and its guns. Can we call it hedonism?

*Third*, Sade's metaphysics claims that nature must be seen as the original principle of death and destruction. He sees nature in terms of the classic atomistic model, according to which the universe is a giant vortex of bodies loaded with energy and *conatus*. The collision of atoms is the truth of nature, and therefore Sade claims that there is no room for transcendental values or gods. He is an atheist. A naturalistic counter-ethic follows. From the principle of nature, he thinks, we can derive a code of conduct for the heroes who are able to appreciate the true science. The main laws of nature prescribe destruction – that is, violent collisions – which are again connected to the psychology of pleasure via the orgiastic experience of nothingness. Murder is the passion which Sade wants to justify in this context. He claims that conflicts irritate and stimulate the mind. Metaphysics is an important part of Sade's philosophy, simply because it explains his psychology of pleasure and leads us to the heart of darkness – evil itself. Nevertheless, the naturalistic ethic is an interim stage.

*Fourth*, for Sade, ethics proper is the field in which conventional virtue becomes vice and vice becomes virtue. Two different interpretations can be given to this paradox. According to the first interpretation, social life and the role of a person are such that virtue does not pay off, although vice does. In the Aristotelian manner, virtue is a mean between the scarcity and excess of what is *prima facie* desirable. When a person is too virtuous, as it were, he acquires characteristics which are not exactly wicked but are harmful defects of personality. Insufficient or false virtue, on the other hand, is also dangerous. But who doesn't shade into one side or the other? For Sade, the golden mean of virtue is so narrow that one never hits it, and much of what Sade wrote is dedicated to proving this thesis. According to the second interpretation, all cultures support different and mutually conflicting values. This relativism can be shown by means of comparative anthropology; to support it, Sade himself uses empirical data in a bewildering manner. He tries to sketch a blueprint of an ideal society of villains, so there is a return from ethics to a parody of the civil contract. The narrative circles back to its starting point, and parody provides the contents for the later stages of philosophy.

The true Sadean problem is not at the surface of his ethics. As I shall argue, the problem is that after denying all enduring values except violent pleasure, Sade must nevertheless postulate the existence and validity of something like objective values. The truly wicked person wants to commit crime, and nothing stimulates him like mischief. But to be able to do so he must first define crime, and for crime to exist there must be laws and values. A criminal, vicious person violates natural laws and moral laws. Therefore vice logically entails the existence of virtue. I do not think that Sade is content to rebel against the subjective convictions of the people he loathes. Neither would he be interested in producing merely undesirable consequences; they tend to be unknown or irrelevant to the Sadean agent himself. He needs to break his own true values and annihilate the valid laws of religion and morality. This is what destructive nature tells him to do, and in order to enjoy it he needs something to be destroyed, namely, virtue. Therefore, two conflicting sets of genuine values must exist: those which one transgresses and those which one really aims at. How is this possible? That is the problem that faces us when we try to understand the nature of evil and the wickedness of the will. In order to answer it, we must turn to Sade's idea of style, by means of which he attempts to bridge the two aspects of the mutually incompatible moral theories.

The *fifth* and ultimate level which Sade creates is that of style, or what can be called his aesthetics. The text works not only as a pornographic story, a scandalous novel, or an incoherent philosophical treatise, but also as an instrument of torture which is directed by Sade against the reader. The style is designed to validate the message through the effects it brings about in its audience. Curiosity, fascination, and sexual arousal will first draw the reader in, but if he is successful Sade will replace them in the end by terror, disgust, and aggression against the narrator. The style is intended to work as a self-validating pragmatic theory, or as an insult which reaches from the narrator towards the innocent reader. The text which discusses evil may itself be an evil thing, and therefore also a valid account of wickedness. It involves stylistic devices like repetition, metaphor, and the structural fragmentation of the text. An account of the style of terror and its pragmatics of disgust is the essence of any interpretation of Sade that tries to make sense of his enigmatic enterprise. My own approach to Sade is through his fiction of evil. I shall not discuss hard facts, since Sade's stories hardly create the effect of verisimilitude. In his fiction everything is unreal. Even in this sense the Divine Marquis is a subversive writer.

Sade does not exhibit any weakness of the will, self-deception, moral negligence, or even error. He aims at subjective pleasure and objective harm with perfect self-knowledge; he really cares for his pet counter-values, and he is ready to suffer imprisonment and censorship in order to entertain his readers. This is why he is divine. He exemplifies the wickedness of the will through the very fact that he struggles to sabotage any idea of what Hannah Arendt was to call "the banality of evil." The ultimate recourse of countless helpless victims, including those who were persecuted by the Nazis, has been the idea that cruelty is a small, gray, boring, and undistinguished thing. As such, it not only lacks value in itself but value for any others; it is unrewarding to the agents of evil themselves. From this standpoint, even the most powerful cruelty would be a matter of the agent's error and psychological weakness. Sade's project is to combat any such notion. He paints wickedness as a strong and grand phenomenon which provides glory and spectacle, and entails all the opportunities for enjoyment, creativity, and satisfaction. Certainly, the attempt to break all the norms is somehow related to an individual's freedom and creativity. It is, however, mainly related to subversive action. Wickedness becomes a new type of problem when it is taken beyond the limits of banality.[10]

The idea of the banality of evil is a novel effort to claim that evil is without value; it does not evoke the tautology of condemning evil because of its nature as an intrinsically undesirable thing, or evil-as-evil. On the contrary, the accusation of banality projects the nature of evil upon an aesthetic and emotive medium, which creates the impression that something informative has been said. One ends up condemning evil because it is characterized by banality, a negative feature in all cases, but one not usually associated with things like the description of the nature of evil. Something of the same type of strategy, but with an opposite result, is involved in Sade's own aesthetics of style, in which he describes wickedness in terms of some new ideas – ideas intended to express its glory and grandeur.

Sade himself might agree that evil is banal, but only if the evil involved is the kind of official violence practiced by the state (which provides, after all, many of the most familiar examples of cruelty). By its own lights, the commendable feature of such violence is supposed to be its impersonality; its cruelty is only a bureaucratic control measure among countless other equally impersonal methods. Since rational bureaucracy is a tool which must be used according to formal rules, any personal enjoyment of its effects must be classified as a malfunction of the machine. Sade's counterpoint is an obvious one: namely, that cruelty should be enjoyed. To him, the banality of evil would simply mean that evil without enjoyment is indeed boring. As opposed to the banality of public violence, Sade privatizes violence and makes it a personal attribute. Even state cruelty could only be enjoyable, he thinks, if it managed to create an unjust distribution of power which led to the realization of one's own ends. Evil should be de-banalized, he seems to be saying. With him one thus approaches an uncharted territory.

Philosophers have scarcely proved that the glamor of vice remains an impossibility throughout all contexts of cruelty. Sade argues that it is possible; he does so by telling a story of the solipsist mind which directs its gaze inside upon its own libidinal landscape and recognizes that the scenery is full of terror, violence, and egoistic pleasures. In this sense his story of the Id remains in the state of pure individual and private enjoyment, outside of all norms and values. Such solipsism, in which we are dealing with the privacy of the mind seen from inside, is the theme of my study of Sade, but let us anticipate a little and see how the narrator himself sketches one of his libertine heroes.

Duc de Blangis and his enterprise are described as follows:

> Born treacherous, harsh, imperious, barbaric, selfish, as lavish in the pursuit of pleasure as miserly when it were a question of useful spending, a liar, a gourmand, a drunk, a dastard, a sodomite, fond of incest, given to murdering, to arson, to theft, no, not a single virtue compensated that host of vices. Why, what am I saying! not only did he never so much as dream of a single virtue, he beheld them all with horror, and he was frequently heard to say that to be truly happy in this world a man ought not merely fling himself into every vice, but should never permit himself one virtue, and that it was not simply a matter of always doing evil, but also and above all of never doing good.[11]

The surface analysis of this passage is obvious: Blangis is characterized by a rich set of psychological features which explain his actions. His basic motivation is towards pleasure, understood as the private enjoyment of some sensory stimulation. Virtue and ethics in general are seen as barriers to be removed. Values are obstacles, although we shall see later that they are also needed to create subversive pleasure. Moreover, Blangis needs traces of truthfulness as he tries to explain, perhaps only to himself, that his strategy is a satisfactory one – that by means of it one proceeds towards pleasure and not disappointment. A plan of life is accepted which is constituted of vice and which does not utilize any virtue, except inessentially.

The question I would like to raise is whether his negative plan makes sense. It may make sense in terms of a private, egotistical vision of one's own struggle towards the fulfillment of desire. Sade's project aims at envisioning this realm, which has nothing to do with social or structural violence and which therefore presupposes some interesting methodological constructions. Sade does not describe men and women in terms of experience, truth, or veridical evidence. Duc de Blangis is fictional both because he is an invented character and because he could not exist in the world we are accustomed to call the real one. Nevertheless, Sade says something interesting about his life plan. Our task is to see how such a theoretical feat becomes possible.

In Sade's world, even hard facts become twisted as they serve the ends of the libertine heroes. Wounds heal when a miraculous cream is applied to them, men have maidenheads and women ejaculate, people drink enormous quantities of alcohol, and some of their physical features take on superhuman proportions, like those of Minski the Russian cannibal. Yet Juliette shows her commonsense knowledge when she warns that once one starts using opium and alcohol, one must use them for the rest of one's life. Also, some libertines grow old, ugly, and impotent. They are furious about their physical weaknesses, which are explained and described realistically and whose causes are quite clear: they drink too much, practice destructive sex, and are at an advanced age. Sade is also capricious when he is playing with his facts. In effect Sade's world is fictional, and most of all bizarre, even in the deep sense that it could not be mistaken for the real world.

As we have seen, Sade deals with social philosophy, metaphysical ethics, and personal and moral philosophy. Even if these topics are partially disconnected, Sade's ultimate anarchist message comes through: there are no real values or religious truths, social life is a veritable hell, and man is, accordingly, a beast by nature. This worldview is coherent enough in its own way, but also subversive. Sade really wants to destroy values as they are known in the tradition of the good life and religious salvation. He is not a reformist; he possesses no alternative values. Some commentators, of course, have tried to portray him as a reformer. For instance, Lawrence W. Lynch remarks: "In defense of Sade, he seemed genuinely sincere when he claimed that by portraying vice with elans and 'wrapped in the colors of hell', he was contributing to the subsequent avoidance of vice."[12] But Sade's expression of his goals is too equivocal to justify such an apologetic interpretation. He may claim that he has some educational ends in mind when he writes a purely negative parody of all things human and shows how ambiguous our goals are; but this is mostly either irony or self-protection against the censorship laws. It seems better to read him as a consistently transgressive thinker, which does not necessarily entail that he is a consistent writer.

## THE REFUTATION OF OPTIMISM

Sade had plenty of time to study during his life, and he was indeed a well-read and educated person. But it is not known exactly what he read and who influenced him most; and he uses scientific authority capriciously. If we want to place Sade within a tradition, it should not be conceived in terms of the historical and personal influences which shaped his thought, but rather in terms of his spiritual home. This spiritual home seems to be the darker side of philosophical ethics, a kind of neglected vision of human perversity beyond the healing effect of moral teaching.

From an external vantage point, Sade's theory of nature as a destructive principle can be understood as contradicting an absurd but traditional view. It can be called the Pious Principle of Hidden Effects – an optimistic variant of Adam Smith's invisible hand and of Hegel's cunning of reason (*List der Vernunft*). According to this optimism, whatever a person does will in the end turn out to be good, because the world is made to be good (if not quite perfect) and the person is part of the world. A benevolent God designed the universe so that whatever objective a person aims at, he will serve God's purposes, which are by definition good. Let me take an example which is not, in this context, from a standard source. George Berkeley, later Bishop Berkeley, writes:

> we shall be forced to acknowledge that those particular things, which considered in themselves appear to be *evil*, have the nature of *good*, when considered as linked with the whole system of beings.[13]

Berkeley says that there is no alternative to this idea, since it is "forced" upon us. He explains his idea as follows: "We should further consider, that the very blemishes and defects of Nature are not without their use, in that they make an agreeable sort of variety, and augment the beauty of the rest of the creation, as shades in a picture serve to set off the brighter and more enlightened parts."[14] All evil is functional good; or, it is only an appearance that does not exist alone, as a shadow does not exist without light. A wicked person makes visible what is good, and the "idea of some particular pain" which we identify as evil should not bother us unnecessarily. We cannot avoid pain, but luckily there is no real pain, at least if it is understood as something evil.

Bishop Berkeley is an optimist. If we use Nicholas Rescher's terminology, he is an absolute optimist; he believes that "anything bad is, even at worst, only a lack or imperfection – a shortfall of the good." Instrumentalistic optimism would require that "there is actual negativity, but whenever present it serves as a causal means to a greater good."[15] Berkeley is an optimist in both senses, as it is easy to verify. First, some good things appear to be evil, but they are not really evil; and second, defects of nature work to make the picture nicer, provided that they are true defects. Shadows are at the same time both real and transient in the most convenient manner.

Obviously, Sade rejects such a fantastic consequentialist view, or whatever analog of it was current in his time. The principle makes all evil good; the wicked agent must forever fail, and therefore he will remain in torment. Sade becomes angry when he thinks that whatever vice he may aim at, or whatever mischievous plans he may entertain to violate human rights, the results will be good. He seems to recognize that in this happy-go-lucky case the ends must also justify the intentions and actions – which is certainly absurd. The person intentionally does something wrong – this is the starting point of the story – but now it is maintained that he does, consequentially, something good. For Sade, who wants to be evil, this is a cruel fate. The clever demiurge has manufactured a universe where one absolutely cannot go wrong. This intolerable thought drives Sade out of his mind when he struggles to make sense of an alternative, anti-Christian possibility. It may be said that the Pious Principle is a metaphysical analog to the psychology of human weakness, placed in the role of the sole interpretation of the possibility of evil. In all such cases the evil person is merely weak and blind. He is unable to do or to see the good, which after all is there. Sade cannot accept this.

One anarchistic corollary of the Pious Principle is that, since it is in fact impossible for a person to do wrong, he may well aim at what is seen by him to be a set of evil consequences, if this is his preference. He is free to try to harm others and bring about benefit for himself, since all will turn out to be good in the end. Whether his intentions are good or evil, they will benefit others; in this respect, one's intentions are not important.

Sade's world is populated by victims of cruelty who really care, because they suffer even when their private pain is seen in the context of divine benevolence. Actually, such a maximal context may not even exist; there is no well-defined world system whose value one could estimate according to some principle of summation. However, Berkeley's principle is impossible to refute. It contains an empirical point which, nevertheless, cannot be directly checked. The fact of personal pain is supposed to disappear in the wide context of existence, but this event is never observed. In fact, any submaximal section of the world, however large, must display a random degree of pain and evil. Yet this particular truth does not say anything about the value of the totality. The Pious Principle is metaphysical, and as such it exemplifies one of the deepest value-theoretical intuitions of people like Bishop Berkeley. Sade's nature is directly the opposite. In his world suffering does not entail hope. Yet Sade's attitude is far from pessimistic.

Sade is an atheist and needs to dispose of the set of ideas I have called the Pious Principle. Because the enemy is both metaphysical and intuitive, the method of refutation must be at once indirect and persuasive. The goal is obviously difficult to attain, because the target is so deep-seated in Western thought. Sade uses literary techniques to try to make the Pious Principle look unconvincing; he attempts to show that it is vulnerable to empirical counter-evidence and that the principle itself is both cruel and amusing.

We may simulate Sade's own rhetorical technique and also illustrate his method by returning to the stranger side of Berkeley's personality. We know the following hard facts concerning the future bishop:

> Berkeley entered Trinity [College, Dublin] on the 21st of March, 1700 as a pensioner. He was then aged 15.... He was at first a mystery to his fellow undergraduates ... Thomas Contarini, Goldsmith's uncle and benefactor who entered the College in 1701, was one of Berkeley's closest friends. He tells a story of a time when he and Berkeley went to witness a public execution. Berkeley became curious, as a result, about the sensations which accompany the process of dying. He decided to try an experiment on himself, and asked Contarini to be present to prevent the experiment going so far as to make a report impossible. Berkeley was accordingly tied to the ceiling, where he remained until he lost consciousness. Thus Contarini was given no instructions to release him ... Contarini cut Berkeley down, whereupon he ... uttered the memorable words, "Bless my heart, Contarini, you have rumbled my band."[16]

Did Berkeley really believe in his Pious Principle when he pursued the most exotic of all perverse pleasures – namely, the ultimate harm to self of a public, violent suicide? Did he believe that the world would be better because of his death, or did he merely desire to experience certain exotic feelings? Since it is impossible to answer such questions, it is also impossible to exorcise the irony from the event. The most noble of all thoughts, God, and the base enjoyment derived from a public execution, must be considered together in a context where their implications cannot be compared, evaluated, and judged. The result is the irony of being caught between two incompatible thoughts, both of which seem to be enjoyable, although they cannot be. Human folly speaks for itself. I take this example as representative of the Sadean philosophical rhetoric. The fact of irony indicates the truth of chaos.

This story which is told of Berkeley is also a mythical archetype. The same joke which Contarini tells about his young friend can be found in other sources which discuss madness. For example, in the *Encyclopedia* version of the *Philosophy of Mind*, Hegel writes: "Another Englishman who had hanged himself, on being cut down by his servant not only regained the desire to live but also the disease of avarice; for when discharging the servant, he deducted twopence from his wages because the man had acted without instructions in cutting the rope with which his master had hanged himself."[17] This story is a well-known archetypal case of irrational behavior and a model of human folly. However, it contains an even deeper and perverse aspect. The pleasure of dying and the excitement attached to one's last moment attracts Berkeley to the extent that he is driven to experience it. Hegel's melancholy Englishman finds the experience so invigorating that it restores the strength of his former unpleasant self. Sade tells a similar story countless times in different forms and contexts. Death is the moment of truth. However, the key point is the rhetorical one, since the punchlines of the stories mobilize a double association. In the case of Berkeley, the same man who is to be a bishop and serious philosopher, and a lover of the Pious Principle, is like a madman and pervert (at least according to some paradigmatic criteria). In the case of the melancholy Englishman, the melancholy is cured with the help of the man's flirtations with suicide.

Two of Sade's own intellectual heroes were Niccolò Machiavelli and Thomas Hobbes, both of whom he interpreted in the traditional manner to recommend wickedness as an ingredient of virtue. Sade echoes Machiavelli, for instance, when he describes his fictional hero Saint-Fond: "Saint-Fond is a very great minister nonetheless . . . he considers murder indispensable to the maintaining of good government. . . . Did Machiavelli lay down different principles? There is no room for doubt: bloodshed there must be if any regime, a monarchical one especially, is to survive; the throne of the tyrant must be cemented with blood."[18] For Sade, theorists like Machiavelli and Hobbes seem to subscribe to a radical relativity of values, or an actual transformation of value into disvalue for the sake of political survival. Robert Mandeville is another model mentioned by Sade, and he would have appreciated Malthus as well. The pseudo-Malthusian idea of the desirability of the mass destruction of people, as a kind of surplus population, is a recurrent theme with Sade, who promotes murder and opposes procreation. Malthus's *An Essay on the Principle of Population* did not appear before the year 1798, but similar ideas were popular before that time.[19]

## THE DEFINITION OF PERVERSITY

In accepting a set of ideas that can be dubbed the Poe-definition of perversity, Sade inverts the optimistic Pious Principle so that now everything leads to evil ends. In his fiction, if not in his life, he utilizes the relativity of values in full and maintains that the world is such that only vice pays off. The Poe-definition of perversity, formulated by Edgar Allan Poe in his essay "The Imp of the Perverse," can be stated as follows: the perverse person does what he should not, just because he should not do it. So formulated, there is some problem with the objectivity of values, since with Poe's Imp (and its Sadean parallel) the existence of perversity presupposes true values and knowledge of them as its own necessary conditions. Both the Imp and Sade need to know what they should not do, and to do that they need to know what the values are.

In his essay, Poe starts by criticizing a teleological and functionalist concept of the mind, which is an Aristotelian notion. According to this, the psychic mechanism is geared to attain certain intrinsic goals, or to work in a certain manner which is good. The mind is a black box whose contents can be read from the results it is designed to produce. Moreover, those alleged results are anchored to some goals which, in their turn, can be inferred from the holistic concept of nature and the knowledge of its creator. The concept is teleological; all processes which do not serve the proper ends are aberrations, weaknesses, and errors. The weakness of the will, or akrasia, seems to explain much of human folly. The mind naturally aims at the good, and akrasia explains why something else is realized. Yet this is a mistaken view, Poe says. Empirical observations indicate that the human mind contains features which cannot be understood as mere weakness and error.

The teleological and functionalist conception of the mind implies that the mind has intrinsic goals, and any distraction from them is only accidental. However, in Poe's words, there is no "preconceived destiny of man." On the contrary, empirical scientific observation, or "induction," shows that the mind works according to principles which cannot be understood functionally. They do not serve rational ends. Therefore the mind, according to Poe, can also be seen as a self-destructive machine whose spontaneous processes do not exhibit any higher design like that of the Pious Principle, and must therefore be classified as evil. The proper attitude towards such goals is, perhaps, Poe's own sardonic laughter.

Let us explore what such perverse goals are. We can almost hear Sade's voice when Poe writes about his crucial inductive discovery as follows:

> Induction, *a posteriori*, would have brought phrenology to admit, as an innate and primitive principle of human action, a paradoxical something, which we may call *perverseness*, for want of a more characteristic term. In the sense I intend, it is, in fact, a *mobile* without motive, a motive not *motiviert*. Through its promptings we act without comprehensible object; or, if this shall be understood as a contradiction in terms, we may so far modify the proposition as to say, that through its promptings we act, for the reason that we should *not*. In theory, no reason can be more unreasonable; but, in fact, there is none more strong. With certain minds, under certain conditions, it becomes absolutely irresistible.[20]

As we shall see, Sade uses an anti-Aristotelian model of perversity similar to Poe's. Their two philosophies may suffer from the same type of weakness. In Poe's case, the term "irresistible" in the quotation above seems to indicate the presence of mere akrasia, which has no place in this context: one wants to do good, but one is unable to resist some contrary drive. Poe also claims that perversity entails the lack of any motive whatsoever, but even this can be challenged. Actually, Poe wants to replace the teleological goal – a motive in its own right – with the causal concept of an efficient force which drives the agent forward toward his doom. Poe suggests that no motivating reason, value, or goal can explain this strange possibility.

But what examples does Poe give of perverse motivation? There are several, the first of which concerns a speaker's "earnest desire to tantalize a listener by circumlocution." Although he wants to please and is able to do so, the speaker succumbs to the temptation to irritate and involves himself in a disastrous performance. The speaker acts against his own good intentions. This first case resembles the familiar Aristotelian case of the weakness of the will.

Poe's second example concerns a person who has an important task to perform before a deadline, but waits until it is too late. Here we may think that he did not even consider doing the work in time. In his attraction to the disaster, he avoided it from the beginning. The third case involves the fascination of danger, in which one is compelled to break a safety barrier simply because it is there. The fourth and final example is the fate of the narrator himself, who writes from death row after being condemned for the murder of a rich relative. The narrator says he simply wanted to break the status quo of success and well-being; he confessed just because he wants to confess.

The Poe-definition of perversity demands that "we perpetrate them [evil deeds] merely because we feel that we should *not*." This type of claim, especially the motivational clause "because we should not" deserves to be analyzed and compared to the akratic approach, which it certainly resembles. Poe does not quite convince his reader that he has described a new, anti-Aristotelian mental phenomenon. Poe should show that personal disaster is the agent's best option. If it is not, his cases concern akrasia, understood as the agent's choice of his second-best alternative. For example, suppose safety is one's first concern and yet one jumps into an abyss. In Poe's scheme, the fall itself must be the best choice. The temptation not to jump can then be understood in reference to the elusive desire for safety, which must be sacrificed. Certainly, one may feel regret because one is unable to get the second-best value, as well as the primary one.

Instead of going deeper into this technical issue at this point, let us merely note that the Poe-definition of perversity is present in the work of other authors, even before the time of Sade. An example is Erasmus's notorious *Ichthyophagia, or Concerning the Eating of Fish*. In it the Fishmonger responds to the Butcher's alarming proposition that a new law will allow the consumption of meat without religious restrictions. The Fishmonger claims, predictably (but somehow surprisingly), that when it becomes permissible to consume meat, there will be an increased demand for the less desirable foodstuff, fish.

> *Butcher*: What I tell you is too true for jesting. But please tell me how you are assured of a better trade in the light of this [new law].
>
> *Fishmonger*: Because people by nature are more desirous of that

which is forbidden to them.... When they are free to eat flesh, they will eat less of it. Then there will be no entertainment greater than the eating of fish, as it used to be in the past. So I shall be glad if there is a license to eat flesh. I also wish the eating of fish was prohibited; then people would desire it more intensely.[21]

The Butcher also claims that "when it comes to a choice between two things, one being better than the other, we commonly choose the worse." The Fishmonger agrees: "No, if he [a priest] neglects to say his prayers on the appointed hour, he must be excommunicated; but if he is a usurer, or guilty of simony, he goes scot-free." These examples seem to concern inconsistent value systems rather than choices, even if the discussion starts from the problems of choice. But the message is clear: some choices are perverse, and our expressed values are inconsistent with our judgments of real worth. People give preference to alternatives that are less than ideal, all things considered.

In the passages from Erasmus one finds the same confusion between perversity and akrasia found in the case of Poe. On the one hand, Erasmus states that what the person knows is forbidden is for him more desirable than anything else – this is perverse. On the other hand, he says that we prefer our second-best alternative to the best one – which is nothing but akrasia.

The core question concerns the characterization of perverse values themselves. Let us propose a thesis about motivations: that wickedness interests those perverts who are without akrasia and who also know what they are doing. The Sade-problem in ethics would then be this: how can a person subscribe to the Poe-definition of perversity without at the same time creating a new set of personal preferences? If he cannot, his counter-goals may be perfectly agreeable, even if they happen to express novel values. The corollary of the problem is that if Sade promotes certain values in order to violate them, how can he avoid the accusation that he is akratic, that is, that he chooses according to his second-best preference? If this happens, the person is not perverse. Combining both cases, we can ask how a continent person can remain wicked – i.e., not endorse a set of values which is different from the original set, but is still a fixed collection of assumed values. If the person is not akratic, he seems to make a mere error.

Of course, Sade himself is no ethical reformer. He is not inventing novel values. He wants to avoid the Pious Principle and promote value-relativity. How can he achieve something like this? He does it by presenting a non-Epicurean view of aggressive and submissive pleasures and by denying the conclusion to the effect that viciousness is in fact a value. He aims at confusion and nothingness.

# 2

# THE MEANING OF PERVERSION

We need conceptual tools to allow us to talk more technically about evil as it emerges from a certain kind of psychological mechanism, namely, from the wicked will. A wicked person wishes vicious actions to take place which will result in some harm or injury to the victims. In the conventional sense of the term, he will be guilty in bringing such things about; yet he may refuse to accept any measure of self-condemnation. In everyday experience we are familiar with such a phenomenon, and say that wicked persons are somehow alienated. This negative attitude of alienation may be philosophically misleading, however; we think we know what wickedness is, but when we analyze it the conviction tends to vanish.

The phenomena in question are elusive and slippery in terms of the analytical language of action theory. It is difficult to understand how plain evil can motivate anybody or, for that matter, dominate anyone's imagination. Evil may not even be a coherent idea. Perhaps it is the mere absence of the good and disappears on independent scrutiny? One often entertains strange and impossible thoughts if one finds them stimulating. We may also call fantasy, imagination, and fiction wicked on the grounds that idle ideas of evil predominate over other mental contents. Thomas Hobbes formulates a similar point: "An Anatomist, or a Physitian may speak, or write his judgement of unclean things; because it is not to please, but profit: but for another man to write his extravagant, and pleasant fancies of the same, is as if a man, from being tumbled into the dirt, should come and present himselfe before good company."[1] In the same way, evil may be a mere aberration of the subconscious mind, an idea one may occasionally call up to stimulate the bored ego. Alternatively, such thoughts can also be the painful compulsions of a distracted mind.

For example, suppose S does x, which is called evil by others, simply because S wishes to refute the opinion that x is bad by doing x. In this case the opinions entertained by others, however negative, are independent of S's subjective values. If S errs, he does something evil while aiming at his own good. In such a case one may say that the decision represents the person's own good, which happens to violate the good of others. Had the agent fully understood what he aimed at, he would not have done it. Sometimes a person is morally blind or is an egoist; hence his inability to observe the good of others. Alternatively, his reasoning does not take into account the universality of moral norms, and this mistake explains his wicked action: he was not fully aware that he did an immoral thing. Perversity, on the contrary, is a deliberate will to do what is wrong, knowing that it is wrong. Such purely subversive motivation is also exemplified by an agent who acts against his own balanced interests. We call it imprudence, or even self-destruction.

I shall argue that the myth of evil contains a hard kernel. Yet one cannot argue that only if the evil ideas somehow refute their fictional status and therefore demand their own realization – if they are motives – can the person be said to be wicked. It is a mistake to argue that ideas of viciousness turn into vicious ideas because they become personal motives for action. The hard problem is that the term "motive" in its ordinary sense does not make sense in this context. A wicked person needs mechanisms which take him beyond rational choice. Wickedness, unlike moral weakness, does not presuppose choice, as I shall show. Therefore, it is possibly misleading to claim that a person's perverse will desires something wickedly. This may entail that he aims at evil goals; whether these are harmful or merely shameful makes no difference. However, it is true that a wicked person is happy with himself and is content with his own intentions and desires. Perversity, in the sense of Poe-perversity which was defined in chapter 1, is not a source of negative emotions, except perhaps of regret that the person cannot be even more wicked than he already is. To understand what such a strange motivational possibility means, we need an analysis of perversity, together with an explanation of the possibility of the immoral life.[2] We shall ultimately locate perversity somewhere between a causal mechanism and a full-fledged intentional action. A person may choose to do something incomprehensible.

## HARM TO MORAL SELF

I shall first argue that perversity entails harm to self; a wicked person hurts himself through his intentions and actions. It is, therefore, a mistake to think that wickedness could be only other-regarding; if it is, then the notion of wickedness is different from the present concept of Poe-perversion. I shall now explicate these points. Let me first weaken the notion of the wickedness of the will to the point where the agent himself cannot be said to understand that his motives and goals are vicious. In this case there is no question of the person wishing to hurt himself. He may be an egoist or someone who makes the mistake of believing that there is no such thing as the ethical life or, if there is, its principles do not apply in his present situation. He may even be incapable of moral thought; he may be someone Aristotle calls a brutish person:

> we call the lower animals neither temperate nor self-indulgent except by a metaphor, and only if some one race of animals exceeds another as a whole in wantonness, destructiveness, and omnivorous greed; these have no power of choice or calculation, but they *are* departures from the natural norm, as, among men, madmen are. Now brutishness is a less evil than vice, though more alarming.[3]

This description applies to man, too.

Such a notion is not different from the standard psychological one which is borrowed from Freud. Freud explains his concept of perversion by reference to normal sexual behavior, as follows:

> The normal sexual aim is regarded as being the union of the genitals in the act known as copulation. . . . The situation only becomes pathological when the longing for the fetish passes beyond the point of being merely a necessary condition attached to the sexual object and actually *takes the place* of the normal aim, and, further, when the fetish becomes detached from a particular individual and becomes the *sole* sexual object. These are, indeed, the general conditions under which mere variations of the sexual instinct pass over into pathological aberrations.[4]

The medical model of perversion omits the problem of free motivation, namely, what intentions and values guide behavior in its perverse or abnormal mode and help it to overcome guilt, disgust, retribution, and shame. On the contrary, a pervert is either sick or incapable, and accordingly he suffers from a condition he cannot prevent or deflect. Such a person is not akratic but brutish in the Aristotelian sense. The key feature of his behavior is its deviation from the standards of normality, if this can be explained causally. An akratic needs education, whereas both a brute and a Freudian patient need a cure.

We observe here that the modern notion of perversity is sexually loaded, although I want to use the term "perversity" in a much wider sense. It seems that the philosophical context is too general and abstract to allow us to reap profit from psychological literature. Of course, perversity may be an illness of the mind; but again, as I shall show, such a pathological model either actively conceals the main issue or fails to illuminate it. The concept of illness permits society to dispose of the perverse person and of anyone whose mental constitution comes too close to perversity. The classification erects a barrier between the sick and the healthy, and solicits the use of different principles of explanation with respect to each group. The control-notion of morality is not applicable in the present context, though. Indeed, there is no convincing way to understand perversity, if one uses two different canons of understanding, one for the prudent and healthy life, and another for irrationality and psychopathology.

The division of evil into two different categories is evident early in intellectual history. It appears, for instance, in the *Malleus Maleficarum*. We need only to verify how the distinction between utility and intention is applied in the *Malleus*:

> A thing is evil in that it takes away from the good; therefore where there is the more good lost, there the greater evil has gone before. But the sin of our first parent [Adam] brought the greatest loss both to nature and to grace.... But on the contrary side: that which includes the most causes of evil is the greater evil, and such are the sins of witches. For they can, with God's permission, bring every evil upon that which is good by nature and in form, as is declared in the Papal Bull.[5]

Adam's actions created nasty consequences. Also, bad intentions are mentioned as the causes of evil, and this is why witches are so frightening to any decent person. Adam's sin was unintentional but had bad consequences, while witches can do harm intentionally because of their devilish powers.

However, even this textbook on witches fails to give an account of their motivation. We understand that because witches are the devil's own people, they do evil things. Yet this does not explain much. Why do they like to castrate men, for instance, if they know it is wrong? How can they prefer evil to good even though they are aware of religion? Does the devil simply deceive them, or are they insane? The *Malleus* provides no explanation.

In order to shake the medical model, we shall first pay attention to the following analytical distinction. A perverse person's conduct creates harm necessarily, as the result of his action and not only as its consequence. What is the difference here between "results" and "consequences"? Closing a window results in a closed window, and has the consequence of reducing the draught in the room. In the same way, a wicked action always results in harm and may also have harm as its consequence. Or it may even show a net benefit. Since, however, the consequences do not really matter, we are dealing here with a non-consequentialist normative framework. The action is wicked when it breaches values in a more demanding sense than that of brutishness, insanity, and error, so that its (intentional or internal) results are harmful. The (causal or external) consequences do not matter.

In order to understand this further, let us explore two different normative views that may be dubbed "Kantianism" and "utilitarianism." In the first, the agent's intentions determine the value of his decisions. In the second, the consequences of his action to the welfare of others are important. Sade is Kantian in the above sense, and so is his concept of perversion.[6] In his case consequentialism is of secondary interest, although it is not of zero importance. Now, a utilitarian agent may dream of a perfect crime – one that harms others but which brings no loss to the agent himself. He is able to rob without any personal risk. In this case it is impossible to argue that the immoral agent harms himself when he realizes his wicked will. The evil aspect of the crime is, accordingly, defined only in terms of another's harm and injury. The consequences of actions are regretted by a group of persons which excludes the agent himself. If the culprit feels remorse, it is because he sympathizes with the victims.

The Kantian view is different. If one intends to do something wrong, one must understand the situation in terms of one's own values. This means that one knows what is right and wrong and yet chooses the wrong, or evil, alternative. Again, the logical conclusion to be drawn is that the good or even the best option is sidestepped. To do evil in the Kantian universe is to bring about, necessarily, intrinsic harm or injury to oneself; the moral alternative is the best one, and it is freely chosen by an autonomous person. This would not be so if one could use the personal consequences of the action as a compensation by means of which one could deflect the accusation to the effect that the original intention was sub-optimal. Because the (external) consequences do not matter, such an easy possibility does not arise.

If we are allowed to use action-language, we would say that all evil choices produce harm to self, or violate the autonomy of the person (to use a genuinely Kantian phrase). Accordingly, the moral option is the best one, and to deviate from it entails the agent's personal injury in a non-consequentialist sense. The agent sidesteps an option that is to his own good because ethics and responsibility are self-regarding matters. One's freedom is at stake. Thus all evil is self-violation, as a Kantian must argue.

It is indeed important to show that moral perversion, according to its Poe-definition, must aim at the agent's own harm at least indirectly. The argument goes that it is self-evidently true that the person should do the right thing, but he nevertheless desires its opposite and therefore violates the rights and values of others. Because he should not do this, his intentions do not serve his own good in a right way, and this constitutes a violation of the self.

Certainly one can try to dismiss a view like this by arguing that the agent may intend to harm others but not himself, so that the injury to self is only a secondary effect. To counter this last point, I want to direct attention to the fact that even in a situation described in terms of the victims' suffering, the agent violates his own overriding principles of conduct. Perhaps he does not intend to harm himself, but what he wants to achieve can be realized only at the cost of harm to self. Regardless of the actual consequences of one's wicked intentions, harm to self is among the results of the action. The fact that wickedness entails harm to self at the level of the results of action, but not at that of its consequences, has certain far-reaching implications. Sade is a proto-Kantian in his counter-ethics, and I shall argue that such a methodical choice is a necessary condition of the success of his perverse project.

Now, if I am wrong, and moral perversion is not analogous to irrationality in the sense of self-destruction, much of what Sade says – or for that matter, what Freud says – cannot be understood: "A sadist is always at the same time a masochist."[7] Freud suggests the following point. It is easy to suppose that the sexual motive in question is at least partially an agent-centered one, or that perverse acts are performed because of some relevant feelings of personal satisfaction. This must be the case with regard to a masochist, because he is the one who suffers; and if a masochist is also a sadist, the self-centered motivation should accompany the latter phenomenon, too. A sadist seems to hurt only others, but this cannot be true. To hurt others is transgressive in the same way as to hurt oneself. Therefore, what Freud says may indeed be true.

It follows that the sexual arousal that is generated by the two different acts – sadism and masochism – rests on the same self-centered basis. Yet a consequentialist cannot provide an account of this fact. For him, sadism is a pleasure which does not presuppose harm to self. It is the inflicting of suffering on others. Masochism, on the contrary, is a Poe-perversion, because the person wants to be humiliated and hurt. In other words, the fact that a masochist and a sadist are identical does not make sense in terms of the consequentialist ethic; the types of pleasure are unconnected. Because the consequences of sadism and masochism are not similar, there is little reason, on these grounds, to think that they belong together. In terms of non-consequentialism, on the contrary, it is easy to see that both perversions must belong together because they entail the self-destructive (imprudent) results of actions.

When a perverse agent activates his plan, the case resembles a supererogatory one, like saintly or heroic action where a good person suffers in the service of others. It is clear that a moral and a wicked person alike may suffer from harm which results from their own conduct. Yet the cases are radically different. I do not want to explain the difference by referring to benefit versus suffering of others. It seems desirable to understand wickedness as an agent-centered concept, which is the reason why I introduced the idea of harm to self. However, it may now look too weak if his good choices may also create harm to the agent. Obviously, the concept of self-centered harm must be different in the two relevant cases if supererogation and perversity are two different things.

A key difference between moral perversity and supererogatory action seems to be that a pervert deals with harm-as-result and a saint with harm-as-consequence. The latter agent does not breach his own values, unlike the former. Therefore, whatever happens to the saint, he may consider it as a mere consequence of his choice. When a man rushes to a burning house to rescue some children, the burns he suffers are merely accidental (though predictable) in relation to his plan of action. When a hooligan stabs an old lady, he wants to hurt her, which logically entails an immoral motive. The harm is internal to the plan of action.

The problem still remains that if a saint takes risks which count as irrational, then he breaches the personal norms of prudence, and supererogatory choices may again look like perversions. We can, however, sharpen our intuitions and expel the doubts concerning the nature of supererogation by using a distinction made by Hobbes: "many times the injury is received by one man, when the dammage redoundeth to another." Hobbes gives the example of a servant who is ordered to give money to a stranger. If he does not, the "Injury is done to the master, whom he had before covenanted to obey." The stranger suffers damage because he does not get the money; but since he has no rightful claim to it, he does not suffer any injury.[8] In this way a right-violation constitutes harm which is different from mere loss. In the supererogatory case the agent does not suffer injury even if he may damage himself. A pervert suffers injury, even if he avoids all the damage.

In the prudential case, a saint discounts the risks to the degree that he considers the helping of others to be more valuable than his own safety. He may err, but he does not consciously violate his own rights, duties, or even the norms of prudential rationality. If he does, he is a pervert. Brutishness, in Aristotle's conception, is not said to harm the agent himself, but it is a well-known point in the history of philosophy that breaching of values is an intrinsic harm, as Hobbes's "injury" makes clear. Even Julien Offray de La Mettrie – to pick a scandalous author Sade loved – makes the point when he discusses virtue and vice. La Mettrie writes:

> there is so much pleasure in doing good, in recognizing and appreciating what one receives, so much satisfaction in practising virtue, in being gentle, humane, kind, charitable, compassionate and generous ... that I consider as sufficiently punished any one who is unfortunate enough not to have been born virtuous.[9]

Concerning crime and punishment, he maintains that "they [criminals] are sufficiently punished by their own conscience, their first executioner." When an action is done intentionally, a purely consequentialist approach to ethics fails to capture this entailment. The "first executioner" does not emerge. Therefore we should not read La Mettrie consequentialistically in this context. His conscience approaches the Kantian one.

Sade echoes the idea that a person tends to regret his evil deeds. The difference is, of course, that Sade wants to stop the executioner who inhibits one's transgressive action:

> Veritable wisdom, my dear Juliette, consists not in repressing one's vices, for, vices constituting, practically speaking, the sole happiness granted us in life, so to do would be to adopt the role, as it were, of one's own executioner.

Sade claims he knows how one should act:

> you permit me now to indicate the manner of totally silencing that inner and confusion-breeding voice... it consists simply of reiterating the deeds that have made us remorseful, in repeating them so often that the habit either of committing these deeds or of getting away scot-free with them completely undermines every possibility of feeling badly about them.[10]

Sade says, in effect, that vice is an acquired character-trait that allows one to avoid the feelings of guilt, which otherwise follow from evil intentions. Habits, which are learned automatisms, make one act without deliberation or choice on a prudential basis, and – paradoxically – produce harm to self. Poe-perversity is based on an action-generating mechanism which is independent of choice according to one's best option. This is the reason why he has adopted its use and, indeed, why he is devious. The mechanism chooses a bad alternative when it works like a person-external source of causal influence. Thus habits explain the lack of guilt, but not yet, perhaps, the presence of the maximal pleasure to the pervert.

However, the connection of wickedness to perversion can now be stated: the wicked will entails the violation of a person's integrity; and yet to do wrong is somehow stimulating and rewarding, as Sade tries to show. He suggests a mechanism which generates the doing of evil things, although the resulting benefit presupposes at least the agent's imprudence. In other words, without the special reward from the activation of the habit, the combination of the harm-to-self principle and the Poe-perverse behavior could not be understood from the Sadean perspective. We could not say why somebody wants to hurt others, but we would be stuck with the case where the agent chooses against his best prudential values and rights, and is simply miserable.

In order to understand Sade, we must deal with the problem of transgressive behavior. Much of his language is moralistic, and yet he refers perverse motives and their rewards back to the agent himself. One of our main problems will be to try to understand this mysterious reward which follows from Poe-perverse choices, independently of whether they are habitual or not. The role of habit is to make the perverse pleasure possible in the long run, when disgust and remorse tend to extinguish the relevant motives.

## IMPRUDENT PREFERENCE-FORMATION

Certainly what philosophers have sometimes called the state of nature allows one all the freedom one may desire. In the state of nature, all violence is one's right, and as such is innocent. As Hobbes puts it: "in such a condition, every man has a Right to every thing; even to one anothers body."[11] Social life, as a reaction to this anarchy, creates its own logic of normality to the extent that objectivized value judgments emerge – and with them, ironically, the possibility of even more vicious social dreams. One now has something – civil laws, for instance – that one can violate. After morality and law emerge, a wicked person is able deliberately to do things which others interpret as injury to self and which look like mistakes.

The negative evaluation of wickedness of the will implies that the person lacks moral emotions, like remorse and resentment, which characterize guilt and motivate self-corrective action. In other words, the person does not wish to change the world he has helped to create. He may be, on the contrary, happy about what he has accomplished, or he may also construe his own relevant feelings in terms of pleasure. We hesitate. What is at issue here? What kind of fiction are we involved in? Perhaps it is impossible to think that harming oneself can be a source of pleasure and that the violation of moral prescriptions can be a source of satisfaction. If such perverse persons exist, they are truly wicked and bad, but we may see no reason for agreeing that they ever existed, except in fiction.

The normal possibilities of understanding practical reason and action must break down at perversity, as I shall argue. Regardless of this fact, only in the case of perversity do we face the ultimate test of evil. If there is real evil, perversity and wickedness of the will must exist. Otherwise there is only error in its two guises, namely, error that can be avoided and error that cannot, i.e., bad luck and brutishness. The real question is this: what does it mean to choose what one judges as one's worst alternative? To speak of such a choice indicates that, in the darkness of our own atavistic attitudes, we are in quest of a long-lost logic. I shall examine the analytical approach to decisions and try to clarify the issues behind imprudent action. After this we shall return to the mystery of the Asylum Poet and plunge into the realm of subconscious chaos. Prudence and akrasia must be forgotten. I shall try to show how their camouflage works.

To put all this in a more systematic way: suppose that the simple Aristotelian theory of good is valid in the way that it is understood by Hobbes, one of Sade's philosophical sources. Hobbes's claims are typically straightforward:

> The common name for all things that are desired, insofar as they are desired, is *good*; and for all things we shun, *evil*. ... Moreover, good (like evil) is divided into *real* and *apparent*. ... And whenever the major part be good, the series is said to be good, and is desired; on the contrary, if the major part be evil, and, moreover, if it be known to be so, the whole is rejected. Whence it happens that inexperienced men that do not look closely enough at the long-term consequences of things, accept what appears to be good, not seeing the evil annexed to it; afterwards they experience damage.[12]

What is good, for Hobbes, is that which is actually desired, and genuine good is what is desirable in the long run: safety and pleasure. Therefore evil is damage – but never injury – and appears to be a decisional error that is brought about by some kind of ignorance, mistake, or weakness. We are assumed to be weak and error-prone agents. For exactly this reason, it looks strange to say that one aims at something evil, if its only explanation is that one happens to like evil things. One cannot aim at evil, because logically speaking one's aims are the good of the person. All evil seems, therefore, to collapse back into akrasia, self-deception, and negligence. I shall next deal with two of these three alternatives, in order to show that wickedness of will is not reducible to either of them.

To look at these alternatives, let us suppose the following situation. Suppose a person has promised to go home before noon. He understands the idea of commitment, the value of honesty and reliability in social life, and he is also well informed about all the relevant facts. Nevertheless, instead of going home he stays with his friends. Under what conditions does this qualify as akrasia, negligence, or wickedness proper?

If one simplifies a little, weakness of the will, or akrasia, means that due to some lack of personal integrity, and more specifically some failure to realize his intentions, S chooses against what is known to be his best option.[13] Perversity also leads to deviant actions (or omissions), but it is unlike akrasia because no accusation of weakness can be directed against S. A non-akratic, or continent person, intends and wants and actualizes his best action alternative, at least when there is no overpowering unconscious competitor to it. Thus an akratic agent S knows that a given option, x, is his genuine good, and he is fully aware of the facts; yet he chooses something other than x. S does not want x. S somehow rejects the prescriptive or motivating quality of his own best option x and instead chooses something else. This is what I mean by saying S does not want x.

Suppose S's known primary value in his decision situation is x (to go home at noon), and he has committed himself to its value independently of his present wants and intentions. However, S does not *want* x, or he is not motivated to go home. The desire is missing, as we may explain the lack of wanting. At the same time S *intends*, or plans, to do x; which is to say that S's plan of action contains x as its goal. The plan and goal of action are both rational, or they include x as their dominating element. Nevertheless, S's personality is not fully integrated in relation to his present situation. His motives, or wants, are not aligned with his intentions, or plans and reasons. S fails to go home, because he wants something other than what he intends. Consequently, he stays with his friends. S is an incontinent person, at least if judged on the basis of this event.

Let us compare this scenario with one that would involve negligence. In this case S fails to want to go home, but he also fails to form the intention to do so. This double defect is typical of negligence, as I see it. The negligent agent, S, knows that commitment x is his best alternative, all things considered, but he does not want x, and x does not figure in his intentions. Therefore S not only shows less than ideal personal integrity, but he is also plainly irrational. S's intentions are not formed according to his own values. We may hesitate, but we can still call x S's best option, although the element of x is missing from his intentions, and thus x cannot figure in his practical reasoning; x is not even an object of deliberation in the decision environment. In this sense S is indeed negligent of his own values and good.

We can now take up the question of perversity and subversive motivation. In this case, perhaps, the psychological features of akrasia are reinforced to produce virtual negligence, as well as something more. Certainly, a wicked person does not intend to do good. What, therefore, is the extra factor? The answer lies in the fact that our hero does not want to go home because he (enigmatically) wants to harm himself. Therefore, given the features of the case, S's intentions, or plans, now aligned with his wants, though not with his values, should contain a self-destructive element. The difficulty here is that such a harmful element cannot be a new value, stronger than S's value profile. If we do not guard against such a possibility, we shall lose contact with common sense and come close to making perversity a *sui generis* phenomenon. It seems incomprehensible that some persons possess both self-destructive and overriding valuations.

If, however, such new and intrinsically negative values existed, the act of breaching them (and thereby doing good to oneself) would look like a new subversive motive. Any choice of action, based on one's desire to break the highest values, is equally subversive; perversity can entail the breaching of any value, even a self-destructive one. An infinite regress follows from this. If the breaking of a value is a new value, there is no highest value whose violation would guide one's (subversive) choice behavior. A simple paradox of perversion can be formulated: an agent S aims at x; therefore x is his good; but the notion of Poe-perversity applied to S's choices logically entails that x is not good. Moreover, if instead of x, S chooses something else, y, in that case y is his good and a value which he has not yet violated. Two interpretations can be given. First, there are some strange preferences which follow a rule like the following:

(a) xPSy, therefore S acts according to yPSx.

Agent S prefers x over y, but because he is a pervert he chooses y. Such a self-destructive rule turns one's preferences upside-down. The problem is that there is no reason to stop at y. One may turn y around too and end up with choosing x once again. If yPSx looks like the highest preference to S, he should choose according to it, or take x. Such strange cases are not well-defined principles of choice and action.

Second, there may be no preferences at all. Therefore choice cannot follow a rule. On the contrary, the following is the case:

(b) xPSy, therefore yPSx, which is a contradiction and makes S's choice between x and y impossible.

No action results. In other words, perverse S has two mutually inconsistent preference-relations and is unable to act. The first and the second formulation both have a uniform message. A perverse action cannot be understood as a rational choice. Sade is basically correct when he refers to something like habit as the method of overcoming the uneasiness that wickedness creates. According to Sade, habitual action transforms the remorse which is due to the harm to self into the pleasure which follows from breaking a norm. A bad habit is something other than a principle of individual choice. Rather it is a psychological mechanism which produces results that no rational choice can actualize. Such a mechanism is not always the result of habituation on the basis of one's own choices. According to Sade, it is often forced on the person through some more or less violent methods of initiation. However, one's wickedness must produce pleasure and be somehow motivating as well. In other words, if perverse action is based on habit, at least there must be room for desire to continue under the spell of the habit, as I shall show next.

## WEAKNESS AND CORE-PERVERSITY

I shall ask whether the logical structure of the habitual choice of the worst option is that of akrasia or negligence – and if it is not, what is it? Sade's habit-solution to the motivation which explains the wickedness of the will does not automatically solve the problem concerning structure. My answer will be that the explanation of wicked action starts from akratic and negligent action, but one needs also to refer to the pleasure which follows from one's habitual obedience to the harm-to-self principle, or from the reference to inconsistent preferences. In other words, habit explains the action which has an akratic structure, and the accompanying pleasures of transgression explain the acquisition, force, and stability of the bad habit. The best option when taken together with the habit is not the best one when considered independently of it.

Let us call the *core* of perversity that aspect of Poe-perversion which possesses the structure of akrasia or negligence. The point is that this core has a structural aspect which can be strengthened and transformed into real Poe-perversity by adding to it something like pleasure. The structure of perversion is akratic at its core, but the accompanying pleasure is also needed. I shall show how this idea works in due course, but the next task is to show that the core exists.

When we return to our main example, we notice that S wants neither to go home nor to keep his promise. However, his values figure in his intentions in an interesting way. The person is negligent of his own values in the sense that his intentions do not contain them as goals, but at the same time they contain the negations of these values, and in this roundabout manner the person is not all negligent. The values figure for him, if only together with the negation sign. My analytical hypothesis is this: core-perversity is moral negligence in the sense that S's best option, or value x, figures in his intentions, entailing that S has breached this value. S wants and intends not to do x, even when not-to-do-x is a value ranked below x.

Such a hypothesis makes core-perversity negligence under a special description of S's decisions. Take a case of negligence (where the as-clause designates an action and going home is S's best option):

(i) S neither intends nor wants to go home – as he stays with his friends.

Compare this with a different description of the same choice:

(ii) S neither intends nor wants to go home – as he violates his commitments.

Now, two different actions in the same situation are both explained by the lack of the same intention (of going home) and the lack of the same desire. Both cases therefore qualify as negligence, but only one also qualifies as core-perversity. Case (ii) alone mentions a transgression of values. Nevertheless, S violates his commitment simply by staying with his friends, so that in this context proposition (i) logically entails (ii), but not the other way around. A core-perverse action is, therefore, a subtype of negligent action.

The phrase "S stays with his friends" indicates to S how to violate his commitment, but there are also many other ways to do the same thing, i.e., anything which presupposes that S neither intends nor wants to go home. It seems that we can play with such descriptions as much as we like and make cases of negligence also expressions of core-perversion. Every instance of negligence will then look like a hidden intention to break a norm, or create harm to self. Though this is true, it does not yet capture the essence of the Poe-perversion, which is something more serious than negligence. No clear-cut connection between Poe-perversity and its core has yet been established.

Let us look next at a possible connection between akrasia and core-perversity. Suppose that S entertains the following two propositions:

(iii) S stays with his friends, although he intends to go home – as he promised.
(iv) S breaks his promise, although he intends to go home – as he promised.

In an akratic context S intends to go home, but he also does not want to go; and by so doing he will break his promise. It seems that these cases, including (iv), are intuitive. It is indeed possible to intend to do something good and at the same time hate doing it so deeply that one's efficient motivation becomes transgressive. Therefore, the problem is that the akrasia-type interpretation dictates that proposition (iii) logically entails (iv), and in this sense they are intimately related. They are two of the many possible descriptions under which the case is akratic. Nevertheless, (iv) is also mentioned as the core-perverse case.

The violation of an intention may occur in many different ways, for instance by S staying with his friends. A familiar problem then becomes visible, namely, that the subversive desire, even under a good intention, is not really a specified one. S breaks a rule, so that this case can be subsumed under a specific action-description which makes it look like a weakness. Yet the case is also different from akrasia. Even here core-perversity does not seem to have an identity of its own. On the contrary, S wants to do something which is against his good intention, and indeed any action compatible with the one that figures in (iv) will work equally well as a description of the perverse possibility, just as (iii) does. The conclusion is that the idea of core-perversity refers to what is common in all cases of motivated irrationality. They exemplify harm to self, and in this sense they are inadvisable actions.

If one's intuition dictates that Poe-perversity is a more serious problem than either akrasia or negligence, or its own core, it seems that the normal analytical action-theoretical tools do not explicate such an intuition correctly. Sometimes the transgressive motive is indeed a more demanding problem than that of an akratic or negligent action, yet its typical features cannot be seen because both akrasia and negligence entail core-perversity. To counter such a possibility, I shall suggest that a perverse motive must be described from the point of view of its special content. A genuine Poe-perverse motive is a pleasure which follows from habitual wrongdoing and which entails injury to self. It is different from weakness of the will and negligence, because it is not a failure of the agent's particular choice. Rather it is a mental mechanism which successfully realizes one's second-best options. The agent once chose the mechanism and now it works for him. It is easy to see that such an agent is idiosyncratic. In other words, perversity is a twisted approach to self-caused harm to self, following from the perception that one can enjoy one's weakness or even suffering. In this case one's will works because of the violation of values and intentions, and not (akratically) in spite of it.

To make sense of this theory, I want to suggest that when a Poe-perverse person neither wants nor intends to realize his best option, he expresses the need for an additional explanation of psychological facts. Such an explanation does not figure in akrasia and negligence, simply because they are weaknesses. Perversity is not a weakness, but neither can it be explained by means of something which is another value higher than the highest x. The analytical problem of core-perversity can be located just here. It is difficult to understand what such a non-valuational explanation is, if the account must be connected to S's intentions, plans, wants, and motives. Perhaps the only way out is to say that perverse motives are not matters of valuation and knowledge at all. When he thinks of going home at noon, the perverse person does not want or intend to go home, simply because of some emotion aroused by, say, his weakness, or his lack of rationality and integrity; instead, an overpowering emotion prevents him from leaving. In other words, the pervert has the habit of irrationality and he gets his enjoyment from it.

## FACTS OR FICTIONS?

I have conjectured that the perverse person learns that weakness has a stimulating effect on him and becomes habitually drawn towards akratic, self-deceptive, and negligent contexts whose limits he will promptly cross. He has become perverse because he is a person motivated by weaknesses. Poe-perversity is not grounded on failure. More exactly, negligence, akrasia, and Poe-perversity logically entail core-perversity, but not the other way round. Therefore, human irrationality provides only the starting point from which a Poe-perverse habit can be developed.

The pervert has learned that it is pleasant to be irrational, and the habit systematizes his errors. Here we have already gone beyond the limits of philosophical analysis. We must return to the empirical psychology of personality. I have followed Sade by postulating a special emotionally stimulating effect which irrationality and lack of integrity have on a certain type of personality. Accordingly, it is impossible to align Poe-perversity together with, say, akrasia. Akrasia and the other weaknesses do not presuppose any single type of personality. Anyone can err with respect to his values because of some special desires, although only special persons are capable of enjoying their errors.

It is sometimes possible not to care for one's values, because one has a defective character. However, this possibility is not an empirical notion, but rather a logical counterpart of normalcy and of perfection.

Whatever works for us may also fail us. The ascriptions of Poe-perversity, on the contrary, operate in terms of some extra desires which only special personalities possess. In this sense perversity is an empirical notion, and its existence is a hard fact. The possibility of the weakness of the will is a logical problem, while that of Poe-perversity is not.

The person did not want to go home at noon, because he was going to break his promise. He is accustomed to break his promises because of some stimulus-quality in such decisions. But the decision-like event is not guided by another, higher case-specific value. The person just breaks the norm and enjoys it. It is Sade's task to tell a convincing story of this anomic possibility. However, I do not believe that one can develop a non-empirical and analytical theory of perversion. Neither need one stay content with empirical psychology, especially if we accept the proposition that perversion is not an illness which must be dealt with by means of psychiatry. Normative aberrations are difficult to handle empirically, simply because the routines are not pathological. In a sense, this topic defies both strictly logical analysis and simple-minded empirical study, and is therefore disturbing. But it is also easy to understand. A case may sound familiar even when it never seems to be important enough to make it a typical element in our cognitive life. Perversity, as aberration, emerges only in some special case, as when a personality and its environment are strangely twisted together. Knowledge of such idiographic exceptions is outside psychology.

We must try to understand pleasure. I shall suggest that Sade fictionalizes the topic. Some studies on SM – the sado-masochistic sexual subculture – have reached interesting conclusions concerning enjoyable cruelty. This is a case where victims seek painful social positions. SM communities display features which are properly understood as games rather than as reality. The actors in the game want neither to hurt others nor to get hurt themselves:

> Highly formalized, social interaction rituals or ceremonies may bring together individuals who would otherwise be dangerous enemies, without risk of their even being rude (much less violent) with each other. . . . Gay practitioners of SM have developed an etiquette equivalent to that of political opponents shaking hands and eating with each other.[14]

They design complex fictions with rules, values, roles, and mythologies which allow them to stage enjoyable scenes of cruelty. Leather outfits and whips symbolize real weapons of humiliation and punishment. To any external observer this behavior is difficult to understand, since it displays at once a high degree of violence and also tenderness and love. The worlds of fact and fiction are so mixed together that the participants may enjoy thoughts of pain and cruelty along with real violence. The demarcation between love and pain, terror and enjoyment, is not consistently drawn. Only the limit-cases need to be known. Perhaps the details of the rules cannot be clear and consistent, even if they do not express "a confusion of pain and pleasure, but rather of a redefinition of pain."[15] To speak of a definition in this context may be over-optimistic, simply because the scene to be defined is neither that of a laboratory nor of a butcher's shop, and still less that of a family or a law court.

Games are fiction made real. I shall look at some narrative sources to find a convincing rhetorical description of the enigmas of evil. One may grasp something essential concerning the phenomenology of evil by using literary sources which combine philosophical concerns with artistic freedom of expression. We need not only clarity. Sade's fictions of perverse behavior and the attraction of plain evil undermine explanations of perverse action and hint at actual errors and weaknesses behind wicked motivations.

Sade claims that evil cannot be handled in any clear-cut way. To anticipate, the perverse motive is such that the agent transcends the limits of reason while reaching towards mere nothingness. Such a void, or pleasure in the technical sense, is what motivates him. Thus we can understand the meaning of pleasure by first referring to the harm-to-self principle and then by adding to it some empirical (explanatory) facts. The resulting motive is strange, however, and can only be described by fictional means. Moreover, rhetorical plans cannot be turned into reality except by means of games, like those played by the SM-people. Sade transforms those games into theater productions. In the theater even the most perverse behavior may look real, as Sade emphasizes. Indeed, if a factual description is impossible, these are the only available alternatives. Sade's mixed philosophy which combines narrative, theater, moral rhetoric, and philosophical speculation may provide us with a picture of evil. Sade is a writer whose aims are philosophical, whose technique is literary, and whose facts are fiction.

# 3

# NATURE AND THE VOID

"Pleasure is, so to speak, nature's vengeance"; therefore pleasure cannot be understood without nature.[1] Pleasure is a complex phenomenon in Sade's theory, and we have already seen how important it is when we try to understand perverse motivation. However, to maintain that a theory of pleasure presupposes nothing but a reference to nature is to exaggerate; pleasure is a cycle of sensual, cerebral, and orgiastic stages, where the middle point is artificial and thus independent of nature. Yet perverse motivation is first a reaction to natural stimuli, and it must return back to nature via discharge. Sade's word for sexual climax is, indeed, "discharge". The libertine, either a man or a woman, goes off like a gun. "Orgasm" refers to a mental complex which is misleading because Sade wants to be a mechanistic and naturalist philosopher. He deals with actions and reactions, like stimuli and discharges. Of course thoughts and feelings are important but in the end we have a mere discharge, not orgasm. Another important point must be kept in mind, namely, Sade thinks that women climax just like men do. They discharge. So much hinges on this notion that its metaphoric roots and implications must be kept in mind. What we have here is detonation which destroys its own environment. This is important unlike the feelings of pleasure as such. The latter is just psychology. Sade is interested in fiction.

At first sight, Sade wants to be a naturalist and an atheistic philosopher. In his novels the libertine heroes give long accounts of their metaphysical speculations. They place great weight on quite technical and academic points of philosophy in the conduct of their lives; they would be logical positivists if they lived in the twentieth century. For Sade, science makes ethics look like a catalog of unreasonable commands or rhetorical tricks, such as persuasive definitions and noisy exclamations. The principle of nature which governs such verbal behavior is that of universal chaos, death, and destruction, and of the blind proliferation of life. In both of its aspects the world is a vortex of forces which neither display any natural or rational laws, nor show the influence of a benevolent supernatural mind. The injustice of social life and experience in general show that everything leads to destruction and to rebirth in one form or another. Chaos and death also imply rebirth; nature is equally malevolent and productive. The creative aspect is random. Millions of people die, and even more are born.

## THE TWO NOTIONS OF NATURE

Sade's nature is a destructive force whose influence provides the frame for human action and its causal consequences.[2] From the metaphysical point of view, nature is not a static thing, some kind of an external world, but a dynamic principle or force, almost like a living being. It even seems to have a will of its own. Therefore, Sade cannot be understood as speaking of dead matter. Nature appears as *conatus* and teleological principle. However, Sade's laws are unlike those which Thomas Aquinas claimed to exist in nature. Such laws represent some kind of prescriptive facts or universally valid norms that are binding on all and transparent to right reason. Sade's nature possesses no values, but destroys everything. This law of destruction or entropy (if such a negative norm exists) should lead to the mature person's self-destruction. Suicide is a norm which is easy to satisfy and has only a trivial content: kill yourself because death and destruction are everywhere. But Sade cannot mean this. We shall study the destructive principle of nature and the resulting state of nature. Nature annihilates things and thus creates the void; the route, however, is not easy to track. Ruins, as the word suggests, are messy.

Though the use of the principle of nature leads Sade to ethics and aesthetics, this much can be said about its metaphysical aspects. Since the principle represents chaos, or quite literally entropy, it does not leave any room for such principles as consistency of its ends. Sade does not say that the principle is a scientific law of nature in addition to some superimposed anthropomorphic goals and values, so that one could derive predictions and advice from them. Such predictions would presumably be equally valid for all people. To say something like this is to misunderstand the extent to which Sade is a radical and subversive writer. He may speak at times as if the principle of nature were a scientific law of destruction. Nevertheless, this hypothesis is refuted by the fact that such a law applies only to some people and not to others; or to put this point more accurately, its application varies enormously with regard to people with different moral, intellectual, and social statuses. A person may play around with the principle and utilize it for his own personal advantage. A wicked person may destroy others and flourish as well. Such a person may also claim that the principle of nature operates through his decisions, and may benefit from this idea. If, on the contrary, the law of nature is a universal principle of entropy, that of unavailable energy, the wicked person cannot avoid its grip. Moreover, if it is an overriding moral principle, the person should destroy himself, too. According to Sade's own subversive logic, neither conclusion follows. Some people are not destroyed, and by destroying others they may at once follow and transgress the law of nature. According to Sade, all laws and principles must be broken during the course of a wicked career, and this applies to the law of nature too, if it exists. Some of Sade's libertines even want to destroy nature itself. Like tragic heroes, they insist on doing the impossible.

It is easy to admit that the theater of terror achieves a degree of calamity at the fictional level, but the principle of nature may demand the destruction of both the human and the artificial. If this is so, the heroes' struggle for self-preservation and success in life contradicts the norms derivable from the principle of nature. Juliette loves money and an affluent life-style. However, if it is one's natural duty to destroy everything, why does she hesitate and refuse to include her own life in what she means by everything? There is also a weaker interpretation of such an existential dilemma. It denies the existence of teleology and argues that life and death are indifferent to nature. According to this, one should not care about what one is doing; whatever one does is equally meaningless. Under this interpretation, however, it is difficult to understand the source of Sadean pleasure. The human agent would face a mute and blind enemy whose operational principles he cannot understand, and which imply frustration rather than enjoyment. I shall discuss both interpretations, although my conclusion will be that the latter is the one that Sade has in mind.

A sharpening of the second interpretation of nature can be suggested: natural laws and the principle of natural activity constitute a myth (the term "nature" here designating the essence of the world, or everything that is real). Thus we get rid of the question of the meaning of laws, which otherwise represents an insoluble problem. Sade himself does not entertain a pseudo-scientific theory of these things. On the contrary, he alludes to the myth of the natural which destroys. As a story with veiled meaning, the myth covers all that is essential about life. In this sense the principle of nature is an allusion to the truth that the world is chaotic. In other words, (causal) consequences of actions are uncontrollable, unlike (intentional) results which represent what is artificial in the social environment. In this chapter I shall attempt to elucidate Sade's vision.

The allegorical interpretation of Sade's nature reveals the foundation upon which the rest of his philosophy is erected. Everything is random, so that whatever one enjoys is a matter of scavenging, or of indiscriminately consuming what happens to be available. The world is a giant corpse upon which man feeds. A scavenger is a restless wanderer who can never afford to stop; he has no power. Therefore, whatever he produces or consumes is waste, like excrement, as Sade emphasizes.

Such is the scavenger's view that emerges when we are clear about the metaphysics of nature itself. This study will lead us towards the second approximation of the psychology of pleasure – its cerebral mode – understood as a revenge of natural boredom upon innocent victims who represent nature under their guise of virgin innocence, or virtue. Pleasure, which is nature's vengeance, is transformed into reaction towards nature: the intolerably uncontrollable sensual irritation is directed against innocent victims via pain and mental anguish. But this presupposes mastery over what is natural. The result is a skillfully built artificial world. The avenger will ultimately turn into a predator in his social life, because there he can track down his prey. The human development is from scavenger to avenger to predator. It leads from shit, through murder and torture, towards discharge. Coprophilia, necrophilia, and nothingness illustrate the three stages of man's cosmic fate.

Sade's concept of nature must be understood as the map of a road from vulgar materialism to hell. External atoms and forces are transformed, step by step, into the myth of evil in man. D. H. Lawrence illustrates perfectly the Sadean struggle against nature in this mad urge to destroy everything meaningful. In *Women in Love*, Birkin, who has been ill, has been traveling in France. Ursula, depressed, walks at night by the pond, upon the mirror-like surface of which the moon is reflected. Birkin suddenly emerges, like a *deus ex machina*, and confronts the female symbol of the moon, bright and well defined. He fails to understand the situation that he discovers. "There wouldn't have to be any truth, if there weren't any lies," he says. "Then one needn't assert anything." Therefore he wants to destroy the lie which is facing him, the simple, well-defined, bright image of womanhood:

> And he was not satisfied. Like a madness, he must go on. He got large stones, and threw them, one after the other, at the white-burning centre of the moon, till there was nothing but a rocking of hollow noise, and a pond surged up, no moon any more, only a few broken flakes tangled and glittering broadcast in the darkness, without aim or meaning, a darkened confusion, like a black and white kaleidoscope tossed at random.

What is clear and transparent cannot be changed, but it cannot be stated either. Birkin behaves like a madman. Yet rage brings him beyond language, as torture does, and satisfies him. But the moon always comes back: "a distorted, frayed moon was shaking upon the waters again, reasserted, renewed." Lawrence suggests that the pure feeling devoid of language and truth is like the paradisal bird that can never be netted. The moon can be broken up, but it will return exactly as it was. Nothing has been changed, because nothing has altered; the processes of nature are beyond human malevolence. They are illusory reflections of a reality which is deeper than the probes of experience and language. At the same time, the myth of nature, in the Laurentian allegory, is the essence of woman.[3]

A Sadean person turns his rage upon things which he can neither control nor violate. Therefore Sade's pseudo-materialist metaphysics has no scientific basis other than its dynamic force, which produces some random causal consequences. Its basis is also strictly anti-religious. In his revolt against Christianity, Sade dreams of a principle of nature which is the negation of all things Christian. In this dream, there are no gods, and nature itself is the pantheist and counter-Spinozistic evil. Sade's nature tends to acquire the features of an object of worship, as if Sade himself fought a losing struggle against such an anthropomorphic idea. He wants a dead nature, but nature's forces also require attention and respect. Sade never quite shakes such a pseudo-teleological interpretation of nature, however hard he tries.

The simplest possible interpretation of Sade is in terms of the concept of nature that makes the world external to the individual. As a pseudo-materialist, Sade would agree that nature as such is eternal and indestructible. But that fact offers him no personal consolation. All things die so that something else may be born. Our souls perish. According to this simple interpretation, only matter and force are real, and that is why they cannot die: under the blind forces of life and death nature just changes. Nature destroys and procreates all the time. In the Sadean view, creation itself is chaotic because it can neither be controlled nor utilized. Whatever is born represents an enigma and even a threat.

## NATURE AND VALUE

Sade's anxious gaze focuses on forms which come out from the dark, and flicker and vanish without allowing him to grasp them. Whether one wants to call something birth or death is quite idiosyncratic. Murder and the refusal to procreate are the two great natural vices, so that the act (murder) and its omission (refusal to procreate) are interchangeable. Murder is creative, since it produces a new state of affairs, death, and a corpse. Non-procreation is more negative, because it results in absolute nothingness. Nothing happens, so that omission is directly associated with voidness. Murder creates death, work excrement, and the refusal to procreate an empty slot in the structure of being. There is nothing else to consume but waste, yet it can only be consumed at the cost of repetition, which leads nowhere. Since nature is chaos, no moral directive can be derived from it. Nothing can be learned from confusion. However, it is clear that Sade also gives nature a didactic role.

The logic of the simplest principle of nature is clear in Sade's writings, but that is not the complete story. Why does Sade want to take nature, which is a randomizing device, as a practical guideline? Perhaps he refused to tolerate learned and calm argumentation about the principles of hell, or about the irony of living well. The relation between nature and Sade's ethics is the same as that between philosophy and orgiastic pleasure. The heroes start their truth-seeking philosophizing in the best scientific tradition. After getting their ideas straight, they are ready to proceed to crime, which produces mad rage and virtual insanity. Accordingly, the principle of nature is the first stepping-stone on the way to ethics proper. Ultimately, the libertines care about neither the metaphysics of nature nor its permissiveness. They hate it, like they hate philosophy; yet because the heroes confront nature as the symbol of what is negative and chaotic, they cannot alienate themselves from it. They are perverts. Sade moves from an alienated nature towards its immanence within the person: external chaos is represented by sexual climax and discharge. By means of a myth, nature is ultimately defined as transgression. This myth of being defines what libertines are.

The destructive principle is not impossible to understand. Sade needs an overarching view which provides support for his anti-moral and narrative fiction. He achieves this by stipulating that whatever human goals and values there may be, they will ultimately lead to suffering, death, and destruction, and to the multiplication of things. The world is shit – the symbol of uselessness – since nature is a random device, independent of human goals and intentions. One cannot control or even follow nature. Such a principle unifies his metaphysics of materialism, his atheism, his hedonism, his life in prisons, and his theory of the subversive literary style. Everything can be understood from a single point of view, which therefore looks attractive to Sade. At the same time, nature as a general explanatory scheme cannot lead us far into the realm of terror.

The simple and basic principle of nature is either random or causal; therefore it cannot be teleological and value-bound, except deceptively. Nevertheless, Sade derives certain key aspects of his normative ethics from nature, by saying simply that because nature destroys, we should destroy too. But sometimes he refuses to draw this conclusion, asserting instead that if a person understands the meaning of the principle correctly, he can destroy without being destroyed. In this way, the principle offers a justificatory argument for the wicked person, and shows him a way out of the maelstrom of meaningless suffering and death. Moreover, the laws of nature may even be utilized instrumentally for one's own benefit. Such a far-flung interpretation, which Sade announces repeatedly, indicates that nature has a deeper meaning than a blind materialism may allow.

The principle of nature is deceptive, though. Since natural processes lead to their proper ends, it looks teleological, and this should be taken into account. The world is what it is, and humans must recognize this and live accordingly. The argument continues: human beings are natural creatures, and therefore the principle of nature applies to them. When people live their lives, they behave as highly motivated, destructive, and violent animals. People find the fulfillment of their mature desires in the life led according to the prescriptions of violence. Yet they are nothing but bloodthirsty scavengers who consume whatever dirt emerges from the processes of decay. Nature's promises are deceptive.

Nature is cruel and the lot of man is tragic, because contrary to what may appear to be the case, nothing allows people to be violent. That would entail the control and exploitation of nature, which they cannot achieve. The violent animal fails to destroy, because nature provides only waste for him to play with. Instead of being what he is, he becomes a scavenger. To consume what is already consumed – shit – is to share what is decomposed and without use or function. This is the essence of circularity. Therefore Sade's counter-ethical problem is to show that to consume waste is orgiastic. Anyone who can prove this coprologic theorem deserves to be read. Jane Gallop writes about it: "The turd, like the corpse, ought to be left behind in any universal process."[4] A pervert refuses to honor this intuition. He plays with the corpse and consumes the turd. He starts from circularity and proceeds, via repetition, towards self-transcendence, which is the truth of the natural world and therefore also of orgiastic self-destruction. I shall return to this idea later in the book.

As a result, two major principles clash in an uncompromising manner: the unpredictability of nature and the prescriptions of wickedness derived from it. According to the first, we must destroy and be destroyed at random. According to the second, we must break all the laws, since this is the sole satisfying thing from a perverse perspective. Whatever principles exist must be broken. Finally, the libertines will enjoy social success, and become wealthy, influential, and famous. In a confusing manner, social success follows from a wicked life plan. Self-destruction is not on the agenda. Destructive nature is deceived by those immoral people who join its forces and avoid their natural fate. Thus the world is inconsistent and not moral at all: it is impossible to formulate anything like a regular principle of nature, since as such it must be immediately broken.

Here there emerges a deeper level of the principle of nature, or a myth of the human essence. A person creates contradictions by violating the norms and laws, and this is his sole satisfying possibility. The project of the wicked life is ultimately expressed in terms of the norms of inconsistency, incoherence, and the absence of personal integrity. A wicked person is required to break even the laws of wickedness and destroy the source of destruction itself. This is his perverse pleasure, and the satisfaction of his own natural character. Since one cannot realize these plans, a scavenging attitude is the result. One consumes whatever happens to be available. However, scavenging is a restless, eternal search-process. It implies lack of power and leads to disappointment and hatred; and begging, in turn, necessitates revenge. To be an avenger one must manipulate a victim, like a predator does, but with a merely negative and self-denying attitude. Yet predation already entails a relative freedom from nature.

The ultimate success is achieved in the artificial world of social life, and established via a civil contract. There one is able to forget hatred, and aim at one's own controlled pleasure. Nevertheless, a Sadean person always struggles against his nature, which condemns him to passivity; although he, as a libertine, tries to be busy, he cannot avoid the need for apathy – meaning rigor, decisiveness, and calmness – when facing any horror.[5] His pleasures are rigid. His atrocities are repetitive. His work is predictable and thus not creative. How can destruction be otherwise? Such is Sade's ultimate challenge to morality and religious thinking. Can we make sense of such a life, when Sade claims that it is an ideal? My answer will be: only in fiction by means of literary style.

The problem which Sade now faces may be put in the following terms. The principle of nature explains why libertine heroes enjoy their perverse pleasures so readily. Their actions are part of a destructive and meaningless process. They aim at nothing, or at the void. But why should destruction appear as a stimulus to them? And how can they be socially successful in a jungle? Philosophers as they are, they should know that there is nothing to destroy or to gain in the long run. Excluding discharges, all barriers are mere illusions; in nature nothing can be destroyed or achieved. All activity becomes pointless. Though Sade may have an explanation for the perverse pleasure, he cannot account for its occurrence and long-term existence. If barriers existed, their collapse would provide some excitement for people, but nothing resembling such obstacles exists. Everything is just unavailable energy. In order to discover a coherent view, we need to go into the details of Sade's metaphysics. We can see where a scavenger's momentary pleasure comes from, if not the reason why the heroes enjoy lasting social success. In other words, if nothing matters, why should one enjoy it, and how can such nothingness lead to social success?

The point must be stressed, however, that the principle of nature says almost nothing about sex. This asexuality of nature is important because nature is the principal metaphysical explanation of pleasure and motivation, and therefore it follows that sex is secondary in importance to death. However, a goal is still needed, so that one cannot drop the term "orgasm," understood as discharge and orgiastic pleasure, from the Sadean vocabulary. It is really not a sexual term, but more a general expression referring to a natural process, or a primordial release, of which the sexual feeling proper is only a pleasant approximation. Sex may be important, but regardless of its status as the good source of liquid discharge, it cannot express the truth about pleasure to its investigator. The key term for Sade is perversity. Sade is first and foremost interested in murder, both as an action (killing) and as an omission (no procreation); and perversity is primarily related to killing and death, and only secondarily to sex. Sade is not interested in sex if it is associated with love. Only perverse sex interests him, but that is secondary to his interest in destruction. The rhetorical links between death, sex, and discharge, are provided by the language of crime and cruelty.

Metaphysics, the science of the ultimate truth, has no room for anything less than the complex forms of the annihilation of life. A set of nested allusions is involved: the void is confusion, indicating active and passive killing as well as the blind proliferation of life, and all this is both natural and enjoyable. The bitter truth is that it is emptiness alone which drives people towards activity and artificial constructions. They can find true happiness, but only if they can simultaneously reach the void and realize their values. The irony of this plan is our inheritance from Sade's discussion of the myth of nature, which he takes to be our own essence.

Sade's fundamental presupposition is that we need to be active. Why are we not complacent, then? Perhaps the sole answer is that by killing God, Sade creates a new god, nature, which is still to be conquered. Even the dead God is an enemy, because nothing can replace Him. The void which He leaves behind haunts Sade and drives him to cross the limits beyond which the void itself waits. He struggles to be active in realizing his negative ends and counter-values. Sade's ethics and utopian speculations can be understood as a rebellion against nature from within, by means of artificial constructions. Language, pleasure, and society are all results of work whose purpose is to show that the Sadean person is a genuine predator, an active seeker of his own pleasure. The final meaning of nature is, therefore, given in terms of what is artificial in a person. Beyond this is the ultimate non-experience which follows from discharging, or orgiastic pleasure which is nothingness. Therefore nature is but a stepping-stone back to itself.

## THE SCAVENGER

In *Juliette* the Pope is the key spokesman of nature. He is the indication of Sade's link between nature as a living counter-god and Sade's anti-Christian atheism. The Pope worships the wrong god, nature, when God is already dead. In this way atheism can be seen as a subversive rhetorical element. When Sade breaks the grammar of things, making subversion universal, his blasphemy becomes one of his sins. But blasphemy itself does not generate too many discharges; religion seems all too verbal. Also, the theory of nature leads to a negative response to religion. However, once the principle of nature becomes a full-fledged metaphysical idea, it contains religion as a feature which the philosophizing person rejects. If everything must go, religion must go too. Yet Sade wishes to retain something of religious emotion – its horror and respect – toward his concept of evil. Moreover, religion does not entirely disappear, since its truth is transformed into nature, which the Pope worships. As we shall see, the Pope is ultimately unable to decipher his own religion. He rejects God, but when he turns toward nature he projects his self-identity onto dead matter, failing to recognize that it is dead. He still worships his own image in a reflecting surface, and by doing so he struggles against the loss of his own identity. Finally, he copulates with Juliette on the altar, as if to beg for forgiveness.

The reason why nature makes man a restless scavenger is that chaos does not support any normative laws or values. And because pleasure is transgression (which presupposes something that can be breached) there is no pleasure in nature. If there is nothing to subvert, no pleasure exists. Man must start building some artificial values, for the reason mentioned. Before this, he must be content with the waste he may find, that is, mere "froth" and "vapor" whose annihilation is hardly stimulating. The key point is that Sade's natural attitude is that nothing is forbidden in nature. He mentions this in many places: "That what we improperly call evil is really not evil at all."[6] But then there is not pleasure either. The only thing to do is to participate in the life of nature, which is to become garbage – a corpse, dead like a turd.

It is worth considering what the Pope told Juliette about the principle of nature when they met in the Vatican. The Pope, the master scavenger, is Sade himself. The joke is that the Pope contravenes his official role as the highest religious authority. The official role is a mask; the Pope lives a double life and presents an enigma. On the one hand, he is priest of a false religion; on the other hand, his message concerning nature is transgressive, defying truth and honesty. The Pope personifies a totally artificial entity.

The record of their exchange covers more than thirty pages and is the largest and richest treatment of the topic anywhere in Sade's work, though much of the ground is also covered in countless other places.[7]

The discussion is not an analytical treatise where the teleological and causal aspects, laws and myths, intentions and consequences are kept neatly apart. The treatment of nature already presupposes much knowledge of perverse pleasure and orgastic life, and although the Pope tries to convince Juliette of something, it cannot be seen at the surface of the text. I shall describe their discussion in detail, ponder its meaning, and try to solve some of the problems which it presents.

The Pope first claims that he can never "retire for the night with unbloodied hands." Juliette then naively asks, "But from where does this monstrous taste come?", to which the Pope replies, misleadingly, that it comes "from Nature, my child, Murder is one of her laws," as if nature were a source of anti-moral commands. Thus the great metaphysical narrative starts like a dull lesson in a dusty classroom. In the very first paragraph, however, a blatant contradiction becomes visible. The Pope presents the following thesis:

> whenever she [Nature] feels the need for murder she inspires in us a longing to commit it, and willy-nilly we obey her.

Next he subscribes to his second thesis, which is incompatible with the first:

> I am prepared to prove to you that man is in no wise dependent upon her.

The contradiction between causal dependence and independence between man and nature can be resolved by arguing either that murder is a natural passion or that it is in obedience to the laws of nature, which nevertheless do not determine man's choices. In other words, an external natural tendency is without causal or prescriptive force, and therefore man is "in no wise dependent upon her." In this way, nature provides man with his character which is, in the Hobbesian sense, a license to do whatever one likes. One's natural inspiration is the recognition of right, and nature kills and destroys all the time anyway.

This simple-minded interpretation of Sade's Pope is grounded in historical fact, and as such the message is not surprising. Hobbes's view provides the boundaries which Sade must transgress if he wants to be wicked and not just a Hobbesian. Concerning man's independence from nature, Hobbes's position is like that of the Pope, although they draw different conclusions from it. Hobbes says,

> The Desires, and other Passions of man, are in themselves no

Sin. No more are the Actions, that proceed from those Passions, till they know a Law that forbids them: which till Lawes be made they cannot know: nor can any Law be made, till they have agreed upon the Person that shall make it.[8]

Sade refuses to nominate a law-giver. Therefore nature rules absolutely, providing the human agents with their entitlements but not with their corresponding duties. For Sade, everything is permissible.

Again, the Beast of Malmesbury expresses the point perfectly when he repeats that "Nature hath given *every one a right to all*. ... And this is what is meant by the common saying, *nature hath given all to all*. From whence we understand likewise that in the state of nature profit is the measure of right."[9] According to such a view, the traditional natural law theory is nonsense. One cannot find any normative principles in nature. On the contrary, in the state of nature anything a person wants is right and good; nature has no normative content which is not projected on it via civil laws and conventional moral codes. Of course, Hobbes fears death, unlike the Sadean person, who refuses to honor even that final constraint on decision-making. Though Hobbes forces an ethic upon the human race, Sade does not. He does need additional arguments, however, to surpass Hobbesianism.

The Pope's next thesis is that "no earthly creature is expressly formed by Nature, none deliberately made by her." Nature is said to be, at most, productive in the causal sense of being creative, not in the teleological sense. It is without purpose. One is inconsistent if one thinks that the human body is more valuable than that of a lamb, although "to appease his gluttony he roasted the lamb entire on a spit ... this gentle and peaceable lamb." Of course, the animal has no value for itself, nor have its virtues any appeal to the Pope. It is absurd to think that a man is better than a lamb, even if both were created; but in fact neither is created, and therefore both are totally without value. Then follows a potentially misleading cosmic illustration: "All are the results of her laws and her workings ...; very different creatures probably inhabit other globes, the myriads of globes wherewith space is freighted." This should be read as referring to random production. All these things are, accordingly, without value; they are like the "froth" and the "vapors" which result from chemical processes and evaporate into the air. "This steam is not created, it is resultative," the Pope maintains, in order to make a sharp distinction between the *causa finalis* and the *causa efficiens* in nature, where only the latter obtains. Nature is a vortex of causes, and different worlds are like different gases. Since nature does not create, it has, for this very reason, no intrinsic value.

The Sadean grand theory follows. The truth is:

> Man thus has no relationship to Nature, nor Nature to man; Nature cannot bind man by any law, man is in no way dependent upon Nature, neither is answerable to the other, they cannot either harm or help each other.

This strong thesis holds that man is only a contingent result of natural causes which he is unable to modify. Causal consequences are uncontrollable in two directions: man cannot control nature, but neither can nature control man. Nature has no plans for man, and the laws of nature do not bind him from without, because man is a natural thing himself. Whatever man may do is according to nature; and according to his essential nature, too, his actions are natural. Nature sets no limits on him, and his actions defy constraint. Certainly some plans cannot be realized, but Sade does not consider them constraint, because plans are whimsical anyway and have no positive role in human life. Nature does not answer; the universe is silent. Man is an automaton, prone to moral apathy. This may not yet be a full action-theory, but it is an approximation to what Sade thinks.

Immediately the Pope seems to forget all he has said, because in presenting the next set of ideas, concerning human propagation, he argues as follows:

> If man destroys himself, he does wrong – in his own eyes. But this is not the view Nature takes of the thing. As she sees it, if he multiplies he does wrong, for he usurps from Nature the honor of a new phenomenon, creatures being the necessary result of her workings. If those creatures that are cast were not to propagate themselves, she would cast new entities and enjoy a faculty she has ceased to be able to exercise.

This looks like anthropomorphic nonsense in relation to the thesis of man–nature independence which he stated earlier. The Pope appears to assume the existence of genuine human error. But when we read that "our multiplication . . . is therefore decidedly detrimental to the phenomena whereof Nature is capable," we see what he means. Perhaps he intends to say that man's efforts are not needed, or that the attempt to correct natural processes leads only to illusion. To try to realize one's plans, in the sense of a value, is to lapse into error and become guilty of self-deception. The only purposes one may fulfill are those which aim at nothing and lead to inconsistency, confusion, pain, the void. These orgiastic goals are natural.

The fundamental truth is therefore that man and nature are indeed independent of each other, so that any laws against killing or the duty to reproduce cannot exist. Nature takes care of that, and if it does not, the extinction of the human race is of no consequence to nature, or to the individual who will be already dead. Therefore man need not take seriously the alleged duty to marry, reproduce, and take care of his offspring.

The Pope refers continuously to nature's tendency to produce new individuals and forms of life. Little attention, however, need be paid to the Pope's Sadean figures of speech here. Of course this is not creativity, but blindness. Nevertheless, one may think that the Pope implies that nature is not just destructive. Perhaps the new forms of life represent hope and recovery. Alas, destruction and multiplication are equally blind and violent. Both processes are the opposites of human hopes and planning. Most importantly, the blind increase of individuals is part of the maelstrom where things are torn apart and rejected. When something big becomes fragmented, the result is a multiplicity of small pieces; because this is without logic or meaning, one may ironically call it creation. It makes little difference whether the Pope speaks about destruction or the emergence of something new.

The Pope's message is clear. Because nothing disappears for good from nature, therefore nature is greater than man, who is bound to hate both it and his own vulnerable condition. One needs to keep in mind, however, that he describes only the first step towards a philosophy and that his basic point is thus all too simple. That man and nature are totally independent of each other is such an abstract idea that it cannot carry the counter-ethical doctrine as far as Sade himself wants to go. Because Sade cannot achieve anything according to plan, neither can he obtain pleasure, except randomly or via self-deception. This double problem remains: how should one get rid of scavenging, and why must one not deceive oneself? Therefore, most of the sermon must be regarded as empty rhetoric.

The Pope next develops a rudimentary naturalistic ethic which allows the audience to understand the problem of self-deception. This proves to be the direct opposite of a motive to be virtuous. Any planning utilizes values and truths, which means that one aims at one's own good. But since there is no good in nature, the result is self-deception. This is bad because it cannot be enjoyed. A self-deceiving person does not understand his own vice. It is a missed opportunity simply because a self-deceiving agent cannot exploit the case in which the values "we regard as virtues become crimes from her [Nature's] point of view." In the same way, killing, negligence, and cruelty look like virtues if they are seen as something they really are not. At this point we must leave the realm of the Pope's simple theory, which maintains the independence of man and nature along with the Hobbesian right to everything.

Not only is a person entitled to wrongful action, but he is also motivated towards the exploitation of such a possibility. It is indeed a long step from the idea that all actions are permissible, and for the same reason totally indifferent to man, to the thesis that the ways of nature somehow attract and motivate man. What is this motive like? Somehow the Pope's ethics should explain the thesis to the effect that virtue is something which must be avoided; it is like vice. But because vice should be cherished, we are faced with some kind of mere mockery of moral discourse, from which no sensible directives seem to follow. Values will disappear because normative language and theory are unstable. Virtue and vice flicker and vanish as they appear at the same time as something similar and different. As Bataille would put it, one is a parody of the other.[10]

The Pope says that "all the laws we humans have made... necessarily conflict with all of hers [Nature's]." This entails that the criminalization of murder and the requirements of marriage and reproduction are opposed to the principles of nature, which are mainly destructive and only secondarily formative: "And there is the sole cause of this immensity of successive creations: each of them consists of a repetition of the first principles of exhaustion or of destruction." The two crucial words are "repetition" and "exhaustion," which have a key role throughout the Sadean aesthetics and ethics. Their instability entails the circularity of life and, ultimately, its emptiness.

In a figurative, uninformative sense, nature can also be called malevolent. What this means is that its victims observe that nature is really a chaotic process without any intrinsic telos. Its energies are more geared to destruction, the negation of its own contents, than to anything creative. The Pope may take this as an atheistic idea, simply because God is supposed to be a creative force capable of destroying His creation. Nature is different: "In all living beings the principle of life is no other than that of death." Therefore, religious ethics are unnatural.

The argument proceeds stepwise and establishes a connection between destructive nature and human motivation. The first step repeats the idea of following nature:

> So rend away, hack and hew, torment, break, wreck, massacre, burn, grind to dust, melt.... Unable to please her by the atrocity of a global destruction, at least provide her the pleasure of local atrocity, and into your murderings put every imaginable foulness and horror, thereby showing utmost docility in your compliance with the laws she imposes upon you.

In this way the Pope insists both on the desirability of the natural life, and on the main reason why all this is true: "atrocity in crime pleases Nature, since 'tis according to this factor alone she regulates the delight to provide us when we commit a crime. The more frightful it is, the more we enjoy it; the blacker, the fouler it is, the more we are thrilled by it."

The second step follows: since man himself is constituted according to the destructive principle of nature, the Pope must be understood as speaking not of the external nature but of the inner life of man. His psychological language refers directly to human motivation. Man is evil in the same sense as nature is destructive, and therefore he enjoys everything that is a crime, as the Pope says. He argues that "Cruelty in man is simply an expression of his desire to exercise his strength." This is explained by saying that "we are born to serve as blind instruments" who are driven forward by the search for excitement and pleasure. Man is both a natural creature himself and motivated by the laws of nature. Man and nature may be normatively independent of each other, but man's motivation stems from his essence.

Instead of taking too seriously such ideas of evil as an imitation of chaos or as man's debt to nature, I shall suggest a solution to the question of why one is vicious: it is because nature is a random process without purpose, and man is a natural thing too. Whatever aims one may posit, they are subject to luck and contingencies. Moreover, such factors are fundamental and unavoidable. One sees that ethics and its virtues are too risky to warrant adoption. They represent mere self-deception and akrasia without compensating pleasure. In his novels Sade tries to prove this truth by showing that the consequences of virtuous action are detrimental. Vice, however, may lead to success, because the evil person is a predator rather than the prey. The latter role is one Sade strongly rejects. This discloses the consequentialist side of the picture: vice brings about optimal results and virtue is risky. Perverse intentions, however, have a different foundation. They rest on the joy of conscious injury to self, the only way one can escape nature's grip and enter the void. The scavenger turns into avenger.

The Pope concludes his talk by displaying empirical examples of crime in historical and primitive societies, and by letting the voice of majestic nature speak for itself. The first sentence is a fine Mosaic joke, especially if read in the proper theatrical manner:

> it is writ in my laws that ye all destroy yourselves mutually; and the true way to succeed therein is to harm thy neighbor without stint or cease. Whence it cometh that I have placed the sharpest bent for crime in thee; whence it is that my intention be that thou render thyself happy, at the expense of whosoever it be.... So form or destroy as thou wilt and at thy ease; tomorrow's sun shall rise just the same.

Although man is part of nature, man and nature are totally independent of each other. Again the contrast between creation and destruction is taken up and found to be meaningless. A natural ethic leads man to desperation and apathy.

Murder and sex without procreation are all a person is left with. This cyclic process resembles consumption of waste. Thus nature ensures that man avoids virtue and it puts no constraints on this process. Nature's attitude is one of indifference. Though the best way to get pleasure is to play the game, one should not think that this alone changes anything. Sadean teachers always emphasize that since nature does not care what we do, human beings are alone in the world and at the mercy of their neighbors, who are all greedy for their private pleasure. The result is their cruelty to one another. How can Juliette like such a message? Juliette may be happy about the fact that her neighbors are her enemies, but how can she still love it if she becomes the object of cruelty herself? Juliette welcomes these truths in the name of her personal liberation, and she goes on to explore the promised land. The features of pleasure, however, are purely negative, consisting in both killing and being killed.

## LUCK AND TRANSGRESSION

In its own way, Sade's philosophy of nature is coherent and interesting, at least if read as a totality and without too much attention to details. Pain, cruelty, and murder are powerful motives simply because human beings are parts of nature which always destroy each other; thus we act in harmony with her. However, if this is so, the social symmetry required for survival remains an enigma. Sade argues that the French society of the Old Regime, the society he knows best, is unjust in exactly the sense that crime pays off there while virtue does not. The virtuous Justine soon learns this fact: "Great God, I cried with much bitterness, then it is impossible for my soul to give vent to any virtuous impulse without my being instantly and very seriously punished for it!"[11] Her misfortunes, though, depend neither on physical nature, nor even on human psychology. It is possible to imagine small and isolated societies which struggle successfully against the cruel laws of nature. A utopia may exist. Yet Sade's point is that virtue is always a risky strategy, because it leaves a person vulnerable to the greed, treachery, and cruelty of others. If she wants to take proper precautions, she must become wicked herself. Virtue is not even pleasant. A good person will follow the norms whose goal is at best peaceful coexistence, or mere obedience to custom and tradition; but it is likely to mean that one becomes a professional victim who lives through others' efforts to mold her body like clay. No learning will ensue. Justine never comprehends this fact. As for Juliette, she knows that "each murder is a commentary and critique of the others, each demands improvement in the next," so that a whole career is formed and she can become an artist with her life. Of course, even Juliette might become too victimized to survive; but this is always a contingent accident, bad luck, whose occurrence can best be avoided by being as evil as possible.

Wickedness entails harm to self as the result of one's action; yet the consequences tend to be beneficial. Virtuousness produces harmful consequences which effectively negate all good intentions. Sade's argument is that by harming herself Juliette assumes a natural position. She is in harmony with the destructive principle of nature and therefore she is a source of calamity. Justine, on the contrary, remains as a mere object because her plans defy what is natural. Because she does not harm herself – she is good – she must remain in the passive position; at least, this is how I read Sade. In the existing social order things normally go well for the cruelly enterprising person. If she is killed, Sade seems to argue, she must take this as another trick of nature. The ironic fact is that only harm creates benefit. Nature is chaos in the sense that it frustrates and mocks at practical reason. Juliette's inconsistency pays off.

We have seen that nature provides Sade with a model of real life that is at once destructive and pleasant. Through a series of cruel acts, one finds that union with nature which is an orgiastic experience. If one can transcend the factual and physical obstacles which reality produces, life is the feeling of the void. Through destructive action, one shows one's power in changing the world, and also achieves an intensely pleasant state of mind. Originally one is alone in the world, since no religion or ethics can offer guidance or consolation: neighbors are either victims, "fodder for earth," or potential enemies whose wickedness is a threat. If certain social unions are possible, they work as parodies of the civil contract, since they serve only one's personal interests. The weakest members of coalitions are sure to suffer. Nevertheless, such societies have their own important roles, as we shall see.

Perhaps the most important lesson to learn is that pleasure must be understood as transcendence, as the crossing of limits so that one enters the void where all is permissible, nothing matters, and nothing can be achieved. Only through crime is transcendence transformed into transgression, the feeling of the total void. Murder becomes a commentary on earlier crimes, and repetition is the key to the plot of the play. Ethics is not concerned with such a void; on the contrary, it is concerned with a careful redefinition of things, and their social control. It is the minimization of caprice. Good aims are well defined, and therefore (to Sade) they are not worthwhile. Evil things, on the other hand, are incomprehensible, and thus are pleasant like discharging or jumping into the void. Sade refers to wickedness as irritation and to pleasure as destruction: a person who faces an incomprehensible danger feels a strong phobic emotion. It is like the torture by the rats in George Orwell's *1984*; the torture exploits Winston's worst fears and changes his life, even if the rats never touch his face.[12]

Franz Kafka's "In the Penal Colony" illustrates the Sadean attitude towards the mystery of nature.[13] In the society of the penal colony, the inhabitants believe in a primordial law-giver, called "the former Commandant," who has given them the law. In social life, as it is, knowledge of the law is partially corrupted. Yet some principles are self-evident, like "Honor thy superiors!", "Guilt is never to be doubted," and "Be just!" They use a complex machine which writes the name of his crime all over the victim's body with glass needles – justice is transparent. The victim slowly learns the name of his crime by reading the text of wounds on his body: "Nothing more happens than that the man begins to understand the inscription, he purses his mouth as if he were listening." Finally, the dead body is thrown into a pit.

The infernal machine in Kafka's story finally breaks, so that the victim never learns the name of the crime and therefore cannot die; he escapes without illumination. The officer in charge made a mistake by tying himself to the machine, as if to learn the name of his own crime, which led to the breakdown of the sacred mechanism. According to his own principles, he must be punished. He has failed to convince the visitor – who may be his superior – of the justice of the system, and guilt cannot be doubted. But he knows too much. He understands that he is guilty, which the victim of the Kafkaesque natural law never does. Therefore the spikes merely pierce him so that he perishes without the enlightenment he seeks. From the perspective of Sade, who was also fond of machines, his mistake was that he thought he could understand his own failure and compensate for it through his death. He should have understood that the luck of the criminal is a catastrophe without intrinsic meaning. All actions must aim at the sheer pleasure which is transcendence. But the officer is logical. He reaches his own false nothingness – which is devoid of liberation – when the senseless mechanism refuses to throw him into a garbage pile: "no sign was visible of the promised redemption."

It may be asked why Sade (or the Pope) does not commit suicide, since nature is perceived to be such a devious guide. The answer is: first, because nature does not require anything from them. Second, their pleasure is the experience of the void, which resembles death. Third, all life is merely metaphoric in relation to nature, which alone is really real. They are already dead.

This last point is particularly important. At the simplest individual level the principle of metaphor entails that all libertines simulate the life of nature by destroying as much as possible. But they, unlike nature, also love, reason, deliberate, unite, and struggle to avoid death. In this way they play a game whose name is nature, and whose rules specify that they know the total isolation of nature. It neither prescribes nor answers questions, and whatever they do has no effect on what is real. The sole alternative is to find the way to ultimate transcendent pleasures through some fictional means – stories, narratives, stage productions. Life, including the society of the Old Regime, becomes a mere play. Sadean heroes have no real hope of being successfully wicked, because they know nature does not care about them. They need substitutes, like the Sadean theater of pain where they enact pleasure.

The truth of pleasure is the act of discharging; everything Sade says is a reflection of this one reality in which he believes. When the Pope kills, he feels something quite close to nature, but which has nothing to do with it. Therefore he must try to repeat and perfect his act. In his fury, he tells a story of what it feels like to live a genuine life in society. What he cannot do is to become happy, or to achieve something. Thus he is only wasting his time and other people's lives. But he can do nothing else.

# 4
# HEDONISM IN PSYCHOLOGY

Sade's view does not need to reflect scientific truth in order to be of interest. One can say, on the contrary, that his vision is attractive perhaps just for the reason that it deviates from reality. Sade does not deny facts, but transcends them. Therefore, veridicality is not the only virtue in philosophical theory.

As for Sade's psychology, it certainly strikes the reader as being patently false. We are accustomed to attributing falsehood or truth to things like psychology because we feel that it is something more or less fixed; we feel that we cannot re-create ourselves in the same way that, say, a social organization can be re-created by us. But even if psychology is not a field of artifacts in the same sense as sociology, that fact alone does not guarantee its immunity to fictional alterations. In this context we shall see that Sade's ideas of pleasure and personal identity are at once strange and illuminating.

Sade aims at giving a description of the person as he is and an explanation of why he acts in such strange and surprising ways. After accomplishing this much, Sade is ready to argue normatively that the behavior he describes is authentic and not alienated – something anyone can, and should, aim at. The descriptive theory of personal psychology seems to make it possible to justify cruelty and aggression. If psychology makes such features pathological or deeply irrational, their acceptance as free action would become superfluous. Therefore, the question of the reasons for developing such a psychology as Sade's can be answered by suggesting that Sade's psychology aims at showing not only what a civilized person *prima facie* experiences, but what his authentic nature is. This goal he achieves through certain symbolic features embedded in the stories that people tell about themselves. In this sense both Sade's psychology and especially his concept of authenticity are normative. Their norms are related to metaphysics, to the theory of natural life, and also to the life of nature.

I shall first describe the constitution of the Sadean personal identity through attributes which are related, on the one hand, to the agent's intentions and, on the other hand, to his passivity as a target of actions. Next I shall provide an account of pleasure which is an avenger's joy of doing harm to his enemies, and to himself too. Such pleasure is without transcendence and therefore mixes value with bitterness. Sadean heroes need the social life – the artificial social world – before they achieve true enjoyment, and this is the solution to the riddle of libertine friendship. The fact that in nature any agent is only a scavenger creates frustration and the desire for revenge. I shall suggest that psychologically such pleasure is very different from socially constituted enjoyment. The argument for this proposition will proceed in terms of the rejection of the categories of the natural, which cannot be mastered, and the adoption of those of the artificial, which can be utilized in the production of pleasure. Accordingly, my argument will fork into two branches, one dealing with the ethics of pleasure and the other with the logic of the social contract. After that we shall deal with Sade's style, which shows his reader the path of redemption.

## PERSONAL IDENTITY

Personal identity can be construed in two ways: in terms of the characteristics of an agent, and in terms of what happens to him. Ideally, these two aspects are mutually exclusive, as Sade seems to think. A mature agent is not an object, but only a subject. His victim is a pure recipient without an identity of his own. Such a separation between direct and ironic identity, however, cannot succeed in psychological terms. It takes place only in a utopian social order – an artifact created by means of a social contract. In order to succeed in understanding what a person is, we need to discard all our conventional ideas of psychology. Sade's analysis starts from nature, and this is equivalent to saying that we should utilize premises of incomprehension and nothingness, as well as those of destruction and terror.

To understand the Sadean person we must look first at his/her constitution from the point of view of personal identity. To do so is to crack the cosmic shell of nature, so that from its uniformity an individual emerges ready for action. The definition of the polarity between nature and personality is first displayed (to move like a scavenger), then defined (to tear apart like an avenger), and finally used by Sade (to enjoy like a predator). Sade's basic motive is to keep the distance between opposites as minimal as possible, so that a person remains both rigid and independent, his pleasure coming from nature but his action remaining as his own. The link between them is constituted by the fact that the thought and the theory are the pleasure itself. Roberta Hackel writes in her insightful study as follows:

> The Sadean character's essence is only defined in terms of moral as distinguished from physical attributes, just as he exists in a moral milieu as distinguished from a physical setting. Descriptions of localities are cursory. Psychological motivations are all reduced to penchants toward good or evil.[1]

I shall follow this lead, not in Sade's short stories (as Hackel does) but in his clandestine novels, which are even more extreme in their description of people. It is true that Sadean heroes are not psychologically well-defined characters, but rather constellations of evaluative and prescriptive attributes. Though such a fact is easy to verify in Sade's novels, it is difficult to explicate properly; it pinpoints the more general problem of attempting to say what a well-rounded personality is. Sade refuses to tackle this issue. Instead he approaches his characters from the outside, grounding their moral attributes in what they are in the habit of doing. Even such first-person narratives as that of Justine follow this rule. Juliette tells what she did, in the same way as Justine relates what happened to her. But Juliette's narrative relates what has happened to people around her because of the interactions she has initiated, and Juliette becomes a person in a fuller sense than Justine. Only Juliette produces results; Justine herself is a result.

The following illustrates the implications of Juliette's thoughts: "'No,' I demurred, preoccupied with a thought I could not drive out of my head, an ill-defined premonition, 'no, I believe I will drink a glass and talk with Durand rather than fuck. Besides, I am menstruating, and feel a little out of sorts ... I simply wish to chat.'"[2] She feels depressed. Here we observe a Juliette who – rather uncharacteristically – exhibits a conventional personality, in contrast to those Sadean subjects who refuse to define themselves in terms of personally felt emotion and reason. The reader briefly identifies with Juliette, who corresponds to the reader's own picture of himself as a human being who is confronted with the problems of life. This feeling disappears quickly when the reader recognizes that Juliette is indeed in great danger. Her deliberation means that she is becoming a victim herself. She must get rid of the gaze and start acting again.

Sade offers his readers heroes with whom they cannot identify. In a gallery of mutually exclusive types, each person represents a conglomeration of attributes without any change within the person or connection between the different types. Persons are rigoristic and unified, but only through the pleasure they seek. But pleasure means transcendence, and thus depersonalizes its subject. The sole interesting exception to this rule defining the uniqueness of persons is education. Aside from the change wrought by education, Sadean personalities are so firm that they do not qualify as identities in any conventional sense.

The personalities are divided into two broad classes: the strong and the weak. Typically, it is the sadistic hero versus a helpless victim. The metaphor is that of physical labor which produces results which are at the worker's mercy. Through his initial emphasis on hard work, or pain, a perverse tinge comes to Sade's narrative; his own desperate efforts at masturbation in a prison cell are twisted into the mastery over products like shit, sperm, or a corpse. What is first a token of reluctance is turned into the celebration of a victory over a fluid medium. Sade's problem is that hard work and pleasurable discharge never quite fit together. The lord and his slave resist unification, however transcendent that may be.

As to the question of the relationship between persons and nature, the problem is that Sade requires both that his heroes be independent of nature and that they behave according to its prescriptions. Such persons are described in terms of their general functional propensities and their particular individual features. The general functional propensities include the size of the penis, the availability of orifices, the vividness of imagination, and degree of cruelty. These relate to what one is capable of doing as well as to what one actually does. Age, social class, profession, marital status, and beauty are examples of particular features. All are assigned mainly to victims, and are fixed characterizations of the uses to which such persons are put. Descriptions, which focus on stable features of the body and mind, are used to indicate usage. Passivity belongs to an object which is characterized as without action-propensities – unlike the hero, who is constantly represented as pure activity. Of course, even the heroes may be described as particular individuals, but this serves to indicate their availability for categories of victimization. Even the heroes can be betrayed, abused, mutilated, and killed. They are neither clean nor mature, since they can be described and the description itself changed. This entails harm to them. Accordingly, the strongest of the heroes become indescribable, as if they were pure act, the libidinal Id, identifiable solely in terms of the results it produces according to its desire. The victims, on the contrary, are mere matter which needs form in order to exist at all. Their egos entail peril.

For the details of personal identity, I shall use the gallery of types in the *120 Days of Sodom*. There are two classes of primary persons: the actors (the four libertine friends) and the four object persons or subjects of debauchery (the friends' wives and daughters). The former are active recipients of the marks of actions and operations; the latter are passive carriers of them. It may seem that all are well defined and have their identities grounded on a rich set of features; all, for instance, have proper names, physical features, social backgrounds and active propensities, tastes, and virtues. The same technique is also used in *Justine*, and is equally deceptive there.

A primary hero possesses both a factual and a moral identity, with the former much richer than the latter. We know that Curval was "born as a great gourmand and drunk . . . [and it has been] ten years since Curval has ceased to discharge his judicial duties." In this sense his identity is fixed: it cannot be swapped with that of, say, Duc de Blangis, who has not been a judge and was not born under similar circumstances. Yet, as Sade makes clear, Curval is now an older man, his judicial role is over, and the echo of his past can no longer be heard. Even the memory of his immature past has more or less vanished:

> Curval was to such a point mired down in the morass of vice and libertinage that it had become virtually impossible for him to think or speak of anything else. . . . This disorder of mind . . . had during the past few years given him an air of imbecility and prostration which, he would declare, made for his most cherished delight.[3]

This description shows why his past identity, constituted in terms of its social roles and memories, has all but vanished. No longer existing as a self-contained person, Curval has become fluid. To try to control, punish, or violate such a non-person is simply meaningless. Only his name and his body are left for his enemy to play with. Since the name is conventional in the sense of being changeable with others, it would seem that only the body identifies the individual Curval. At the same time, Curval is so ugly and his body so rotten that he is not different from the victimized secondary persons. Because the body is passive, it is a source of danger – it must be destroyed. Yet in Sade's mythology the body is not an identity-constituting factor, as we shall see.

In his role as pure anti-moral agent, Curval is similar to all other libertines. All libertine scenes are repetitive; they can be eliminated, multiplied, and rearranged as one likes without any loss to the narrative. In the same way, Curval is like any of the other characters who disappear and reappear without a clear pattern. In *Justine* and *Juliette* such things occur all the time. The structure of these novels dictates that each new monster must go through his nasty rituals, just as Justine must go away and meet the next rake. From the point of view of the narrative, the persons are all freely interchangeable and have no identity of their own. They are characterized only in terms of what they want to do. A new actor with similar values can take their place without any loss to the story. Neither vice nor violence offers a descriptive arsenal which fixes the dramatic personalities so firmly that they become irreplaceable.

Just as anti-moral and active propensities do not permanently individualize a libertine, so too with the primary victims. The psychology of the wives at Silling is given as follows:

> To all these amenities Constance joined a fair and agreeable wit, a spirit somewhat more elevated than it ought to have been, considering the melancholy situation fate had awarded her, for thereby she was enabled to sense all its horror, and doubtless, she would have been happier if furnished with less delicate perceptions.[4]

Constance is described as an ideal victim who fully understands her peril, and is therefore able to suffer. Because, unlike Curval, she thinks and understands, she alone is fit to be unhappy. Her name, Constance, signifies her natural capacity to suffer. She is the embodiment of the psychology of passivity, both in the sense of a *tabula rasa* and *ex nihilo nihil*. Because she understands what comes in from the outside world, she is unable to initiate actions: she is empty. Defined in terms of pain, she does not exist without her tormentors.

Justine also, as primary victim, is capable of thought:

> The courtesy of this young man, who was in no sort indebted to me, brought tears to my eyes. Kind treatment is sweet indeed when for so long one has experienced nought but the most odious. I accepted his gifts, at the same time swearing I was going to work at nothing but to put myself in a way to be able someday to reciprocate.[5]

Because her suffering is meaningful, one can be sorry for her. She comes very close to being real.

Unlike Constance and Justine, who are primary victims, a secondary person does not think or feel. He or she is defined only in relation to the primary persons. Such persons enter the social context at Silling from the outside, either because they are hired or because they are kidnapped. Their background is explained by the heroes who are responsible for their presence at Silling. They also have physical features which are either the objects or the results of debauchery. They have no personality traits unrelated to libertine procedures. In fact, they are pleasure machines, and have exactly the same degree of identity as any machine. Most of all, they do not have their own plans, desires, or fears. They have neither wit nor sensitivity. Though they may scream and talk, they do not deliberate, evaluate, or judge. In this way, even their suffering becomes meaningless. They are simply pierced and cut to pieces like dead matter; or they are dismantled as if they were automatons regular as clockwork.

These secondary entities are divided again into two major classes: the active and the passive. There are the four active fuckers who possess animal minds and large members, like the one called Assbreaker. Those in the active class represent labor. The passive class consists of the victims – kidnapped boys and girls, and the four ugly old female servants. The young will soon be destroyed; the old are mute memories of the horrors of life. These classes are meant to designate the future and past tenses, respectively, and Sade's message is that all tenses have the same content. The boys and girls will suffer in the future; the servants have already suffered in the past. As victims of cruelty, they bear its physical marks:

> Marie was the name of the first one; she had been the servant of a notorious brigand quite recently put to death on the wheel, whipping and branding had been her penalty. She was fifty-eight years old, had almost no hair left, her nose stood askew, her eyes were dull and rheumy.[6]

All these pseudo-persons are freely interchangeable, so that if they drop out of the story, nothing changes.

The four storytellers at Silling are constituted through their language and memories. They are active in the sense of being creative, but only in relation to their audience. Sade describes Madame Desgranges by saying, "her soul was the depository of all the most unheard-of vices and crimes." She is defined in terms of memories with which her audience is not yet familiar. In a sense, she is defined contextually by the very specification of what the members of the audience do not know. If they knew, Madame Desgranges could not exist. Her mind is stimulating because its workings are unexpected.

The storytellers are quite remarkable persons, since they represent not destruction but the creative preservation of what has been true. By conserving the past, they reach a high degree of invulnerability to violence. Perhaps this is the result of their spiritual character. Sade's novels do not offer many other examples of this tendency. In fact, the storytellers represent Sade himself under the guise of a female ego. The fuckers, on the contrary, are merely physical beings, ready to act but, unlike the storytellers, dispensable and vulnerable to counter-action.

In conclusion, I would like to suggest the following criterion of personal identity in Sade's narrative. In all fiction, the story as a whole is changed into another story if one genuine identity-carrying personal description is changed to another. Or the story may simply stop there and remain incomplete if the character is altered or missing. This is not a threat in *Justine* or *Juliette*, but it is a threat in the *120 Days of Sodom*. If Justine disappeared in the middle of her adventures, the story would merely be shorter, but not incomplete. The story of Justine is so repetitive that her personality cannot be fully defined. If one of the four friends at Silling becomes unavailable, any one of the remaining libertines can take his place and the basic story remains the same. Their identities are weak, but together they are informative. Without some of them, the narrative does not reach its climax. In *Juliette* both the heroine and her story are rather strongly defined, although Juliette herself may be replaced by a villain without cutting the story short. *Philosophy in the Bedroom*, however, works like an ordinary novel in the sense that both the main characters and the plot are strong. Madame de Saint-Ange cannot be dropped in the middle without cutting the story short and making it incomplete.

## WOMEN

Obviously anyone can be a Sadean hero. The choice is free, as the cases of Justine and Juliette show. In the same way, no fundamental differences between men and women emerge, despite the claim of some interpreters of Sade. For instance, Lawrence W. Lynch has argued:

> If women have no sexual dignity in Sade, we could also say that they have no physical identity. Justine and Juliette exist only in

terms of their relationship to males. Furthermore, women have no civil or monetary rights. . . . It seems that Sade envisaged two types of women. They are either prostitutes. . . . Or, women can be enslaved by men and submit to eventual murder. . . . Juliette may be freer than the other females in Sade, but she must continually rob and kill in order to survive.[7]

It is indeed true that in the end Juliette is still dependent on the fortunes of the Minister de Noirceuil. She is also a whore who accommodates anyone's desires. But these facts do not constitute the whole truth about her. Sade plays with the transgression of sexual roles, and this may entail that women must be similar to men.

Lynch rightly pays much attention to Sade's feminist themes, but the fact remains that no talk of rights makes much sense in the unjust society of the Old Regime. The problem of women in Sade must be seen explicitly against the background of his transgressive project. He paints the most terrifying and humiliating picture of mankind, including women, and does not try to do justice to anyone. Some women are virtuous victims, but Juliette herself loves to kill. The feeling is not misplaced that Sade's depiction of women is rather unsuccessful, but perhaps that is because the stereotypes he is attempting to subvert are themselves unsuccessful depictions of women. In attempting to be subversive in a field which is already conceptually unstable, he seems to struggle.

Sade's women are both helpless victims and brutal victimizers. Sade's trick of playing with extremes works well only with men or when the gender distinctions are altogether left out of the picture. Let me first try to show how traditional the bipartite concept of woman is, and then try to decipher what it means for women to humiliate men – a concept which is a Sadean novelty.

Strong women need not be only witches whose power originates from a strange and unknown source and who are by definition alienated from mainstream society. The *Malleus Maleficarum* is helpful here:

> there are three things in nature, the Tongue, an Ecclesiastic, and a Woman, which know no moderation in goodness or vice; and when they exceed the bounds of their condition they reach the greatest heights and the lowest depths of goodness and vice.[8]

In relation to Sade, this list of dangerous items is fascinating. In his writings, one is crowned by one's own language; men occupy artificial, priestly offices reserved for them only and which may bring them great peril; and his women, unlike his men, are naturally unable to hit the right balance between too much and too little of the good.

Quoting authorities, the *Malleus* specifies that "from the priesthood arises everything good, and everything evil," so that "it is impossible to find either worse or better men than those who grace or disgrace the monasteries." Men rule over the world of the artificial – institutions constructed according to knowledge and values – by applying their practical science. Offices are male even if occupied by a queen or a nun. By contrast, women are free, unconstrained, and natural. Their wickedness is independent of office and power: "there is no wrath above the wrath of a woman. I had rather dwell with a lion and a dragon than keep to house with the wicked woman. . . . All wickedness is but little to the wickedness of a woman. . . . When a woman thinks alone, she thinks evil." A woman is said to be a "desirable calamity."

Men tend to have too little virtue, women too much. But female virtues are also the highest. Here we see the Aristotelian trap in which Sade's victims are caught: too much virtue, like too much benevolence, shows immoderation and is a defect of character. The female virtues are defects simply because they either upset the proper equilibrium of virtues or they lack the master virtue which alone could balance the scale. Sade's women are trapped in the predicament of the *Malleus*: excessive virtue is a mistake which deserves to be punished. One can, however, avoid such a conclusion by saying that female virtues are not moral features, but rather indicators of virginity. Justine possesses too much virtue only in the sense that she never learns; instead, she stays in her original innocent state of ignorance. Her stupidity is incompatible with the balanced notion of virtues, so she remains virginal but not virtuous. Sade uses the term "virtue" to refer not to acquired character traits but rather to natural and uncorrupt features, like innocence and beauty. Such a virginal character is also passive, submissive, and not responsible for anything. Virginity entails a lack of experience and therefore also of initiative. She is outside both the moral and immoral world.

In the *Malleus*, women are compared to animals like lions, indicating that they too are natural creatures. Men are represented as relatively innocent of excess. Their peril results from the importance of their power and their status, which leads them away from virtue. Sade is unable to exploit this traditionalist picture, because his own typical vice is language. His men still have high social status, and his women are natural beasts. Thus his great subversive project becomes boring and suffers simply because he does not want to imagine a utopian social order where women possess the offices and men are natural beasts. On the contrary, Sade exaggerates female vice, making it so overpowering that male official roles look like insignificant insignia. He tries to make female vice so strong that it breaks into the male world of power and offices and poisons it from the inside.

In this way, Sade paints a subversive picture of heroines like Juliette without turning his back either on French society or on the traditional theory of the sexes. The price he pays is that now he cannot get rid of the female essence as traditionally defined without losing his contact with social reality.

Those who claim that Sade's women are only victims do not take into account characters like Madame de Saint-Ange, who teaches the young Eugenie the laws of a good marriage. She clearly assumes that to be a husband is a social role of some power, and her advice concerns how to eradicate male power and female submission. She relates that during her twelve years of marriage she has slept with ten or twelve thousand men. Her contract with her husband leaves the man totally humiliated:

> My husband was already advanced in years when I married him. On our wedding night he gave me notice of his fancies, the while assuring me that, for his part, never would he interfere with mine; I swore to obey him. . . . My husband's whim is to have himself sucked, and here is the most unusual practice joined as a corollary to that one; while, as I bend over him, my buttocks squarely over his face and cheerily pumping the fuck from his balls, I must shit in his mouth! He swallows it down.[9]

The configuration of their positions looks perfectly symmetrical, but actually the husband has been reduced to the role of the passive partner, an object of manipulation. The symbolism of excrement means that he loses his sperm but receives nothing in exchange; he exchanges value for waste. He may have initiated the contract, but it is disadvantageous to him. While the husband's power is turned into passivity, she earns her liberty by means of an act that qualifies as revenge on her husband.

This same scene can also be interpreted as emphasizing the blurring of any difference between male and female roles. They act the same way, their bodies function similarly, and they even look the same. Social norms for permissible sex prevent the creation of such symmetry or harmony, and Sade intends to subvert these norms. For the same reason, Sade constantly praises anal sex, which allows the vagina to be forgotten and makes women similar to men in many respects.

In this subversive project, the real problem for Sade is the male member, whose importance cannot be denied and which seems to justify traditional roles and power differences. Man's ability to penetrate, and in so doing create enjoyment for himself, is a feature which cannot be duplicated mechanically. The penis is a weapon that feels, while the knives and other weapons that Juliette uses can only attempt to simulate the feeling of penetration.

Sade struggles against this difference which violates the ideal of symmetry, and the strategy he uses is to have his men deny the reality of both breasts and vaginas. In Carter's words: "only men are supposed to feel a holy dread before its hairy portals. Only men are privileged to return, even if only partially and intermittently, to this place of fleshy extinction." The temptation is deadly: the Sadean man may return, but then he reaffirms the difference between man and woman. The womb is real, since it offers its own evidence: "in the beginning was the womb and its periodic and haphazard bleedings are so many signs that it has a life of its own."[10] Sade abhors female genitals for a good theoretical reason: it makes a taboo of what man cannot utilize without becoming impotent. Sade maintains that vaginal intercourse is self-castration. The alternative is for man to deny woman, and thus men and women remain bitter towards each other.

What Madame de Saint-Ange achieves is a partial revenge against cruel nature. The turd is the avenging symbol of male penetration insofar as it promises pleasure through one's own anus; it also penetrates the recipient's mouth like a dirty phallus. Here we have one reason why Sade is so excessively interested in excretion, an interest which even Gilbert Lely has trouble accepting in his defense of Sade. The symbolism is the deepest and most disgusting we find in Sade's works: the revenge of castration and the refusal to return to one's birthplace by means of the unclean surrogate of penetration. However, all libertines in their natural condition play with waste, and therefore have reasons to be bitter and to contemplate thoughts of revenge. Nature, liberated Rachel, rejects her own children.

## PLEASURE OR BRAIN

The Sadean mind has a crucial feature which can be understood when Poe's principle of perversity is applied to women: "It has pleased

Nature so to make us that we attain happiness only by way of pain." Only by means of breaking the rule of pain-avoidance can one enjoy sex. However, Madame de Saint-Ange has more to say about the topics of sex and women. She provides a set of propositions which parody prudential and utilitarian thought. For example, she prefers anal penetration to vaginal penetration if the pain can be overcome by means of training, and the arguments should be totally convincing to a utilitarian: "Fewer risks to her health, and none at all of pregnancy," a greater level of pleasure, and (as is made clear elsewhere) no loss of her trade value as a certifiable virgin. By "uniting practice with theory" one can live in a way which maximizes value, expected utility, and pleasure.[11] Some minor handicaps remain, though. Sodomy is generally condemned, and was actually punishable by death in Sade's time. This fact alone, however, cannot change the mind of a prudent decision-maker. If she refuses to practice anal sex under present circumstances, she still regrets it as an unjust denial of the best sexual alternative.

The effect of this parody of normal sex is to make room for the introduction of the theme of pain *qua* pleasure. The axiom of painful pleasure can itself be understood in three different ways: first, "a shared pleasure is a betrayal of the self,"[12] or enjoyment is a zero-sum game; second, it is a necessary condition of pleasure that one suffers before the promised enjoyment, just as hunger precedes an enjoyable meal; third, pain itself is a pleasure. Sade subscribes to the third view in particular. The soul feels excitement when it clashes with what is unexpected or what offers resistance. This is pain in its basic functional sense. Sade takes the soul to be a mere bundle of "voluptuous atoms" whose movement is life, and whose expression of life is their pressure against some other medium. When these voluptuous atoms are combined together in molecules, the result is malevolence. Mental energy is always directed where the resistance is, and the collapse of a barrier is intrinsically motivating. Once resistance is overcome by this energy, it discharges into the void created by the vanishing of the initial obstacle. The image is that of a thrusting force penetrating a medium which opens up, creating a hollow space, and making possible the discharge of energy and matter into the void. This is at once orgiastic pleasure and pain, or suffering in a more demanding sense. As I shall explain, such psychology also leads to vice and crime.

Orgiastic pleasure via discharge can be experienced on at least four separate levels: first, ejaculation (which both men and women can achieve) as a purely bodily reaction; second, irritation, aggression, and rage as the experience of mental confusion; third, the thought of a completed crime as an expression of the moral void; fourth, a breaking down of the grammatical laws of the descriptions of intentions and events. In many cases the last type of crime is the greatest of all acts of violence. Both the style and its grammar are crucial. All these factors must come together as a unity, however, before the authentic Sadean state of mind can be achieved.

Sade is not an Epicurean hedonist. An Epicurean hedonist maintains that pleasure is an actual, experiential, feeling-quality in real time. Pleasure has its magnitude, its opposites, and is also summative. Therefore, a reasonable person will conserve as much of it as possible over an extended period of time, to display his collection to himself so that he may enjoy it. Peak pleasure as such is not very important, simply because it tends to be costly. Any extremes now will hamper the later possibilities. The collection is important. As in the fixation to an atavistic anal phase of sexual development, the person collects all that is somehow connected to himself, as if he produced it and it were a part of his person. Painful things are defined as outside influences to be repressed.

If Sade is a hedonist, he is only a fictional one. Since his hedonism means that the libertine aims at pleasure which signifies transcendence and ultimately nothingness, this makes a mere discharge, detonation, the mark of orgiastic experience. Therefore, pleasure is neither a tool nor an end, but simply an indicator of what we call an orgasm – the orgiastic life is important to Sade as symbolism. An Epicurean hedonist, on the contrary, assigns extrinsic value to pleasure, and intrinsic value to its collection in the long run. In a rather paradoxical manner, he only aims at present pleasure as a means, rejecting any present pleasure which does not contribute towards a final release. Therefore he sees it later in the mirror of his personal history as a picture of the value of his life as a totality. If he is successful, he can be happy that he was happy. Sade's heroes do not want to be happy in this sense.

The Epicurean rule is that what belongs to a person is pleasant and what comes from outside is painful. Pure pleasure, then, does not require external support, and in this sense eating is not an ideal source of pleasure: one must be hungry to enjoy culinary delights, and hunger is an external causal influence on a person. The good life is that which in the end shows the largest collection of internal pleasures. An Epicurean wants to collect such pleasures that do not presuppose dependence on the external world or bring about pain. Of course, if there is a residue of pain, the total collection diminishes in size.

If we interpret these maxims in the strict sense, the only real pleasures are intellectual – reading a book, intelligent company, meditating alone. A person whose pleasures and feelings of love are self-referential becomes a narcissist. Such a strict model must be extended, however, on the grounds that pure intellectual pleasures are connected to more basic physical experiences, without which they cannot emerge. One needs at least some instruments to bring about internal hedonic qualities. One can also argue that the term "pleasure" does not make sense without a bodily component; when one speaks of pleasure, one refers to some kind of physical stimulation which one happens to like. Accordingly, it seems that Epicurean pleasure consists in a harmonious relationship between one's mind, body, and external circumstances.

Some features of the external world can be controlled better than others; for example, sex may be pleasant, but it is difficult to moderate. Food, on the other hand, offers all sorts of opportunities – something for every taste, as it were. Gourmandism can be the essence of Epicurean hedonism once we have lost hope of finding pleasures which are strong and pure. Eating offers pleasure and a controlled social situation (via an etiquette). Not only does it provide a strong bodily experience, but it also offers aesthetic possibilities, even opportunities for artistic creations. Of course, food poisoning, cirrhosis of the liver, obesity, ulcers, choking, and countless other dangers force our hedonist to stay alert and play his game intelligently. A gourmand also exhibits features of animal cruelty by grabbing, tearing apart, and chewing. It seems that the pleasures of the table achieve real-life complexity.

The great celebration of this alternative is in Jean-Anthelme Brillat-Savarin's splendid book *La Physiologie du goût*. Just as Sade's literary works illustrate aspects of the ethics of virtue and vice, as well as Hobbesian political theory, so Brillat-Savarin's essays allow us to see a world devoted to hedonistic pleasures. The table is a metaphor of social order, of human life and its harmonies. The gourmet table gets its meaning from descriptions where everything has its own place, and where etiquette provides the ground rules of enjoyment. Nevertheless, rather than follow this positive clue or pay attention to the brutishness of eating, I shall deal with those personal troubles encountered by the model gourmand in his effort to find his direction in the jungle of pots, pans, forks, tables, chairs, flesh, blood, teeth, and bellies.

Brillat-Savarin claims that his treatise deals with the science of gastronomy, a science which justifies the ideology of gourmandism and explains related psychological and social phenomena. The status of his science is similar to the form of Sade's science of the wicked life. The whole project is an allegory loaded with stories, vivid scenes, and appealing metaphors. It is science only in the sense of a joke: a real philosopher eats, but etiquette forbids him to speak with his mouth full, and that is why we have not heard of him before. Now Brillat-Savarin has found a way of overcoming these obstacles; he succeeds in depicting a universe of eating well in such a way that the result is indeed a whole world. He writes: "Gastronomy governs the whole life of man; for the tears of the new-born child are for its nurse's breast, and the dying man derives pleasure from the final potion, which, alas, he will never digest."[13] Physics is considered reducible to gastronomy by means of rules which relate to the "composition and quality of foodstuffs." Something similar can be said of all other sciences, too. They serve the master-science of the good life. The concept of food has the following meaning: "By food we mean those substances which, on being submitted to the stomach, can be animalized by digestion, and so repair the losses suffered by the human body through the wear and tear of life."[14] Appetite is a "warning device" by means of which we judge that deprivation occurs, and taste is the sense which provides required information about the food.

How do we make contact with pleasure? Taste has its role here too: "Gastronomy examines taste as an organ of both pleasure and pain; it has discovered the gradual increase of excitement to which taste is liable, regulated the rate of that increase, and fixed upon a limit beyond which no self-respecting person should go."[15] Taste is the organ of pleasure which serves functional goals, like the nourishment of the body. At the same time, taste does not contain any restricting natural factors which would prevent a person from exceeding his limits. This is a problem.

The model gourmand dedicates his whole life to his pet values; he substitutes an allegory of living well for reality. He is a widower who creates his own dream universe where his ideals and talents achieve their purest expression. However, he is also a scientist who cannot tolerate fictional worlds of hedonism. Pleasure is real; only his life is an allegory. Since he needs food, he studies this need, and he finds that the sensations of taste are pleasant if they are properly handled. He teaches himself how to maximize the pleasant tone of his taste-buds, elaborates on them, shares his knowledge with his friends, and becomes a happy person. He finds his pleasure both in what is useful and in what is necessary. Nothing compares to the intense pleasures he has found by means of his science. The results, however realistic, are put to metaphoric usage: good eating is life.

Now, the crucial point in this context is that the gourmand must be able to keep both his eating and his life under restraint. First of all, insofar as he must eat well, the culinary code restricts his choices. Then there is the social question of good behavior at table. These two codes control his life. Certain dangers also exist.

The first of these dangers is that of alcoholism. The chapter entitled "The dangerous effects of strong liquor" is as good a description of alcohol-related deaths as can be found anywhere. Brillat-Savarin describes workers in a brandy warehouse who have access to all the hard liquor they want. They start with one glass in the morning, go on to two glasses a day, and finally, after many years of slow degeneration, they "dry up, fever takes hold of them, they go into hospital, and they are never seen again." This happens with a law-like regularity. The person disappears. Instead of death, the malfunction of the body and the patient's disappearance from his fountain of pleasure are described.

The second great danger is that of obesity. Brillat-Savarin discusses it in detail, saying, "By *obesity* I mean that state of fatty congestion in which, without the individual being ill, his limbs gradually increase in volume and lose their original shape and harmony."[16] Obesity is said to injure beauty just as it destroys the natural proportions of the body and makes the face featureless. It prevents one from moving, so that one's societal life becomes restricted. Moreover, an obese person is vulnerable to all kinds of disease. One should take regular exercise, follow a diet, and avoid starches. Certainly, a scientist who knows this is also able to apply his knowledge, even if it means that he cannot eat as much bread and potatoes as he may desire. One must make hard choices and suffer unavoidable losses.

Brillat-Savarin recommends a well-balanced life-style based on knowledge of bodily functions and on judgments of taste; life can be arranged around this nucleus in a permanent manner. Even death is defined in these terms. Brillat-Savarin relates the story of an old lady who dies happily after tasting a glass of good wine. Life on this basis becomes an exercise of style well regulated by means of etiquette, based on knowledge, and conducive to a holistic satisfaction. The crown is social success: your friends love to stay at your home because of your hospitality. Since you simply cannot prepare the meals and eat all alone, no trace of egoism can be detected in this kind of hedonism. You need friends who share your tastes.

However appealing this hedonistic philosophy may sound, it is unlikely that philosophers like Mill and Bentham had something like it in mind when they wrote their famous utilitarian programs. But what else could they have had in mind when they spoke about pleasure and happiness? Unfortunately, Brillat-Savarin's science and values illustrate the good life so very nicely precisely because his ideal gourmand lives in such a narrow sector of life. The picture fails to support an ethic of rights, duties, or social justice. This is to say, an allegory cannot rule in the complex world.

Unlike Brillat-Savarin, a Sadean character does not collect pleasures based on predetermined restrictions which focus on holistic considerations of prudence. How could he? Pleasure as defined by Sade is a clash with a norm already presupposed. Every pleasure means the breaking into the void. The return activates a new episode, or even a new life, which cannot be connected to the earlier one by means of the simple arithmetical operation of summation. Three considerations are relevant here. First, a maximal quantity of pleasure in time is not in itself a physical pleasure, but rather a mere idea of pleasure – at most a source of self-satisfaction and pride. Sade refuses to deal with this. Second, every regulated pleasure is an impoverished pleasure, and Sade loathes non-maximal effects. Third, the destructiveness of extreme pleasure can be controlled by means of self-deception, in the following way. Suppose one eats too much and feels nauseated; or suppose one contracts syphilis, which used to mean certain death. The vomiting can be the opportunity for pure drama, and venereal disease offers countless chances to destroy other persons. Sade claims that because the perverse principle works in the epistemic field, bad luck need not be taken seriously. One may enjoy the privilege of violating both epistemic norms and practical rules. The result is that a Sadean person need not restrain his behavior merely to accumulate smaller pleasures. He maximizes every particular pleasure as it comes, and gets away with it. The Sadean technique is a familiar one: different pleasures are freely interchangeable but not summative or socially shared.

Moreover, the Sadean concept of time-consciousness is different from the Epicurean notion. Sadean time entails circularity. The circles are small but numerous, and time is a set of small circles of real life. Every pleasure is independent of any other pleasure, and after a discharge the person returns to the point from which he started. He achieves nothing, simply because he cannot add more pleasures to the pool of them which he already possesses. The Epicurean concept of time, however, is linear, extending from a person's birth to his death. Because life leads to its end, and after all pleasures are summarized there will be no more, such linearity is terrifying. Circularity avoids this problem, as Brillat-Savarin comes close to admitting. He speculates that all people need alcohol to reduce anxiety about future uncertainties. It has a kind of metaphysical significance as an antidote against the future, or against the painful Epicurean tendency to collect pleasures over a linear period of time. Although his prudential reason tells him that this is where he must live, a person does not dare to look forward. For a drunk, time-consciousness gets twisted and vanishes; so one must drink. Sade plays with similar ideas.

The Sadean person has a large number of independent scenarios of pleasure to work with. Every time he meets resistance, or goes out of his mind or out of his body through ejaculation, he experiences what Sade calls pleasure. This Sadean pleasure abhors limits, because it consists of breaking them. For the same reason, pleasure is not future oriented; it happens here and now, and after its consummation nothing remains.

For Sade, if death is a pleasure, then the whole idea of the summation of pleasures is nonsensical. The sum of all pleasures is something to be calculated after the event, and one cannot make any calculations after death. A similar truth applies to pain and to orgiastic pleasure. It would be foolish to summarize all one's pains and then claim that the larger the sum, the better the life. Because it is experienced pain, such a sum of memories must be a calculus of misery. It does not make sense to say that one restricts present pain so that future pain will be larger. Only at the moment of experiencing it can the pain appear as something pleasant. To restrict pain is to avoid it, and to minimize its total effect. Of course the memory of pain stimulates too, but such a pain, as pain, cannot be maximized. The anticipation of pain may be pleasant to a sado-masochist, but it may be disgusting as well. Sade's characters certainly love to discuss pain and pleasure, but this is because such talk is itself wicked – and therefore a pleasure which is independent of the counter-hedonistic calculi.

Orgiastic pleasures are similar to pain in that they are worthless except at the moment they are experienced; otherwise they can neither be described nor remembered. Here the comparison with a good meal is useful: a good meal can be recalled, say, because of a unique display of dishes. Unlike the case of discharge, where the pleasure is provided by one's transcendence of the sexual scene itself, the culinary pleasure resides at the table. Sexual irritation and rage lead the libertine towards something else, namely, discharge. Having reached it, it is nothing. The gourmand does not leave the table, even in his thoughts. On the contrary, he focuses on the company and the meal all the time, so that he can control his emotions and feelings and find a suitable conclusion to the meal. He follows the script, or the etiquette.

Sade's heroes tend to eat excrement, which they find rather essential: "The little girls' eight steaming turds were arranged amidst the supper's dishes, and at the orgies the competition was doubtless even keener for those of the little boys."[17] This kind of episode can be seen as a parody of the gourmet etiquette described by Brillat-Savarin. Sade writes:

> The rest of that worn and wasted body, that ass of parchment or ancient leather, that ample, noxious hole glistening in its center, this mutilated tit, those three vanished fingers, this short leg that causes her to limp, that mouth destitute of teeth, everything combines to stimulate our libertine pair. Durcet sucks her from in front, Curval posteriorly, and even though objects of the greatest beauty and in the best condition are there before their eyes and ready to brave anything in order to satisfy the least of their desires, even so it is with what Nature and villainy have dishonored, have withered, it is with the filthiest and least appetizing object our two rakes, presently beside themselves, are about to taste the most delicious pleasures.[18]

The two men are "like two savage mastiffs wrangling over a corpse." Sade presents this particular vignette as a riddle and demands, "now give me your explanations!" Significantly, the scene ends when the dinner bell is rung. Thus if we want to understand what is asked we must read the text, disgusting as it is. Sade wants to negate all Brillat-Savarin-type philosophers by presenting his own alternative theory of pleasure. Insofar as man is a beast, doing what is incomprehensible and going out of his mind, this – Sade says – is real life. Everything else is its faint reflection, or its impoverished analog. Sade's pleasures are beyond description, just like nature, and equally difficult to reach.

To summarize Sade's theory of pleasure, three components must be distinguished: sensual, cerebral, and orgiastic. Pleasure often means sensual enjoyment which, as in Brillat-Savarin's case, is neither tainted by any pain nor constituted by reasoning. Reasoning may direct the seeker of sensual enjoyment, but it does not constitute a goal. This is what I call innocent pleasure. Sade is not interested in sensual pleasure *per se*, since he finds it insufficiently stimulating. Sensual pleasure is never strong enough without a cerebral component, as Angela Carter emphasizes: "The nature of [monk] Clement's pleasure is by no means a sensual one; his pleasure is a cerebral one, even an intellectual one – that of the enhancement of the ego."[19] But orgiastic events are different, as Carter herself maintains:

> The libertines are indeed like men possessed by demons. Their orgasms are like the visitation of the gods of Voodoo, annihilating, appalling. Minski's orgasm, that kills his partners, is announced by a ringing yell. Catherine the Great screams and blasphemes. Durand emits dreadful screams and her limbs twitch and thrash. ... These descriptions are those of torture.[20]

However, Carter fails to show that Sade's pleasure is an orgasm and, in addition, cerebral. The theory that the cerebral component is an ego-trip is not right, because "orgasm" or discharge means the loss of the ego and the return to the Id. Carter does not pay sufficient attention to Sade's subversiveness and the self-destruction which is essential to evil.

The paradigm for pleasure is orgiastic, which is indeed pain and torture. Its cerebral component has two functions. First, it makes it possible to understand what it means to breach a value and destroy things. Second, it is required if one is going to be able to achieve discharges in the predatory fashion. One wants a theater, and this is a practical achievement that utilizes science and planning. One's orgiastic pleasure both utilizes science and is cerebral in nature – yet it self-destructs.

## THE AVENGER

The myth of the violation of norms and values is absolutely crucial to Sade. The sequence is always the same: first, a set of closed physical, psychological, and stylistic phases, like a dinner table; then a plan to break out into the freedom of the void, like preparing a disgusting dish; and finally the eating of it, which results in exhaustion and satisfaction, something like vomiting. However, at that point the Sadean heroes have already returned to their original position. Everything has been achieved, and they are calm. Such an eternal return is unavoidable, because behind the barrier there was nothing. The sperm has vanished. In an ironic manner one now understands that the greatest of all pleasures is nothing – and one calms down. The heat of transcendent passion is replaced by a feeling of void, like the immanent emptiness of philosophical chatter.

Such an order of things is evident also in educational matters. Unlike pleasure, wickedness is a good guide. As Juliette says, the libertine must always start from the idea of wickedness and proceed towards excitement and discharge. The wrong order is to start from excitement and rage, and then do the wicked thing. Perverse wickedness must be the motive for performing some acts and not the result of some initial confusion. If one does evil things only when one is agitated, one cannot control one's own actions, and pleasures cannot be found. The agent is neither fully responsible nor totally evil. Because crimes must be started in cold blood, a rigoristic philosophical attitude is important for pleasure. Here we see also the transition from a naively scavenging life-style towards a predatory motive. Pleasure becomes partly cerebral because it requires rigorous self-control, planning, and reasoning. Paradoxically, a mature libertine needs apathy; he needs it because he wants to control his prey. At the earlier stages, a libertine can only do violent things, as if to avenge the harm brought about by his failure to control nature and man.

A Sadean person's authentic plan of life aims at pleasure here and now, regardless of its cost. Some stage is needed, however, so that various aspects of one's life can be unified through one's predatory behavior. The young Juliette goes out with a pistol one night to experience what it is like to kill someone at random. She meets a poor beggar girl who tells her affecting story to Juliette; Juliette promptly shoots her through the head. No artificial stage exists, because Juliette merely trains herself and experiments with her predatory instincts. She goes back to the streets of Paris, outside the walls of the theater of cruelty. Once she is back in her own social world, she has one more story to act out on the stage. She has neither scavenged (she has found her own prey) nor suffered herself (as an avenger does). On the contrary, she has found a source of mature pleasure as a predator.

Now, of the four aspects of pleasure, we are presently interested only in the physical and psychological types. The initial question concerns the description of the proper obstacles to action as seen by the perverse agent himself. The first of them is pain. Just as psychology is related to text, so pain is related to sex. Sex is always an interpretation of pain. Sadean sex is a symbolic activity whose viciousness is connected to pain on the one hand, and to twisted narratives on the other. Sex is also a way of reaching the void through penetration and ejaculation – processes through which one surrenders and loses a part of one's body to another person. Nevertheless, sex is not uniquely important, because the same bodily result can be achieved by means of, say, bleeding or urinating. These are analogous to sexual activity, and Sade indeed treats them interchangeably. Blood gushes out of an open wound, leaving the victim dizzy and exhausted; and it can find its way to another person's body, too. Violence and sex intertwine.

The combination of violence and sex is a familiar literary technique. It is used, for instance, by V. S. Naipaul in his superbly orgiastic account of a killing:

> Her right hand was on the arm swelling around her neck, and it was on her right arm that Bryant made the first cut. The first cut: the rest would follow. Sharp steel met flesh. Skin parted, flesh showed below the skin, for an instant mottled white, and then all was blinding, disfiguring blood, and Bryant could only cut at what had already been cut. She cried out, in tears, in pain, in despair, "Help me Jimmy!"

Jimmy "concentrated on that smoothness and tension until she began to fail," but "there was nothing except desolation."[21] Naipaul provides an example of Sadean pleasure and orgasm in terms which are at most camouflaged sex, but not necessarily even that. Sex is not the paradigm case of pleasure, nor is orgasm an exclusively sexual term. On the contrary, sex and orgasm are modeled according to violence: the body is cut open so that the result is discharge. Therefore violence is independently orgiastic so that sex at most simulates its effects. For this same reason, sex has not much to do with eroticism in the Sadean lore.

In Sade's world, pain comes close to being the essence of pleasure by providing an orgiastic rush into the void through collapsing mental barriers. If pain is inflicted on a victim, the master's pleasure stays at the symbolic level. Sadism is fictional, since only my own pain is physically verifiable. Therefore the masters are ready to suffer themselves. Juliette is happy to accept whippings at any time during her apprenticeship, and at Silling the masters are whipped regularly until their skin is toughened like old leather. The masters enjoy the pain; their victims do not. The masters love the excrement their victim produces and hates. The meal is disgusting, but it is precisely this repulsion that creates the limit whose transgression is the source of what Sade calls pleasure.

It is not only the victims who are violated. The masters experience the same fate. Because the victims are innocent, they are unable to enjoy what they go through; their education is not complete, and many of them will never get a chance to learn. Therefore not everyone is a happy monster. The victims' mental constitution is what makes them suffer without satisfaction, because they do not suffer freely. The masters want to overcome all obstacles. They do not desire to experience anything resembling pleasure in the sense in which the victims use the word. The modest enjoyment of life's little things is declared to be meaningless on the grounds that it motivates only Justine, whose fate is so sad. So-called normal pleasures are either negligently weak or dangerous for the Sadean hero's life plan. Therefore Sade professes to prove that virtue will be persecuted, which indeed happens in the subconscious world of the death-instinct he describes.

All innocent pleasures belong to the life beyond the metaphysical contract which created the wicked life. No aspect of the experience of the Sadean masters should be interpreted along the model of innocent pleasures. When the masters are orgiastic they are madmen out of their minds; their thoughts reach toward forbidden modes, and the results defy the laws of logic and the grammar of the good life. The unity of physical pain, mental rage, and forbidden narratives penetrates to the hidden depths, and have no resemblance to the pleasures of the uninitiated life.

Sade illustrates his motivational psychology in reference to a person's normative ideas as well as in reference to bodily suffering. Just as the person may aim at his own pain, so he may aim at his own psychological torment without bodily pain. One example is a hero who claims that he is a terrible coward. A weak victim is better than a strong one; the former offers a strong moral obstacle, which is more important for Sadean characters than any physical struggle. Supposing that courage is the typical self-ideal of a rich and powerful male, then our hero loves to act in a cowardly way. He commits only safe crimes and is really scared of what he is doing. He is motivated by his negative self-image, of which he is truly proud. Such an example, which utilizes normative concepts in a motivational and factual context, indicates clearly the desperate need of Sadean characters for a barrier. The cowardice of a Sadean master throws up self-created private barriers which must be crossed to experience orgiastic pleasure and the void.

One social corollary of the existence of the perverse goal is that the masters are outside of any social controls. Punishment, persecution, and even torture create an additional pleasant scenario. Because time is not linear, the result is a return to the initial state, or to another stage setting where pain brings about a new discharge. The explanation of the invulnerability of the heroes lies in the fact that the heroes seek a metaphysical revenge, like Captain Ahab; they must get hurt both through their own actions and through the actions of others. They cannot control nature, and hate it; but since they hate nature, they hate themselves. This chain of propositions shows how the pain/pleasure combination works, and also why the Sadean heroes struggle towards something bitter.

In Sade's works, the inward invulnerability of the heroes takes the outward symbolic expression of wealth, social status, and legal power. But as Juliette teaches us, their position is more a result of their invulnerability to the use of power against them than a source of their own power. Juliette becomes wealthy when her education proceeds successfully, and once she is rich and powerful, she can do more and reach even further. She starts from extreme submissiveness and then moves gradually towards a more aggressive position and a stronger identity. Her high social status is a symbolic expression of her hedonistic maturity as a whore. At the same time, her status expresses social injustice.

A somewhat different approach to the riddle of the high social status and great wealth enjoyed by Juliette and other Sadean heroes can be found in the combination of psychological atavism and the nature of pleasure. As Brillat-Savarin writes:

> it is difficult to avoid the belief that the men who lived nearer than ourselves to the cradle of the world were also endowed with appetites far larger than our own. Appetites in those days were supposed to increase in proportion to the dignity of the individual; and a man who was served with the entire back of a five-year-old bull would drink from a cup so heavy he could scarcely lift it.[22]

He also claims that the nobles ate the "most repugnant objects." According to this view, Sade returns to the myth of the original powerful hero, and accordingly, to the modern person's atavistic impulses. Wickedness is the expression of glory, of high social status, and great wealth. Once the person is rich, he has more chance to enjoy his life. As a symbol of enjoyment, wealth is not something which is brought about by vice, contrary to what Sade often says.

Perhaps the ultimate hedonistic problem is the following one. Sade's notion of pleasure may be totally unconvincing as a motivational idea. It may be maintained that it simply does not make sense to suggest that Juliette could be motivated by the idea of overcoming an obstacle, if all she gets in return is pain. Of course, as a psychological theory it does not make much sense. Folk psychology defines pleasure in a twofold way, first by saying that pleasure is something that one likes to feel, and second by saying that pleasure is the motivation or spring of action. Pleasure is construed as a desire, and pain as a typical aversion. By these lights, it would indeed be a contradiction to maintain that a person desires pain.

Sade counters this by saying that although innocent pleasures are something people want if they are uneducated, in a state of normal consciousness, or victimized by others, there is another source of motivational tension which constitutes the ultimate layer of human experience. This is the discharge of aggression that arises through the need to avenge metaphysical frustrations. The pleasure of physical pain is only one aspect of the total picture, and cannot be understood without the help of all the others. The project of perversity and wickedness of will includes the psychological motivation by pain. Even folk psychology must admit that pleasure is merely one of the many different human goals, and Sade's point is that the concepts of pain and pleasure must be radically redefined.

At this point we find the Sadean heroes at their most aggressive. Their pleasures are merely destructive. They cause harm to their victims, from whom they often have difficulties in distinguishing themselves, and they feel themselves deceived by nature, which they cannot control even though it rewards them so amply. This is the reason why pain is attractive to them. They turn in their rage against the only natural entities they think they can master: their own minds and bodies. This revenge, however, is only a transitory stage. They will learn how to create and control an artificial environment which guarantees their perverse pleasures. The first step in this direction is taken by establishing a moral language, which can then be subversively exploited. Through demolishing this morality they can overcome the limits of mere pain as a source of pleasure. Then the heroes are ready to make a social contract and to create an artificial world – a stage – which they produce themselves in their role of predators.

I do not think this aspect of hatred and rage which lies behind Sade's account of orgiastic pleasure has been properly recognized. Somehow the heroes are filled with a dissatisfaction that motivates them, and it is based on the revenge against nature according to Sade's metaphysics. The stage is now set for the appearance of ethics and a social contract, both of which allow the heroes to destroy something they control.

# 5

# THE ETHIC OF VICE

Sade's motivational subversiveness cuts so deep that it may be impossible to understand. One may, *prima facie*, counter this by conceptualizing his efforts as nihilistic projects in ethics and moral philosophy. My feeling is that such an approach is not successful because of the problems we encounter in the case of the principle of nature. To correct this, some loans from aesthetics, or from Sade's style, are needed. At least in Sade's case, wickedness is ultimately an artistic project of shaping one's life in such a narcissistic manner that it will display the features of chaos and destruction. The wicked life will be the story – a vignette of expressions – of what it means to follow the principle of nature in its deepest sense.

The theatrical aspect of Sade's work is the key to these ideas. On stage he dreams of controlling pleasure. Therefore, the process of interpretation must start from the theatrical production of life, or from the artificial frames created by the whorish storytellers at the castle of Silling. The final destructive act is, as we shall see, to read Sade's novels without alienation and irony. Because the unprotected reader tries to decipher what he cannot understand, he will also experience a painful loss. It is dangerous to be naive, Sade seems to say.

Sade's pet strategy is to resort to the baroque richness of expressive forms, and ultimately to inconsistency. At the same time he both hates and adores the injustice in the social world around him. He denies the laws of ethics, but vows friendship and love for his liberated heroes. Moreover, he promotes contradictions and yet wants to tell us a story about them. For him human life is full of inconsistencies in a peculiarly practical sense. But such a creation of a life-world belongs already to Sade's style and its aesthetics.

## PLANS OF LIFE

Before we tackle the enigma of incoherent life-styles from the stylistic point of view, let us review some facts associated with more traditional ethics. John Rawls is an exponent of the view that value is a matter of a person's rational life plan when the person has sufficient information concerning its alternatives and has also mastered the required practical reasoning:

> The rational plan for a person determines his good. Here I adapt Royce's thought that a person may be regarded as a human life lived according to a plan. For Royce an individual says who he is by describing his purposes and causes, what he intends to do in his life.

A plan is rational if it is well informed and consistent with utility theory.[1] In other words, value is defined in terms of good life, which again is a matter of prudent rational choice. According to an extended ideology, which is not exactly the same as the Rawlsian theory, a person chooses his own moral career, which in turn makes possible cooperation, a meaningful life-style, personal integrity, and the achievement of one's own goals. One follows norms which are as simple and as universal as possible. A kind of analog to scientific inductivism concerning theories applied to human life may be suggested. A person is invited to view his whole career as a theory which explains the good life in a social setting. Such a theory must be formulated in a hostile research environment – that is, under epistemic uncertainty and value scarcity.

A person has all kinds of possibilities in life, his choices have unpredictable consequences, and people around him disagree in many ways. The key is to choose the most elegant way of living so that its inherent risks are minimized. Thereby a maximum number of life plans becomes simultaneously possible in a social setting, without serious classes of interest. Convoluted life plans may lead to personal catastrophes exactly as false theories lead to vitiating errors. To avoid this, the personal life plan must be integrated to other plans, so that a smooth personal and social life emerges. One is invited to construct a life just as an inductivist scientist handles his theories, that is, according to the cognitive criterion of evidential elegance as well as that of theoretical integration, explanatory power, and simplicity. Coherence both in theory and in life is the key to their value aspect. I shall first describe the features of such an enlightenment view of ethics and then contrast the results with Sade's ideas, which are romantic or baroque.

A person's life plan must be simple, elegant, and coherent, possessing maximal explanatory power, if it is going to work as a ground for his values. If all goes well, the person may take his own values to the bargaining table, a universal forum where people participate. There one reaches an agreement with others to the effect that some values are shared, some are reserved for private use, and certain residual items are discarded. A person may not want powerful coercive capabilities among his bargaining chips, because he understands that they will be eliminated at the table on the grounds that not all can have them, and thus they are risky. He is not entitled to cruelty as a value because it is dangerous to others. The most basic values – those that will be in every bag when the players arrive at the table – we call initially "basic rights," then "human rights" after agreement is reached. The variable elements in life plans we call "factors of welfare," such as the conspicuous consumption of goods and exposure to art. Certain items are rejected, including pornography, blood sports, recreational drugs, and the pleasures derived from harming others. In addition to well-founded rejections, a number of taboos are also created, such as nudity and dirty words, so that room for personal values is located between the limits constituted by rights and taboos.

Now, every individual needs his own life plan, because otherwise he has nothing to sell to others. Competitors must perceive their lives as being dependent on it so that they recognize the person and make concessions when facing his demands. Therefore, one's streamlined product must also display certain crucial features; otherwise it may become so awkward that it will be simplified at the bargaining table. A person may well save himself from this humiliation by seeing to the plan's initial simplicity. He tries to find a minimal number of items which, taken as his values, allow him to live a life of his own. For instance, he wants to be free, affluent, and capable of both giving and receiving love. Under those conditions, the basic chance of realizing the plan is preserved, whatever one chooses to do and regardless of what the others may think.

The person's life plan is public because of its role in practical reasoning and in the bargaining process. If the plans were private, coherence would not be so important. A person could also amend his plan on an *ad hoc* basis as the occasion requires. However, because he must present his plan to others, it must be at least intelligible, and its rationality makes it such. The next element is the explanatory power of a life plan, in the sense that the plan must make sense of the person's personal desires. For example: one person may subscribe to the values of free time, education, personal independence, and aesthetic enjoyment in order to explain his love of nature. Another person may support the values of technical training, busy schedules, financial independence, and egoism in order to explain a self-centered life-style. In such a case the two explanations of life must be different, because the former value pattern cannot explain the latter goal, and vice versa. Though this is not the same as inconsistency, it is closely related to the integrity of one's career, or the unity of virtues. The classic example of this is that we should not want benevolence without justice, or courage without honesty. The first failure represents foolishness, and the second recklessness. Isolated virtues are worthless.

One cannot refer to the first pattern of explanation above and maintain that the goal is a high-level consumption of goods. This is not an inconsistent view, but only an empirically strange one where the logic is difficult to understand. Why is consumption so important? The explanation of one's life does not succeed. Therefore, the plan of a person's life is designed according to an inductivist model of science, where the object of study is one's own conduct of the business of living. The explanation utilizes empirical evidence gathered from social life and its practices. This is why the model belongs to the inductivist group.

Now, Sade's master project can be understood as a baroque counter-argument against the view that identifies virtue with a coherent life plan, whether virtue is conceived in the Greek sense of the excellence of well-ordered habits or in the Roman and Machiavellian sense of virility, shrewdness, and strength of character. Coherence understood as order and strength is an undesirable quality for Sade, as for any anti-enlightenment thinker. It follows that their life plans cannot be modeled after a scientific theory. On the contrary, to them a person is an individual and his career is an expression of this mysterious uniqueness. The result is a kind of baroque view of thought. The good life and its values are founded directly on character, not on the explanatory coherence which hides individuality. This means that the life plan is neither seen nor accepted at the bargaining table; instead, it is displayed at once by the self-made hero for others to recognize. There is no guarantee that the plan is intelligible to the spectators. Still less probable is their willingness to share such one-sided values.

Even if this lack of coherence entails chaos, that startling result is also welcome. Though in science the lack of coherence endangers understanding and communication, in real life such a danger must be accepted (so long as certain vestiges of communication are preserved). For example, Sade's libertines are fond of social gatherings, and they call each other friends. Perhaps we may say that they need a minimal life plan, according to Sade's philosophy, but the plan has no role in the explanation of goals and intrinsic values. Life plans are merely hypothetical imperatives used as signposts along the road to chaos.

At this point, if Sade wants to reach towards some genuine values, the contradictions of his thought start to emerge through the net he casts. Though discharges and orgiastic pleasure are real, theories are unreal. This can be seen through the periodic changes of theories into discharges and through the collapse back into theory. If discharges are destructive, theory means recuperation. Therefore, a destructive theory is too demanding. It leaves the libertine without a place to which to escape. Because Sade needs his haven of theory, he has no use for moral theories. They are simply too demanding.

Since explanations always generalize, a life plan does not individuate a person, but a type or a case. Therefore, if a person is perfectly moral, he is not an individual but is like any other bearer of these same values. It seems that Sade's counter-ethical point is that moral laws, and the principles of value derived from them, destroy personal identity. (Of course, Sadean pleasure does the same.) At the bargaining table he must be able to retain some idiosyncratic preferences which are so strong that in hard cases he may follow them rather than the shared moral directives. Only on the condition that he becomes unpredictable can he be an individual. Yet Sade does not want to disappear like this; and supported by the idea that the natural world is a principle of energy, pleasure, excitement, and destruction, he fights against his fate. Here, then, is a typically Sadean dilemma: a person faces anonymous destruction within the bounds of ethics (that is, by reasoning like any other good person he loses his individuality); but the only way to avoid such a fate is to rebel and to break the laws of comprehensible thought and prudent action. Such mad rage is the person's only way out of the quiet death which is ethics. Nevertheless, by so doing he does not seem to be able to explain his life as his own. How can he individuate himself if he avoids all explanations? His life plan cannot do it. The ironic conclusion follows that if values and laws cannot work as a plan of life which individuates the heroes, neither can orgiastic pleasure. Nor can self-transcendence achieve this effect. The libertines are identical when they wriggle and scream. The heroes must come back from the darkness in order to tell who they are. They need a philosophy of vice which is not ethics but a method of individuating themselves. They talk endlessly about themselves in order to protect whatever vestige of personal identity they may have.

In a rather profound sense, personal identity, values, and the good life are artificial. They must be created, because by means of them one can explain aspects of one's own existence. Sade's works abound with moral descriptions of friendship and trust between rakes. These persons are not illusory to each other, but at the same time all value explanations are insufficient and restricting, and therefore Sade wants to transgress them. This entails the camouflage of betrayal, cruelty, and nihilism. One cannot destroy what does not exist, which means that good must be manufactured. Of course, the good exists only as a background. It is indeed the interplay between conventional ethics and its undermining by base desires that makes Sade's stories so disturbing to the reader.

Values and moral rules do not explain personal identity for Sade, but they make it possible to enjoy things which otherwise would not even exist. Some laws are broken, others are transcended, and personal identity vanishes into orgiastic pleasure. This is indeed pleasant. Ethics makes possible enjoyment which is denied by the principles themselves. Rigid discipline, applied to others, is pleasant to the masters. On the other hand, such disciplinary rules when applied to the masters themselves must be transgressed. If the rules originate in religion, they are unfounded and will be violated. This inversion produces indirect pleasure, which is not entailed by the rules themselves. Such rules may be thought of as merely useful. Finally, one may transgress one's own principles, in the following way. At Silling, the friends make an agreement not to harm each other or to harm the cooks. Some persons can feel safe, while others feel more insecure. A rule which guarantees safety must be observed in order to create danger to others. In other words, transcended rules have a limited area of application in terms of time, place, and people. Yet another way to transcend rules is by means of self-discipline. Juliette knows that in order to enhance her enjoyment she must experience deprivation. When she finally unleashes herself, her fury is overwhelming. In this case, the disciplinary rules need not be broken, since they apply for only a limited time. Since in most cases disciplinary rules are a nuisance to the hedonist, they must be discarded.

Sade claims that his libertines are free since they live full lives. Of course, such a life is not a life at all in the sense of having a good life and social career. One finds only a concatenation of theatrical episodes, each of which expresses the same points about rest, arousal, and discharge. If we take the theatrical aspect seriously, we need not construct the Sadean heroes' careers as lives in the conventional sense. Because these people are artificial, everything about them is repetitious and episodic: nothing can be explained.

Sadean persons do not look like well-drawn psychological characters. In the background we see their immense wealth and social power, which are produced by their reckless actions in an unjust society. Society's mad order is a background which is tuned up to the level of the heroes' actions and thoughts. Stories of corrupt ministers of justice or cruel priests express Sade's irony, which is not an explanatory notion in some pseudo-scientific sense. In other words, his characters demand explanation (as all characters do), although their bizarre nature makes it difficult to provide one. Certainly no moral psychology of vice is provided by Sade.

A Sadean life is so intense that not much room is left for accusations of incoherence. Philosophical speculation is one thing, but when the debauchery starts it seems pointless to call it incoherent. Like an explosion, such an action follows its own dynamics. Moral criticism runs out of space, because no one even hints at careers that are open to moral control and guidance. For example, if a person only whips other people, his life plan is coherent and his personality well integrated; it just remains unexplained except in terms of psychopathology. The circumstances are too artificial and too theatrical. What is missing is the identity of the torturer. Therefore in his life no conventional ethic applies.

That no persons have identities is one of the main tenets of Sade's counter-ethics. Only a few chosen individuals – the future Nietzsches – are authentic anti-persons. Since they are not individuated, they are uniquely identified by means of the evil stories they tell, their philosophizing, and their acting on stage. All other people are mere objects – junk to be marked or discarded, mechanisms which produce blood, sweat, and tears. In this manner, the ethical ideal of shared human dignity is a basic falsehood. Sade's logic is anti-humanistic.

Sade's counter-ethics describes the principles of living according to a wicked plan, or baroque style of life. The basic rules require one to choose goals which are cruel and deceptive; a judge who hangs people for his enjoyment is the paradigmatic type. One finds the following little exchange of ideas in *Juliette*, where the Minister of Justice, Saint-Fond, goes to work:

"My desires are a bit loathsome, I know, but you are intelligent. I have done you outstanding service; I shall do more: you are wicked, you are vindictive, – very well," said he, tendering me six *lettres de cachet* which required only to be filled in with the names of whomever I chose to have imprisoned for an indeterminate period, "here are some toys, amuse yourself with them."[2]

This episode has inexplicable but decorative moments: a mean minister, a corrupt social order, a cruel apprentice, lust, unknown and unidentified victims, and capricious decisions. It presents an explanatory riddle, since the minister's offer does not make sense. He merely happens to give these dangerous items to Juliette. His plan is simple, but richly decorated. It is at once an expression of his autonomous reason and a pompous gesture. Hence Sade's characters are ambiguous about the categories of the enlightenment and the baroque, logic and decoration.

## THE PARODY OF INVERSION

One must resist a simplified inversion-interpretation of Sade. Even if he says (as he does) that "evil [is] more piquant, more attractive than good," it is not simply a matter that vice is virtuous and virtue is harmful. As I have already argued, what Sade calls virtue does not resemble the standard idea of virtue; he means by it the original state of innocence and virginity. In the same way, what is evil does not constitute a coherent motive. The point is, simply, that all moral motivation is unavailable in the Sadean universe.

If an educated, mature person is vicious, this is not because he aims at something analogous to the good life under the pretext of vice. Sade plays a different type of life-game. He does not imply that there is an ideal world of vice which is a mirror image of the world of virtue. In such a counterpart life evil deeds become profitable, pain pleasant, destruction benevolent, and hate friendship. This cannot be so because the baroque life plan is inconsistent and unstable in time. An evil person needs morality in order to become subversive.

Unlike a good world, an exclusively evil world does not make sense. The inverted world of mirror images must be replaced by a stratified artifice in which virtue is subordinated to vice, and where vice is nothing. Life becomes a theatrical performance, combining destructive nature and the play of life. But a wicked person cannot transcend the stage, because he has no home to go to after the play nor a civil career which replaces his role when he is off stage. He has no life of rational ethics and religious virtue; he has only the cyclic orgiastic plunge into the vortex of nature, which is mindless. Of course, each person pretends to live a good life, too. Since secrecy is an important aspect of vice, crime tends to be hidden. Nothing like ordinary life, or its mirror image, exists at Silling, or at any of those châteaux and churches which Justine visits during her unhappy journeys.

My point is: a virtuous character exists only in a context of virtue, a reasonable social order, and sensible planning. None of these conditions is present in Sade's fictional world. Therefore vice cannot be made virtuous, that is, it cannot take the place of virtue in the core of a person's life plan. Since the person has no reasonable plan, therefore he has no virtues, not even such functional analogies of virtues as might be satisfied by means of vicious actions. The baroque life-style, as one can see, is drastically different from the good life and its virtues.

Of course, it cannot be denied that Sade states in many places that virtue is vice and vice is virtue. Hackel says, "Not only does virtue assume the role of vice, but vice will often assume the role of virtue. The vicious Franlo in *Faxelange* treats his wife with respect. The debauched Granwell in *Miss Henriette Stralson* has several outbursts of generosity."[3] The correct interpretation of such transformations is, however, that the evil world is capricious and out of control. Real values disappear from the scene. Therefore, evil as the mere counter-image of goodness does not get off the ground. Yet if it suits the actors, they may also add more sophisticated conceptual moves to their perverse repertoire.

Expressions like "virtue is vice and vice is virtue" can be seen as tricks when we combine the various ingredients of Sade's thought. Analysis shows such expressions to have a deep-structure incompatible with the surface statement. If a libertine treats vice exactly like other people treat virtue, he may be on the right track, although he is not yet mature. After all, part of Sade's project is educational, as we shall see. It is in the final stages of the training that the novice realizes how deeply his life has changed through following the simple prescription embedded in the mirror image of values. The style of the good life has become impossible, so that this person has entered the maelstrom of destructive nature and of an unjust social contract.

All this can be put in the right perspective by recalling some of Sade's subtle parodies of ethical thought. Madame de Saint-Ange tells Eugenie that for prudential reasons couples should avoid vaginal intercourse and choose anal sex. Following the social convention by choosing vaginal intercourse is the worst option, since it can spoil one's chances for marriage and cause one to contract a deadly disease or get pregnant. If one is interested in self-destruction, of course, these would be reasons for vaginal intercourse; but in this passage, as it turns out, self-destruction is not on the agenda. The context of the discussion of good and bad sexual policy reveals Sade as writing pure parody. The joke is that any reasonable person would be horrified by such advice, especially because he subscribes to the standards of prudence from which the advice seems to follow. According to Sade, prudence is not a self-sufficient attitude, but rather the timid expression of social prejudice that makes people do things uniformly for no good reason at all.

Since much of Sade's moral writing is parodic, it cannot be understood as offering good advice in favor of adopting counter-practices because they constitute a new style of the good life. The worshipping of pain is a parody of hedonist ethics. The philosophical ramblings before torture is applied are a parody of religious consolation to the condemned before execution. Meals of excrement symbolize hard work, with all the effort that goes into it and the waste which comes out. Silling is a parody of the Hobbesian social contract. The great drunken homosexual orgies at Silling are parodies of Socrates in the *Symposium*. Transsexual marriage ceremonies are arranged for the amusement of all: "In celebration of the sixteenth week, Durcet, as a woman, marries Invictus, who enacts a masculine role; and as a man he takes Hyacinthe to be his wife."[4] Ethnographical and sociological reviews of cruel traditions can be seen as jokes on scientific style and the way it is vacuously used to justify policy decisions. Sade's descriptions of officials of state, ranging from hanging judges and priests to the egotistical ministers of justice, are full of the same irony. His stylistic conventions are highlighted in those sections of his writings where he speaks like a strict ethicist and refers to good moral reasons. Sade's argument endorses the baroque view of life and its theatrical interpretations. The explicit reversal of values is a parody of ethical thought, because Sade needs the traditional virtues as they are: they constitute the necessary conditions of moral evil.

## EDUCATING VICE

Among the strange features of the Sadean world is that the heroes can impose a strictly one-sided exercise of power on society. This means that they are able to work out their intentions in a setting where these intentions alone figure. Yet the context is social in the sense that the villains cannot achieve their pleasure without the participation of their victims. But this need is satisfied through the obedience of the subordinate persons to the heroes. One expects the victims to refuse, to plot against the heroes, to rebel, or to fight back before they die. But nothing like that happens. The result is a certain dreamlike quality in Sade's novels. Education allows one to understand certain aspects of such social psychology, as Hackel argues: "The reversal of values is often seen in the educational process that the characters undergo."[5]

Let me compare Brillat-Savarin's concept of right decision to Sade's. The gourmand discusses his pheasant, as follows:

> Every substance has its esculent apogee; some attain it before they reach their full development, such as capers, asparagus, gray partridges, spoon-fed pigeons, etc.; some when they reach their natural prime, such as melons, most kinds of fruit, mutton, beef, venison, and red partridges; and some when they begin to decompose, such as medlars, woodcock, and above all, pheasant. This last bird, eaten within three days of its death, has an undistinguished taste. . . . Cooked at the right time, its flesh is tender, sublime, and tasty, for it partakes of both poultry and venison. This desirable stage is reached just as the pheasant begins to decompose.[6]

The metaphysics is clear. A mature person's desires respect the natural development of things, which vary from case to case. One's peak enjoyment can be reached only when the right time for action has arrived.

The Sadean view is the opposite of this. At Silling, the heroes have ugly, normal, and beautiful victims, all of whom they enjoy in a similar way. The ugly are horrible to touch and the beautiful are shocking to destroy, but since their proper use is independent of time, all these persons can be destroyed indiscriminately without loss of pleasure. For Sade, all limits or considerations of the right moment are merely artificial: "Two servants came up to hold Sophie's legs, and had it been her deflowering hour, never might she have displayed the merchandise to better advantage. But there was yet more to attend to."[7] The time for each specific operation is predetermined, yet there is no question that one time is better than another. The right moment depends on a stipulation and social choice, but not on the nature of the object. In a sense, the libertine's pheasant is the same as his venison or asparagus, since all are freely exchangeable, and therefore dispensable, without loss of pleasure. In Sade's world enjoyment is artificial, something produced by the exercise of power. This aspect is cerebral, controlled, and learnable.

Control is the key word. Since the heroes want to achieve everything by exercising power, everything else is denied its value. This ideology also molds the immature persons around them, who first become initiates and then successful heroes, or moral animals. Now, when we distinguish education, such as that which occurs through the course of Juliette's life, from educational measures, like those applied to Eugenie de Franval and Eugenie de Mistival, we can see how power stigmatizes. But because the stigma is something desirable in the Sadean world, a new hero is born. In other words, special educational measures are applied to passive subjects, who assume the role of initiates. They are given a stigma, which is the mark of power and cruelty. The novices are passive when they receive their training, just like the genuine victims; the difference is that the latter are victimized without the possibility of learning. The social world is thus divided into two casts. Let us see how the training in wickedness works.

In the *Philosophy in the Bedroom*, Eugenie, "daughter of a certain Mistival," is 15 and now ready to receive her education at the hands of the libertines. Madame de Saint-Ange is in love with the girl, whom she promises to meet in private. Eugenie arrives along with some of Madame's friends. Eugenie is at first shocked, but soon she calms down. She is first instructed in the language of sex, all the key terms of which are explained to her. Then she is initiated into some theoretical ideas, like contraception, adultery, homosexuality, and incest. Some demonstrations follow, and finally she herself is allowed to experiment. When she is ready, she receives her own playthings – her own mother, as any Freudian understands. Her graduation proceeds by means of cruelty to her mother, after which she is fully initiated. Everything happens in one day, which shows how strange the Sadean concept of time is. During this day she changes from a timid child to a beast.

Education produces in Eugenie the first clear insight into her own nature: "I adore you; you will never have a more submissive scholar."[8] She shows much promise and understands her own vulnerability and passivity. These are Sadean virtues. The second stage is reached when she says, ridiculously: "I too might be able to confess to feeling a few dispositions to viciousness." But at this point her instruction is already complete. She knows the truth and can reject the wrong ideas presented by Le Chevalier. She instructs the listeners:

> You triumph, Dolmance, the laurel belongs to you! Le Chevalier's harangue did but barely brush my spirit, yours seduces and entirely wins it over. Ah, Chevalier, take my advice: speak rather to the passions than to the virtues when you wish to persuade a woman.[9]

Eugenie feels an impulse to cruelty, knowing herself sufficiently well to give advice to men. Education has involved information, theory, and experiment. The submissive victim's cruelty is now actualized. Originally mere wax, she has now received her proper form. Such education has nothing to do with edification. Proper instruction alters Eugenie's psychology in a manner which does not take into account either the resistance to, or the rejection of, doctrine. None of Eugenie's earlier convictions have left a permanent mark on her character. In a true Platonic manner, false opinions are shadows which vanish when the light is shed on them. She is now incorrigible.

Certainly Sade understands that initiation is supposed to do something impossible, a fact that should not surprise us. The same enigma can be found in other ethnographic contexts, such as the traditional Sambia life in the New Guinea highlands. Male initiation, which includes forced nose-bleeding, teaches boys that a master must become like his victim. He must first carry the stigma of what is evil before he obtains the status of a mature person. As Herdt writes:

> Masculinity is deceptively powerful by virtue of its negativity: the suppression of women in public affairs, and the stylized castigation of feminine qualities in men's public conversation or activities. Secret ritual, the *private force* lying behind masculine behavior, is altogether another matter. The logical paradox of Sambia thought and speech is that secret male ritual takes some of its most powerful symbolic imagery from the supremely feminine. For example, menstruation: men simulate in themselves nose-bleeding, which they culturally and consciously relate to menstruation, as the very well-spring of masculine vitality and strength.[10]

In the same way, a Sadean hero enjoys the possibility of being like his victim – but only because it is perverse.

Perhaps one should focus on the Platonic trend in Sade's thought and say that Eugenie's innate ideas of lust and cruelty are awakened in the appropriate circumstances. Her education is an initiation or baptism into the cult of vice which she already knows. All she needs is a trigger, and the energy erupts. This also suggests that the results of education are natural rather than artificial, chaotic rather than structured. Education does not create anything new, but explicates Eugenie's innate propensities. Sade's world is dualistic, divided into victims and heroes, and the flow of action is unilateral, from heroes toward their victims. While some people are like inert but sentient matter, other people learn. Such an interpretation makes the initiate a natural being, a scavenger, which cannot satisfy the Sadean requirement of maturity, power, and wickedness. The artificial world where one can be a free predator is still at least one step away. Eugenie pretends to know how to enjoy life, but she has as yet no idea of how to control the destiny of others. She is not mature. Therefore the only thing she has in mind is to get revenge against her mother, whom she perceives as a tyrant and an obstacle to her and her father. Without her friends she is reduced to mere scavenging at the barren table of nature.

The second Eugenie, Eugenie de Franval, receives her training from her incestuous father, who follows the model of Rousseau's *Emile*. The girl is separated early from her mother, and provided with fresh air, the chance to exercise, beautiful clothing, and other amenities. She matures nicely and becomes ready to undergo her initiation through the rites of education. The pattern of those rites is already familiar. She receives her stigma of vice through her realization that immorality is the truth of social things.

However, when Eugenie is brought up the right way, she indeed loves her father and allows him to seduce her without a trace of resistance on her part. She is able to reject what Freud calls the horror of incest. From there she proceeds towards crueler ideas. By this Sade intends to demonstrate once again that all innocent moral thought represents merely the life of the unformed mind, a mind which offers no resistance whatever to the powers of the corrupt mind. The weaker spirit takes the stamp from the stronger one. As such, its original virtue is deceptive. The uneducated mind is a medium without a form of its own, and the libertine has nothing to gain from the activity of the victim. She is a merely passive being whose thoughts and actions are random and meaningless. The libertine creates his own worthless company as a shadow – a mere reflection in the mirror of his mature mind. As Eugenie's stature grows, her independence advances.

Finally, the solitary hero emerges at the end of *120 Days of Sodom*:

"an exceedingly wealthy, very powerful lord, very harsh, very cruel, his heart is of stone." He is the rare sovereign man that Georges Bataille declares Sade's characters to be.[11] He represents the final stage of the development of an avenger, a person who faces nature, but not without the help of theatrical context. In many ways this unnamed man is a remarkable fictional creation, and more remarkable because *120 Days of Sodom* is an unfinished work. Its last story, the "hell passion," is both detailed and illuminating. The man exhibits perfect power, self-control, wisdom, and seriousness of mind. Every fortnight he acquires fifteen beautiful young girls, rapes them, sorts them into groups according to the tortures they must suffer, and throws them down into a cellar. He follows them there and reaches his climax through masturbation while gazing at his victims. As the corpses are buried, the man anticipates the next session. His action is boring, predictable, repetitive, controlled, and cruel. The man is a type of divine judge whose justice gives everyone what they do not deserve: "Everything is ready, all the tortures are in motion, and they proceed simultaneously, amidst much noise."[12] This is the end of education.

Unlike the educated people, the victims are animals to be butchered. The final scenes of *120 Days of Sodom*, for instance, are taken straight from a slaughter house. Paradoxically, the victims do not seem to suffer even in the eyes of their torturers, because they are not persons and they cannot fight back. Every victim is the ultimate one in the sense that he does not even form the intention to struggle. Sade's text does not allow the reader to sympathize with the victim, except in special cases like that of Justine.

The utopian social order at Silling lasts only for 120 days. After that the survivors go home. This indicates how all social life – according to baroque principles – is only a show; it makes sense for a while, but then must be dissolved. If we do not interpret the message like this, we are driven to the utilitarian conclusion that Juliette's education will bring her fame and fortune that otherwise would be out of her reach, and that she will be able to cheat destructive nature and create a life-style which is both wicked and conducive to personal values. But this cannot be so. Juliette learns that caprice is the final state of affairs, so that when she lives accordingly she joins in what is real, that is, natural. With full consciousness she becomes part both of orgiastic nature and of an unjust social order.

## LOVE

The fact that subordinate persons in Sade's writings have nothing to give to their tormentors is relevant to a criticism of Sade's ethics, understood as a hedonist theory. Many important pleasures – such as love – cannot be achieved by the heroes. But in order to understand Sade we must reject the traditional view of love as an emotion or desire which a person directs towards another. Hobbes expresses this traditional view in *Leviathan*: "That which men Desire, they are also sayd to Love . . . So that Desire, and Love, are the same thing." Such a view which identifies love and desire is not only too limited, but it inverts the direction of the love-relation. In its proper sense love entails personal acceptance, devotion, safety, and the guarantee of the mutual exchange of feelings. It is one person's token of devotion and commitment to another, a kind of quest for a joint identity between people. To achieve this, one offers himself to the other person; and if the process is mutual, the result is a valuable social bond. We may distinguish between some subtypes like mother-love, brotherly love or friendship, and sexual love.

Love may be compared to pleasure and respect in the contexts of buying, selling, and acquiring entitlements. In the case of pleasure, as Sade knows, this is something one can buy or take by force. However, one cannot buy sexual love without turning it into prostitution. That money does not buy love may be denied, but in that case we are witnessing a confusion between buying and deserving. One tends to think that the rich and the famous deserve affection, and we find it understandable that they are admired, respected, and even loved.

As Sade insists, one can deserve admiration and respect – but not love. Like a bishop, an affluent person may call himself respectable and claim that social respect is his proper entitlement. But an affluent person may want even more. In the counterfactual mode he may say: "Because of my personal characteristics, if you do not respect me you are wrong." By so doing he would claim for himself the right to be what he is, so that it is a mistake to deny his status. People do things in order to be respected. They receive education and take an office because of a relentless desire to justify the sentiments of respect and admiration; and they are right in so doing.

Thomas Hobbes puts forward a formulation of this neglected aspect of honor in virtue-ethics. For him, power deserves to be admired, and this entails a genuine claim to personal virtuousness. Hobbes's illuminating argument proceeds in several steps. First, "The

Power of a Man, is his present means to obtain some future apparent Good." Second, "The Value, or Worth of a man, is as of all other things, his Price; that is to say, so much as would be given for the use of his Power." Third, "The manifestation of the Value we set on one another, is that which is commonly called Honouring." Fourth, "To pray to another, for ayde of any kind, is to Honour; because a signe we have an opinion he has power to help." Fifth and finally, "Nor does it alter the case of Honour, whether an action . . . be just or unjust: for Honour consisteth onely in the opinion of Power." All this applies to Sade's heroes and their achievements, which Hobbes would call "Rapes, Thefts, and other great, but unjust, or unclean acts."[13] Such things can be honored, because they express power which one needs. As Hobbes puts it, the ancient gods were villains, yet they were honored by human beings. In this special case even the Sadean heroes are virtuous when they are admired by their friends because of their power. The heroes honor each other, and are also respected by their victims. Moreover, even if they were not respected, they should be, simply because of their wealth, self-control, stamina, and cruelty. But is it love?

Love does not follow the logic of such a paradigm of entitlements as honor. One cannot argue that one should be loved or otherwise there is a mistake. It does not make sense to say that I know you love me, but if you do not, you should, because otherwise you are making a mistake. One may make such claims in regard to power or honor, but any normative claim to love is nonsense. The only thing that makes sense to say is that persons who deserve respect are in fact often recipients of love, too. Such a proposition is not a normative one, however, but merely a description of cultural modes which people happen to know well.

The slogan "love is a gift" means that a person needs to be open for love, that is, at least he is not offering money, power, or services in exchange for it. If one offers money to a person who wants to give a gift, the gift-relation will certainly be eliminated. One does not buy gifts. The positive side of openness is related to factors like the information flow between persons, mutual respect, a general willingness to accept something from others, and the courageous acceptance of risks. Especially detrimental is the demand that one should be loved; any respect or admiration that is received in return may then be mistaken for love. In addition, gifts may be thought of as imposing an obligation on the recipient. This may be true, but if a person is loved, no obligation to return love is created. Because love is an offer, it may always be rejected. The only obligation concerns the loving person's commitment to the good of the recipient of the love.

Mutual love forms a network of gift-relationships which also entails a strong ethical bond. Many of the best features of social life are based on such gifts, and we could not possibly manage without them. Tending to dismiss this truth, we deceive ourselves into believing both that we deserve what we claim from others and that what we give creates obligations from them. We may further argue, falsely, that we have earned what we have by means of clever bargaining moves, or perhaps by manufacturing so much that it makes us special. The truth is, one can only beg for love, like one begs for any other gift.

The topic of the gifts of love is too large to be developed here in any further detail. My purpose is merely to make room for a criticism of Sade from a less obvious angle. It is not easy to criticize a writer who wants to be wicked. It is not probable that he would agree that love is important. Why should he care? If there is love, Sadean revenge is made unnecessary, even without the introduction of an artificial world of repressive power. This looks desirable; but it is not enough if love does not promise unconditional orgiastic pleasure. And that it cannot do.

Sade's view of life does not allow us to understand interpersonal fulfillment. Certainly, if power at the social level is sufficient for Sade, he is beyond criticism. But for those who do not want to go as far as Sade does, the idea of a gift-relationship may offer relief against the threat of a lonely, short, and brutish existence. Since he aims at total control, he must also deny the value of love and affection, though not of respect. We can understand the Sadean position better if we think as follows. A person may be successful, but if others deny him their love he can only try harder. Unlike respect, affection and love flow from the others toward the agent. Therefore, some good things like love are gifts which may be begged for. Sadean heroes are often admired and respected; indeed, much of their cruelty can be seen as the demand for respect. Since violence is a claim to the right to be admired, anyone who does not pay homage to them is simply wrong. But they are never loved. How could they be? They refuse to accept a gift from their victims.

A commercial analogy works here: in many emotionally significant cases, a person tries to make a purchase of feelings in a market which is already saturated. It is a seller's market in which nobody is eager to sell. Nothing one offers as a payment will work, and the person must beg. Sade misses this analogy because he hates it. For him the social world is a field of raw power where strong persons encounter passivity and inertia. The strong never have the chance of getting a share of love and respect, though this is neither wanted nor offered, except between powerful people who assign some instrumental value to such feelings in order better to exploit their victims. In the social world as it is normally understood, even the strongest individuals need love and affection, not as a means to something else, but as an intrinsic value. Sade's world, on the contrary, is strange exactly in this respect. He talks about pleasure in a manner which at the same time evokes the paradigm of unhappiness.

In effect, for Sade pleasure and happiness are two different things. One can acquire pleasure through stimulating one's senses, but happiness results from an exchange between free persons. Sade does not care either for such love or for happiness. This is not surprising, because he recommends wickedness. But I would like to show what Sade misses when he claims that love is a virtuous illusion. Justine and other characters in his stories suffer endlessly because of it. Sade dismisses the balance between the desire to be loved and being strong-willed, which is so important in ethics.

A genuinely virtuous, or anti-Sadean, agent attracts the softer emotions and may expect to receive love and respect. Sade's reaction to such an event is dramatic. As we know, he claims that virtuous self-presentation is a trap. If a person is virtuous, he begs for acceptance and is thereby likely to victimize himself. To try to make a favorable impression means that if other people do not buy the impression, the virtuous person is in trouble. Not only is he disappointed, but he is also at their mercy. This is Sade's point against the ethics of virtue: you beg for love, but by so doing you only harm yourself. The only worthwhile pleasure, he feels, is what one can buy (as through prostitution) or take by force (as through robbery). Loving, however, is dangerous. In giving gifts, the person commits himself to a recipient whom he cannot control by means of his actions. In this sense the loving person makes himself vulnerable.

Mutual fear is evident between libertines. The mature Juliette finally poisons her friend Clairwil. Madame Durand says:

> Listen to me, Juliette; and having heard me, reveal nothing. This island in Dalmatia . . . this Princess Christine, this voyage . . . dear girl, had you taken it you were doomed. It was all a trap set

by a woman whom you believed to be your dearest friend. Clairwil! She plotted your death. She covets your wealth.

Juliette takes her due revenge without hesitation:

> The meal was served us; I had taken my decision. To be the dupe of Clairwil's tales, this was absolutely impossible.... Into the first dish I handed Clairwil I slipped the poison hidden between my fingers; she took a mouthful, swallowed, swayed in her chair, and fell, emitting a single furious scream.[14]

Betrayal is the peril hidden in any Sadean friendship.

Sade's own view is that of a person who rejects the idea of waiting for the gift of love from other people. As a result, the whole ethical world looks distorted, strange, and terrifying in Sade's novels. Instead of the eternal promise of love, his world is dominated by the fear of denial, deception, and treachery. In his fear, the weak person is haunted by the thought of the necessity of striking first. Every friendship has an unconvincing aspect, because betrayal promises so much pleasure. At the same time, however, Sade's stories are full of the praise of genuine affection between the rakes. Friendship, trust, cooperation, and love turn into their own parody. Though the destruction of friendship and love is a wonderful source of cruel pleasure, yet it is dismissed only because of the negligible joy of keeping them intact. Since friendship happens to be virtue, and love is prized by the Christians, the cohesion between the libertines is one of the most surprising elements in Sade's philosophy. In order to explain this, we must study the meaning of the civil contract in Sade's fiction.

The view of certain social goods as gifts allows us to understand the tremendous force of social conventions, as well as the fierceness of Sade's rebellion. If one cannot earn the value for oneself, one can present oneself so that those gifts can be given to one. What open positions a person may assume depend on social life, history, and conventions. Therefore, the only thing a person can do if he wants to be happy is to see that he is there when the ultimate goods are distributed. The reason why he is so helpless against social conventions and norms is that the openness of his position is defined through them. He must follow the etiquette, whatever it happens to be. Of course, a real moral hero may be oblivious to other people's evaluations, but the result is a supererogatory ethic that is truly cruel. The only substitute is the narcissistic self-admiration of a person who assigns to himself a unique moral status.

This fact also makes us see the ultimate peril in Sade's position: loneliness. The last, solitary man mentioned in *120 Days of Sodom* is far from being the ultimate hero. He is too lonely. Unlike ordinary humans who keep themselves open to the gifts of love and are ready to take risks and suffer inconveniences for it, the Sadean heroes arrange their lives so that their pleasure is their own product. Artificial pleasure is manufactured by them. Even when successful, they are only workers.

Sade's text can be understood as a remedy for lost affection. If virtue is the ultimate trap, only narcissism may save the person from loneliness. He projects his own self onto the flesh of his victims and enjoys his own image there. The revenge of being forced to beg is the denial of the possibility of satisfaction. Accordingly, one maintains that the only good thing is the person himself. To do terrible things to others is to enjoy one's own personality in a self-externalized form. The stigma imposed on the passive world is the monster's gift given to his own admiring self.

The hatred Sade's heroes feel against their victims is understandable when one considers the disappointment the heroes go through when they are threatened by loneliness and the bittersweet medicine of narcissism. They hate their victims because the victims never provide them with the fulfillment of desire. The agonizing thought that the victims are elusive takes at least two forms: first, they die and escape; and second, an ever-larger number of persons should be destroyed without reaching an upper limit. Clairwil wants to know what Minister Saint-Fond does to his victims before they die. Saint-Fond confesses that religion still troubles him so much that he cannot be quite sure that the immortality of the soul is a fiction. He tells Clairwil: "in order to bar the victim from celestial joys, it is necessary to have him sign a pact, writ in his heart's blood, whereby he contracts his soul to the devil; next to insert this paper in his asshole and to stamp it home with one's prick; and while doing so to cause him to suffer the greatest pain in one's power to inflict."[15] This sends the victim to eternal pain in hell. Otherwise one can never be certain that the victim has not escaped his tormentor. But after all, the stratagem is based on theistic reasoning, and it would be difficult to see how a strictly atheist reasoning could reduce Saint-Fond's pain of losing his victims for good. Moreover, his fears are countered by a merely theoretical lesson. Unlike pleasure and pain, philosophical certainty is not a gut-feeling which is real while it occurs. Theory is dangerous, and a good dialectician could create havoc even in the libertine mind, assuming the libertine's life plan is based on rational argumentation. If it is based on the joys of blasphemy, of course, this is a different matter.

Mass murder is also an important but inconclusive pleasure for Sade's heroes: "From a terrace Olympia and I surveyed the disaster, frigging ourselves as the conflagrations spread. By evening the thirty-seven asylums were all in flames and the dead already exceeded twenty thousand."[16] As Juliette knows, nature makes human life insignificant, and when the fire has gone out, new pleasures must be found. Therefore, in Sade's world pleasure represents the endless work of Sisyphus, or of modern industrial production: repetition combined with the vain hope that we never need to beg for what we can produce ourselves. Yet we cannot manufacture it all, as Sade sometimes realizes when his characters fail to get an erection, or when they dream of mass murder, or when they would like to destroy nature itself.

Because the production line of debauchery is limited, the result is repetition and exaggeration. Jane Gallop reads some texts as referring to whoring, a kind of counterfeit love:

> Eugenie, the pupil, like Juliette the slut, stands ready to bear the imprint of the other. Empty of any wish or idea of her own, she becomes aroused by the contact with the other's desire or thought. Counterfeit: contra-facere, make against, make by the application of pressure (by something placed) against the object-to-be. The authenticity of a coin is founded upon its fidelity to the paradigmatic form of that coin. The most authentic coin is the best copy, the truest counterfeit.[17]

Such is the sad conclusion discernible in Sade's story of the work ethic: stigma, not gift. But the mature Juliette has her own will, and the villains are sovereign.

The Sadean avenger indeed has his reasons to hate both the natural world which he is unable to control, and the social stigma of love which he cannot yet share with others. Sade turns to the artificial world of the civil contract and interprets this as theater. He aims at power and the control over pleasures. The endless struggle against disappointment can be avoided in the company of friends. This entails both civil contract and artificial social relationships. Therefore social relationships, admiration, and love are less essential than instrumental. They are needed not because of heroic identity, but because of the pleasure which is devoid of natural disappointment. Gallop stays at the level of the categories of what is natural, and seems to forget both the need for social laws and the stage of the Sadean theater. There the civil contract creates both artificial love and fictional pleasure. Thus Sade explains what it is to be a true predator.

# 6

# THE PARODY OF THE CIVIL CONTRACT

Sade's rampant egoism dictates that "everything hinges upon the total annihilation of that absurd notion of fraternity" and that "between your self and some other self no connection whatever exists." This negative idea is in contrast to the vows of fidelity the rakes exchange: "the two friends, clasping each other, were fifteen minutes exchanging avowals of sincerest friendship, confidence, and devotion."[1] Fifteen minutes is a long time to hug. They are genuine friends. However, it is also true that they never sacrifice their own good to that of others.

These confusions indicate that they accept a social contract which is, ideally, successful, since it divides the world into predatory heroes and passive victims, guaranteeing that no mix-up occurs. According to the stipulated criteria of value, the heroes can identify not only themselves, but also their victims. Some people are taken to be wretches who do not deserve devotion or love. Also, friendship between the libertines now becomes possible. Because of the social contract an artificial world is created. Such an artifact is so well planned that self-sacrifice is never needed. It resembles a secret society or a theater stage where the perfect plans of cruelty and horror can be realized. All the social vice becomes enjoyable to the friends. The earlier imperfections of the cruel life can be corrected, ironically, through its free celebration. The Sadean world is an inverted version of the construct suggested by Thomas Hobbes and Niccolò Machiavelli.

Hobbes wants to perfect the primitive social order by recreating it by means of the right science, so it will show all the rational features of civil laws. Nevertheless, the proper state of nature never existed, because "there had never been any time wherein particular men were in a condition of warre one against the other." But many similar chaotic conditions have been known, especially during and after civil wars. Sade seems to agree that the chaotic state of nature never existed.

He refers to different social systems, historical as well as contemporary, as examples to be followed in France. The implication is that they are all civilized compared to France. For Sade this is to say that they are cruel and unjust, but not absolutely so. His social project aims at perfecting the horror inherent in social life. Sade's France is like Hobbes's Indian nations. Hobbes says, "The Savages of America, are not without some good Morall Sentences . . . but they are not therefore Philosophers."[2] Who are the Sadean philosophers, and how do they reason about social artifacts?

The artificial social order appears in Sade's writings at two different levels. First, in *120 Days of Sodom* he designs his own (explicit) utopia at the castle of Silling. It reappears in *Justine* as the community of the four violent monks hidden in the church of Saint-Mary-in-the-Woods, and in *Juliette* as the secret society of pleasure, the Sodality of Paris. Second, throughout his works he sketches a full-blown (implicit) social order of authority, coercion, and social stratification. This system supervenes on the real world of the Old Regime but is not identical to it. The first approach is easier to interpret than the second, which lies embedded in the rather chaotic material in Sade's books. I shall give an account of both, since without his social philosophy no picture of Sade can be satisfactory. However, I shall deal only with his fictional writings and leave aside the revolutionary political pamphlets.

## SOCIAL CRITICISM

In *Philosophy in the Bedroom*, there is an interesting exchange between Dolmance and Le Chevalier. Dolmance, who represents the truth, opposes the large-scale republican program of politics. He explains that the younger philosopher has got many of his points right, except the following all-important thesis: never trust your heart. He believes that intuitions are worthless. Through the views of Le Chevalier, Sade makes it clear that no cultural universals exist in the field of social manners and moral convictions. On the contrary, everything is a matter of caprice or stipulation. The emergence of the basic social order is not founded on any reasoned theory of man and motivation. Sade tries to prove this by reviewing social life in the light of socio-historical and anthropological research. In doing so he attempts to demonstrate that whatever the French think to be unjust or revolting is always accepted somewhere else. Most significantly, this happens in the primitive stages of social life, which are closer to nature. For example, he says that "The blacks of the Ivory Coast and Gabon prostitute their wives to their own children," which is supposed to show that the taboo about incest is not valid universally. The Pope is familiar with the following ethnographical fact:

> Egyptians, Arabs, Cretans, Cypriots, Rhodians, Phocaeans, Greeks, Pelagians, Scythians, Romans, Phoenicians, Persians, Indians, Chinese, Massagetae, Getae, Sarmatians, Irish, Norwegians, Suevi, Scandinavians, all Northern peoples, Gauls, Celts, Cimbrians, Germans, Bretons, Spaniards, Moors, Blacks, all of them individually and generally have slain human beings upon the altars of their gods.[3]

Therefore, says Sade, what the French think of their own morality means nothing. Starting from the nature of man as an orgiastic being, a valid theory of value must be built on a psychological basis.

Of course, Sade's anthropological views count as parody. In referring to the rapes, murders, and robberies he finds in anthropological literature, he reproduces evidence which is wildly counterintuitive. Nevertheless, a long line of ethicists, including Edward Westermarck and John Mackie, have thought that such evidence must have some epistemic value. In the light of Sade, Mackie's skeptical "argument from relativity" may not look convincing.[4] Sade shows that any such position can be turned into a joke which rests on the connotations of perverse practices.

Sade needs a clean slate on which to write his favorite story of the pleasure of cruelty and the pain of pleasure. On his way towards hedonism, he argues to the effect that all human practices are equally acceptable. Le Chevalier reads the following soft-hearted view from a pamphlet found in the streets:

> Revive your trade, restore energy and markets to your manufacturing; cause your arts to flourish again, encourage agriculture, both so necessary in a government such as yours, and whose aim must be to provide for everyone without standing in need of anyone . . . let other people observe you happy, and they will rush to happiness by the same road you have traced for them.[5]

This kind of edifying argument sounds odd because the pamphlet has already defended stealing as a legal way of establishing a higher degree of economic equality:

it [theft] furthers equality and, what is more, renders more difficult the conservation of property.... What are the elements of the social contract? Does it not consist in one's yielding a little of his freedom and of his wealth in order to assure and sustain the preservation of each?[6]

Murder, incest, and many other mischiefs are also defended. Since these principles are not fully coherent, a thinker like Dolmance is able to show that they fall victim to one's idea of social comedy:

I should like men, gathered in no matter what temple, to invoke the eternal who wears their image, to be seen as so many comics in a theater, at whose antics everyone may go to laugh.[7]

All values, all gods, are human creations, and as such they are ridiculous in their claim to truth and authority. Le Chevalier, who professes to be a true philosopher, commits the typical philosopher's blunders.

One of Sade's central methodological principles is that based on comedy. Dolmance, who knows better, applies it to the plain truth, which is nothing but the familiar Poe-principle of perversity applied to social structure. He says: "In a word, is it possible to compare permissible pleasures with pleasures which, to far more piquant delights, join those inestimable joys that come of bursting socially imposed restraints and of the violation of every law?"[8] This is Sade's own transgressive theory of "delights born of apathy," which are contrasted to "those you get of your sensibility." The point is clear: whether stealing and murder are legitimized or not does not matter. Whatever laws and moral values one may recognize, whatever decisions they prescribe, the greatest pleasure always results from the strict violation of the law. Therefore, the problem lies in the possibility of understanding the nature of the law to be breached. If there is no law and no crime, whence the possibility of violence and pleasure? The social contract establishes laws which may also be broken; and since crime and vice are only metaphors for the void, breaking the law entails confusion and death. This is also pleasure.

The social state of nature, familiar from political philosophy, plays a double role in Sade. The concept designates the Hobbesian idea of the original condition of society. Its first meaning is that man's natural situation is determined by the society in which he lives. Its second meaning is specified by Sade, echoing Hobbes's own words. Sade writes:

But you will say, thence we will be born in a state of perpetual warfare. Excellent! is that not the perpetual state of Nature? Is it not the only state to which we are really adapted? All men are born isolated, envious, cruel and despotic; wishing to have everything and surrender nothing.[9]

No Hobbesian social contract works, because the weak lose everything to the powerful, although the powerful do not need any concessions from them. For the strong, the mutual struggle is advantageous, because one deserves what one is able to grab. This is the Hobbesian picture of the original condition of man, though of course Hobbes claims that all men are equal in strength, at least in the sense that no one individual can protect himself from all the others. Because Sade does not appreciate this feature of Hobbes's theory, he thinks that the strong will win. Alternatively, one may say that since Sade does not care, it is immaterial who gains.

Sade represents French society as approximating a social state of nature, because it is a perpetually unjust social order. Its violence is thinly camouflaged. Here he differs from Hobbes, who locates the state of nature in a fictional world or in distant times and places. Hobbes refuses to portray his own world as a mutual life-and-death struggle. Sade, on the contrary, is bitterly aware of the dangers inherent in the existing social order: "Friends, I said, people united through so many similarities of disposition and outlook ought never separate, and when they have the misfortune of being prisoners together they should join forces to break out of the bondage to which human injustice has reduced them."[10] Therefore, the state of nature, understood as the original condition of man, is indeed something intolerable, and men should join forces against it and make a new social contract to establish a better social order. For Hobbes, natural law is an element of the state of nature, but it cannot function well there. The social order must be established before the natural law will work efficiently via the civil laws of the commonwealth. Sade thinks, in principle, in the same way. The virtual state of nature – contemporary society – must be transformed into a utopian society with a libertine life-style where the cruel laws of nature are unleashed.

Social life is terrible for Sade because its potential violence and wickedness can be suffered but not utilized. His new social order must exploit nature in a systematic manner. Sade, in fact, inverts the Hobbesian project so that the ideal society will be crueler than the original one. If French society is indeed unjust enough to be called a hell, then this situation can be corrected by means of a new social contract. It will make life even more unjust, but also more enjoyable to the libertine mind. In this artificial new environment, the avenger can control things, and become a predator.

## UTOPIA AND BEYOND

Sade suggests that all existing social orders, ranging from historical states and present primitive cultures to his own France, are equally savage. No evolution or historical progress exists between the types of societies. Because all of them are in the social state of nature, they are all evil, but blindly so; therefore their life cannot be meaningful. At most one learns that all moral norms are conventional and even void: what is mandatory in France is forbidden somewhere else, and what is incomprehensible is practiced: "'Daniel', the Pope went on, 'informs us that the Babylonians cast unfortunates into hot ovens.'"[11] Sade wants to establish a new social contract between his libertine heroes in order to make injustice and cruelty artificial, for when it is artificial it can be controlled and enjoyed without bitterness of mind.

In his *120 Days of Sodom* Sade invites his readers to join him in the quest for a kind of paradise or utopian social order; it is to be established in the isolated castle of Silling in the snow-covered mountains of the Black Forest in Germany. For its inhabitants it is to be not merely a castle but a whole world, a commonwealth of the wicked. Once the libertines are in Silling, no one can leave or arrive. The external world ceases to exist; only the rooms and halls of the castle exist. It is as if the inhabitants were on an island; they are surrounded by frigid air and frozen water. Food and drink are supplied from the cellars, and the existence of food is taken for granted. It is used but not destroyed. The kitchen is not part of the social life, and the chefs and cooks are not visible.

After Sade has bracketed the world, the social contract can be established within. As indicated earlier, this society consists of four libertine friends (Sade's heroes), their wives (who are also the friends' daughters), old women servants, a harem of little boys and girls (who are around 12 years old), female prostitutes who act as storytellers, and what Sade calls fuckers – young adult males who are beasts possessing little intelligence but a strong sexuality. The heroes want to make a civil contract which will create order from chaos and guarantee that their own desires will be satisfied. What constitutes their good depends on their personal features, which are assessed according to Sade's psychology.

## THE PARODY OF THE CIVIL CONTRACT

The friends are not the only members of society subject to the covenant, for others are under their power. No higher coercive authority exists, not even a God who would ultimately judge their deeds. Their task is to move out from the original state of nature to civilized, though criminal, life by means of a free social contract. In fact they move from a pseudo-civilization towards a utopia, or super-civilization. The result is a stratified social order.

After leaving the state of nature, the members of the group find themselves in a pre-contract situation. In actual fact, it is just an empty house and a group of people. Of course all these persons have their own backgrounds and relationships to each other; they are not perfect strangers. The heroes are rich, but also old, corrupt, and often physically weak. The storytellers are happy and self-confident. The fuckers are stupid but strong. The wives are timid and submissive. The children are scared, and so on. Prior to the arrival of the members of the group, many words have been spoken and agreements made. The children have been bought or kidnapped; the storytellers have been hired. All this activity, however, belongs to the ordinary social life, that is, to Sade's France. It is only when they reach the empty and isolated castle of Silling that they truly reach the pre-contract position.

The group has a number of alternatives open to it. Most of the participants know the peril they are in. But for some reason no rebellion breaks out. In the initial power vacuum anyone who knows how can rule; and the fuckers or the storytellers, for example, could seize power. But each person carries with him or her the remnants of the original state of nature. Thus, unlikely as it may seem, the heroes stay in charge and Sade proceeds to describe the final contract. According to it, life and welfare do not matter at Silling, and one should realize that this is the case. The social contract is made and can now be inscribed as a set of statutes and rules properly enforced by the fuckers. The heroes, whose power is unchallenged, decide on the constitution. The covenant is formed through tacit consent, because nobody disagrees or protests.

The utopian laws are strict indeed. They include rituals specifying when and how to go to bed, to eat, and to treat each other. In fact, the social life is constituted through etiquette and taboos. Subordinate persons are assigned to the friends, either permanently or on a rotating basis. The duties of the storytellers and the old servants are as specific as the duties of workers. The law also specifies deadlines for what can be done to the victims. The rules and laws are enforced through violent punishments, except when the heroes agree not to touch each other.

Also, the storytellers are given some guarantee of safety, although it is not clear whether they should trust it or not. Since the heroes' mutual relations are based on trust and compromise, they are supposed to know that cooperation serves their interests best. They cannot win by taking undue advantage of each other.

Sade's logic seems to be that because the heroes are free to do what they like, they will trust each other. If this is so, one has certainly come a long way from the blind search for mere orgiastic pleasure. But what is the social life and how is it kept stable? According to the Hobbesian classification, Silling is a mixture of a commonwealth established by institution and by acquisition – that is, by covenant and conquest. As such it is different from the Sodality, which is grounded by covenant alone, and from the church of Saint-Mary-in-the-Woods, which appears to be based on conquest.

But why does no one rebel against the cruel and sovereign friends? The reason is that acceptance of the social order is the only way of guaranteeing personal survival. Any breaching of the rules will lead the rebel to expulsion into the bitter cold outside or to a mutual struggle for power in which there would be lacking even the minimal degree of safety which the victims have under the contract. Even the children realize this. They may lament their fate, but they cannot do anything about it. They live in a society "where the Sovereign Power is acquired by Force; . . . when men . . . for fear of death, or bonds, do authorise all the actions of that Man, or Assembly, that hath their lives and liberty in his Power."[12] Hobbesian logic reigns at Sade's Silling. If they are rational, the victims should stay where they are. They are citizens and therefore they do not rebel.

In his interpretation of Sade, Philip Hallie postulates a psychological account of the victims' inability to resist cruelty. Hallie thinks that the victim is fascinated by his torturers. He says:

> the paradox of cruelty is this: the destruction of men . . . is both readily justifiable (in terms of stimulation, economic or social need, etc.), and totally unjustifiable. . . . The paradox appears also in the victim's mind and actions: she dreads her destruction, and is fascinated, both by her destroyer and by the very act of destruction. . . . But what the paradox does to the victim is rather different from what it does to the victimizer: it does not make a self-deceiver or a hypocrite of her – it paralyzes her, renders her even more passive than she was before. It enchants, enthralls her, makes the will of another her law.[13]

Hallie's explanation is misleading, however, in regard to what happens at Silling. Sade's point is normative, not psychological. The new social order at Silling is such that regardless of the participants' feelings (fascination, etc.), prudence dictates obedience to the lords. If one happens to be weak, one should obey, because the truth that one is weak must be taken seriously. One is unable to rebel successfully, or to form an independent plan of the good life. Hallie's analysis does not take this normative aspect of the situation into account, but instead supposes an external spectator whose gaze reveals something the victim herself misses.

Those at Silling all go to hell without resisting because it is part of the life at Silling. Though the point may not be well founded according to our ordinary life experience, the refusal to resist has an important message: the social order keeps people in its spell. The civilized life has its own iron logic which blinds the citizens to any alternatives. Those on the bottom rung of the social ladder go to their doom quietly enough. For those on top, their caprice has one last limit: that one does not betray one's own kind under normal conditions. The etiquette of social life is binding on all, Sade seems to say.

To follow Hallie and postulate a psychological factor in the victim's fascination with cruelty is to miss Sade's essential point, namely, the parody of social life. Once we take parody into account we can see how deeply Sade's philosophy cuts. Hobbesian and utopian political theories produce a social order which is hell. Sade's irony shows how far a lawful social order may go towards enslaving its citizens without giving them either a motive to escape or a method of doing so. It is a trap.

The social order of Silling can be seen as a kind of family. Sade's ideas on the arrangement are not much more frightful than those of Hobbes; they are just more detailed. Let us look briefly at Hobbes's account of the family – first in the state of nature, and next in a commonwealth – in order to see how cruel this arrangement is.

According to Hobbes, the child in the state of nature belongs to that person – his mother – who first has power over him. She takes care of him on condition that the child does not become her enemy when he matures and grows stronger. The mother becomes the "lord" of the child because she enters into a covenant with him on counterfactual grounds: because it is the only guarantee that the mother will not kill him immediately, the child would accept the pact if he understood it. Hobbes writes: "For else it would be wisdom in men, rather to let their children perish, while they are infants, than to live in their danger or subjection, when they are grown."[14] Next, when the male-dominated political order emerges, then the "society of bed" is replaced by an order in which man is the lord of the woman, and therefore also of her children. All this is grounded not only in feelings of gratitude, but on a covenant.

At Silling a parody of the contractual family is created by the establishment of a social order in a typically philosophical manner. While its form is law-governed, the functioning of the system is described in terms of silly and cruel pleasures. Family love, trust, and mutual help are transformed into their opposites. Hobbes has already done virtually the same thing, but it is left to Sade to highlight one of the critical problems of the social contract theory of justice – namely, that regardless of what happens within the bounds of the contract, the best alternative is to keep the treaty intact.

Juliette, the cruel woman, becomes a member of the Sodality, a secret society whose purpose is to perform all the debaucheries one can imagine. It is a kind of temporary and restricted utopia in the sense that one does not live there. Only the president is permanently in residence. Yet the bylaws are clearly defined and strictly enforced, and this is not all. The Sodality is embedded in the threatening state of nature, so that the secret society resembles an island. It is an outpost of civilization and its unjust plans of life. Certainly, the Sodality is a philosophically less interesting arrangement than Silling. In the Sodality the young victims are confined to cellars and do not participate in the normal life of the society. At Silling, the victims are active all the time. Because the Sodality lacks Silling's complex social arrangements between different classes, its lords and victims can hardly be called citizens. The victims are mere prisoners.

Nevertheless, the forty-five laws of the Sodality are of some interest. They specify who can be a member, what it costs, the penalties for a violation of the rules, and what the rituals are. The activities of the Sodality consist of sex and torture, of course.

As part of its social contract, the rules of the Sodality say, "Rejected by the world, these outcasts [criminals] will find consolation and friends in a society which recognizes their value and will always give preference to their candidacy" (§ 17). Moreover, "Under no circumstances does the Sodality intrude or interfere in government affairs, nor may any Member" (§ 43).[15] The Sodality represents the negation of the state. As such, it invites people in from the cold, and also prevents them from returning. The poorer members are also entitled to reduced membership fees, an indication of the fair play within this organization.

Besides the societies of the Sodality and Silling, Sade provides a third example of civilized life in *Justine*. A small society of four monks of the Benedictine Order occupy the church of Saint-Mary-in-the-Woods and a connected, secret house behind a maze of walls and barriers. Justine, the virtuous fool, is taken to the house as a prisoner after she has entered the church to go to confession. The monks have a harem of kidnapped girls who are forced to participate in the life there as victims and servants of the monks. The basic setup is much like that of Silling, though not quite as detailed and systematic. However, Sade does describe carefully where the people live. Because he is creating a new world, its geography is important.

The statutes are as follows: "The monks regularly sleep every night in this pavilion, they return here at five in the afternoon and go to the monastery the following morning at nine, except for one of the four, chosen daily, who spends the day here.... We will soon see what his duties are." Also the victims learn what awaits them: "Failure to rise in the morning at the prescribed hour, thirty strokes with the whip," and so on.[16] Again, a social order is created, presenting the opposite of life outside. In this case the monks come to the house because of their excessively vicious nature, and they also return to the external world, even to the highest social positions. The Reverend Father Severino "had just been named the General of the Benedictine Order by His Holiness," and it is while he is away that Justine is able to make her escape from Saint-Mary-in-the-Woods. She simply climbs the wall and disappears from the fortress. According to the laws of narrative form, because she is finished she is free to leave.

## THE THEATER OF PAIN AND PLEASURE

In the cases of the Sodality and the Four Monks, the political implications are not as clear-cut as they are in the case of Silling. Silling deals with citizenship and sovereignty, while in the other two cases the focus is on cults and civilized life in an otherwise unspecified political context. The ideal social order is always seen as a system of principles which can neither be universally applied nor accepted in the vulgar state of nature. Only in a properly restricted realm can the friends satisfy their lust (with lust here presented as the ironic expression of the culture and its life-style). Nevertheless, in both the political and the cultural cases strict rules and their application define social membership in an artificial world.

Sade's social systems serve the one end of satisfying the heroes' lusts. Life at Silling aims at the pleasure of the friends through the work and suffering of others. The method by which this is achieved is most interesting: at Silling the key is the expansion of the person's imagination through narratives, combined with experimentation and the living out of all possibilities. The system is regular, efficient, and varied. Strict rules of conduct and ritual form a background to the variety of forms of pleasure in the foreground. This rigid order is necessary to vary the pleasures. Silling resembles a production plant where the daily operations are carefully listed and where any attempt to confuse the order is properly punished: "And so, as we have just indicated, one subject is dispatched daily, in the following order..." Nevertheless, it is variety that plays the main role. Against the background of routine and ritual (eating, sleeping, punishing, having sex, making decisions), variety takes two forms: real and imaginary. The real aspect consists of oppositions like philosophical/orgiastic, beautiful/ugly, weak/strong, aroused/calm, ordered/chaotic. The imagin- ary structure consists of narratives which allow people to share each other's lives. This fictional material is then translated into the language of real variety. The bridge between them is the theater; the fulfillment of the good life is itself a stage production. In the theater of horror, disgust, and aggression, they all "dance to the music of pain." This is why they need storytellers.

However, because variety consists of a limited number of simple dichotomies, such a translation from imagination to reality cannot succeed. The result is a riddle, perhaps even a tragedy. The friends are always threatened by impotence, a symbol of fear and of panic, which they struggle to avoid. They are ready to kill for a discharge. They exchange the expiration of a life for a discharge of sperm. In this way, the new social order serves not their pleasure, but their salvation. In Silling they worship nature, and as a consequence they live.

The symbolic goal of the civilized life is the pleasure of those who are capable of enjoying it. The key task is to create variety by translating the creatures of the imagination into the language of reality by means of stage productions. The standard etiquette is set aside momentarily; the workers erect a stage and direct a play; the masters join their victims and slaves, and all create something new. This means that the heroes must surrender their power. As masters of life and death, this is no longer enough. Those who control the narrative exercise control over the rakes. The storytellers become ritual rulers worshipped by the usurpers of force.

The storytellers are professional whores who have seen all aspects of lust and perversity. Madame Duclos enters the throne first. Duclos looks like Edgar Allan Poe's "shrouded human figure, very far larger in its proportions than any dweller among men. And the hue of the skin of the figure was of the perfect whiteness of the snow."[17] In her relentless search for the ultimate evil in man, she sounds like the chorus of Sophocles' *Oedipus at Colonus*, who chant:

> Look for the man! Who is he? where's he hiding? –
> where's he gone, rushed away, where now?
> That man, of all men on earth
> the most shameless, desperate man alive!
> Look for him, press the search now
> scour every inch of the ground![18]

This is what the whore accomplishes when she acts as the collective storehouse of wisdom and vision. She masters all the stories and myths of "simple passions," her memory is collective rather than individual, and she is both untouchable and indispensable. This is how she enters her throne:

> The three storytellers, magnificently dressed as upper class Parisian courtesans, were seated below the throne upon a couch, and Madame Duclos, the month's narrator, in very scanty and very elegant attire, well rouged and heavily bejeweled, having taken her place on the stage, thus began the story of what had occurred in her life, into which account she was, with all pertinent details, to insert the first one hundred and fifty passions designated by the title of *simple passions*.[19]

The throne is located on the stage, from which the unmoved mover controls the petty scene below her by means of her limitless memory. It is derived from the collective experience of all the whores of all the ages. Sade writes:

> she was placed like an actor in a theater, and the audience in their niches found themselves situated as if observing a spectacle in an amphitheater. . . . At the back of each niche was a little door leading into an adjoining closet which was to be used at times when . . . one preferred not to execute before everyone the delight for whose execution one has summoned that subject.[20]

At Silling, a hero has the choice between public control and private enjoyment. But the place where everything starts is the public stage, which carries the throne, which carries the whore who possesses all knowledge of vice and its pleasures: "'One moment there,' said the Duc.... 'Would you provide further information upon two matters: first, have you ever had any news about your mother?'" The friends are curious and therefore dependent on the woman.

Of course, reality must be avoided. The storytellers tell stories which may be true or false, but it doesn't really matter which. What matters is that the four women have something to tell: narratives which are first carefully classified and then assigned to different days. Thus time is another factor which works as a regulatory background and frame. The flow of days is all-important as a symbol of the personal life cycle. One of the whores, a high priestess of the ancient religion of perverted pleasures, relates one story a day, picked according to the appropriate classification. Since the story is magical, the narrative truth makes even the heroes her slaves. They follow the plot as if it were a command. The story stimulates their passions and drives them forward; it is a drug taken regularly and in large doses.

A storyteller has free access to novelty and variety. The theme is explored thoroughly even when it deals with simple pleasures such as eating excrement or anal sex. Everything possible is brought up, told, and explained. The stories are shared by the listeners as if they were real-life possibilities. Because the grammar of routine and conventional etiquette is broken, a new twisted grammar emerges where the relations of people, ideas, and things are contorted. The real problem is how to make all these strange things happen, and how to enjoy them.

For the translation of what is imaginary into the language of reality, careful preparations are needed. The victims of translation must be ready and the circumstances right. Both private quarters and a public stage are needed. The masters perform a translation which in principle is to be shared in public. The main effort takes place on the stage, where the audience is invited. That creates no problem at Silling, where the laws regulate this duty too. Art is coercive. But private quarters exist as well. A master may retire there with another person, because imagination and language are also private affairs. One needs time to think, and to withdraw behind the curtain is the same as to think things over. Yet privacy is an enigma which other people can neither share nor understand. Sade is not a behaviorist who makes visible all that the masters do when they translate the stories into the theater of civilized life. Since life is not a mere performance, it contains

# THE PARODY OF THE CIVIL CONTRACT

a private, intentional, and deliberative element. Such a private residue of what has already become public must always remain. A scream from a private chamber is at once the ultimate mystery and an assertion of individual freedom.

In other words, the publicity of the stage is the subversive transformation of privacy into a public medium. The secret life backstage is the same as the phobic horror of being alone in a dark place. The dialectic is between shameful disclosure and nameless horror. Some things are awful to see; others are frightening when hidden. In a subversive manner Sade inverts the normal cultural pattern and makes violence private and sex public. According to the familiar Christian taboos, the order must be different. Violence is to be both shared and experienced at its emotional and sympathetic level. Sex is to be enjoyed privately, subject to shame (real sex in public) and jealousy (imaginary sex in private). One wants to know why a person screams in pain, while one resists the same temptation in the case of sex.

The extreme level of control achieved by means of social etiquette is directly comparable to a stage production. Sade's account of table manners, meals, dishes, and drinks is important exactly in this respect. But his etiquette is turned around to serve ends which should normally be rejected, as in the case of Minski, the Russian, whose staple fare consists of human flesh. Sade's parody concerns social life in general, so that its point is directed to the extreme restrictions we accept in order to find some hidden pleasure. At Silling, the social system is an etiquette of the grand table, aimed at the pleasures of the stage, where people devour each other. They feed the children fine foods in order to keep their excrement delicious. They must also control their toilet behavior so that their treasures are not wasted.

In the story of life at Silling, as in all Sade's descriptions of life, the action is constrained by the stage. Life is artificial, and therefore enjoyable. Everything takes place in episodic scenarios that are based on planning and manufacturing and come from a theory. In the *120 Days of Sodom*, Sade makes it quite clear that the civilized life is a stage production and that its laws are those of the theater. It is a presupposition he will never reject. The stage accommodates a performance where something like the following takes place. The story depicts a complicated social situation where a person is brutally raped. The masters are interested, then amazed; they understand the point, and they get excited about it. They decide to try it out. A scenario is created in which one of the resident victims is raped while everyone else watches. The interpretation takes the form of a question: what would

I have thought and felt if I had committed the original crime? Once this is answered, by means of a rape, the scenario is finished, and either the storyteller proceeds with the narrative or the heroes withdraw to eat and drink. They experience how it feels to be a predator who locates his prey, stalks it, and kills it. This is why they need the theater.

The excitement is created both by its novelty and by the difficulties the heroes experience. The theater looks less than interesting, once we realize that the heroes have 120 full days to carry out their program. For thirty days they bathe in urine and dung, stubbornly refusing to try anything else, and bravely fighting off boredom. Even the first episode of the first day is catastrophic. First, Duclos omits some details from her story, like the size of penises, which makes it impossible for the President and the Bishop to visualize the person the story is about. Second, after the missing information is supplied, the crime in question is just pissing and kissing. Yet the Bishop suddenly wants to retire to a private room with a couple of victims. While the others wait patiently, the Bishop emerges, dissatisfied. He wants to punish his slave, and refuses consolatory sex; and as they all laugh, Duclos continues her story. Though they are competent, their performance needs fine tuning. They do everything they can to create real interest.

The masters have beautiful children, ugly old women, and everything in between. They feel pain and fear, or ecstasy and delirium. The masters may assume either the role of aggressor or victim, but there is no trace here of a complicated dialectic of submission and aggression. The food is always good. The masters' own condition varies between erection, ejaculation, and exhaustion. The variables are simple and few, so that their range of values follows no normal distribution. The play must be, of necessity, schematic. Ultimately they produce mere sketchy line-drawings, like the murderous passions which are summarized at the end of Sade's *120 Days of Sodom*. Of course, one can argue that the book is an incomplete draft, never finished because of Sade's prison conditions at the Bastille. I would suggest, on the contrary, that the book cannot be completed. Life at Silling is artificial, from which it logically follows that certain physical limitations must exist concerning what can be done.

The last narrator, Madame Desgranges, tells simple stories, but ones which would be hard to physically act out at Silling. For example, she describes a man who "would flog, then later kill the woman by depriving her of sleep" – a story which would take a week to finish at Silling. Some scenes, like no. 123, are labor intensive; others, like no.

125, would be difficult to arrange because they require six pregnant women; or they are technically demanding, like no. 127, which requires a special collapsible ceiling. These advanced horrors are accompanied by the friends' attempts to cut their victims to pieces.

Since Madame Desgranges rejects the maxim of veridicality, there are no requirements that her stories have accurate details. It is not even sensible to demand that one should be able to visualize the people who carry out their murderous passions. Desgranges penetrates right into one's subconscious imagination, where the motives that are present are depicted by Sade as a long list of horrors. But the greatest of all passions are also the most abstract; they cannot be translated into action on a stage, nor are they something one can enjoy. With the last storyteller, the whole theater becomes meaningless. She goes so deep that nothing can be done after hearing her stories, and the friends are left alone, gazing in amazement. They are now powerless. Sade concludes: "Wherewith Desgranges terminates her contribution; she is congratulated, toasted, acclaimed, etc."[21] Her status reflects her achievements. As Sade says: "etc."

## THE FALSIFICATION OF PHALLOCRACY

The politics of pleasure and cruelty at Silling appear in a surprising way when the issues concerning women are highlighted. Silling is a complex social arrangement of means and ends. The libertine friends have a definite goal in mind when they establish their artificial society. They build a theater because there they can dance to the flutes of the storytellers. Although the friends have all the coercive means at their disposal, the storytellers also wield power. No social life at Silling could go on without their narratives, and they are correspondingly influential. In fact, the four prostitutes are the necessary ingredients for the whole enterprise.

Jane Gallop provides an interesting discussion of women, sex, and male domination in her study of Sade, Jacques Lacan, and Luce Irigaray. She seems to argue that Sadean sexuality is anal, like that of psychoanalysis and even of some feminism. It is marked by its phallocracy: dry ideas, tight arguments, penetrating inquiry, and most of all, the need for unilateral control. She writes: "All penetration, considered to be sadistic penetration of the body's defensive envelope, is thought according to the model of anal penetration. The dry anus suffers pain; the penetrated is a humiliated man."

Gallop says that Sade is unable to handle the issue of menstrual blood, even though the libertine loves blood and wounds:

> Menstrual blood is not a wound in the closure of the body; the menstrual flow ignores the distinction virgin/deflowered. . . . The white virgin is necessarily sullied from without. In sadistic science there is no place for menstrual blood, for the latter marks woman as woman (virgin or not) with no need of man's tools.[22]

Sade panics and therefore stays quiet on the whole topic. Gallop quotes Irigaray: "For, whatever his libertinage, his transgression of all prohibitions, menstrual blood remains generally taboo for him."

The argument is that a man wants to control the flow of blood, which he does by cutting flesh open; he hates uncontrolled periods, and Sade fails to deal with this in his philosophy. Her periods are the sign of the female's natural freedom. The phallic power of the male necessitates the subordination of women, but this natural freedom both threatens this system and male solidity itself. Gallop says: "The solidity of his virile organ cannot risk cuntamination with anything so alien to it."[23] Women are alien creatures. Gallop describes how Madame de Saint-Ange fights her alienation and comes close to becoming a male figure in the course of her debate with Dolmance. But even she must reject phallocracy if she is going to succeed as a woman, Gallop argues. She says:

> the vagina . . . has a juicy receptivity which makes penetration not painful, but a free flowing exchange, leaving no solid borders to be violated. The vagina flows before penetration. It does not wait for man to break its seal, but hospitably prepares a welcome for his entry.

The anti-anal result is fluidity as the denial of pain and control. A Sadean heterosexual rape scene denies all these essential elements of fluidity.

Gallop's thesis about Sade's anal science and the lack of control which it entails looks less convincing if one carefully reads the constitution of Silling. Where the phallic power of the male friends is at its strongest, it is also the most illusory. Paradoxically, the system is ultimately anti-phallic. The society of Silling is highly exploitative of women, more so than any other system mentioned in Sade's stories. Because the friends hate women and the vagina, they are for pain and anal sex. But at the same time they are dependent on their storytellers, who are characteristically female and anti-phallic. If we apply Gallop's ideas of femininity to them, we see that they are the antithesis of phallocracy and its anal logic. They are open and flexible, welcoming and juicy: "Fluidity has its own properties," as Gallop puts this important discovery.[24] If the essence of the feminine logic entails its fluidity, then the whores possess it.

The female storytellers at Silling mention periods, so it is a mistake to maintain that Sade could not accommodate this subject in his writings. One should read the *120 Days of Sodom* and not mainly the story of *Philosophy in the Bedroom*, as Gallop seems to have done. It is true that Sade hates menstruation because it cannot be controlled, but one must keep in mind that Sade mentions at least three different passions in which menstruation figures. First, blood is involved in the passion for filth. Duclos tells a story in which "for more than six weeks Guerin absolutely forbade my sister to wash"; he enjoyed the menstrual blood as he enjoyed all "impurities." Later, menstruation is compared to shit, spittle, and unwashed feet. The libertine is punished by being forced to eat all this dirt; if he fails to obey, he will be flogged by women.

As I see it, Silling is the place where the power of phallic science is both confirmed and transcended. Its truth is affirmed by what the friends do, but there is a way out in the stories which are fluid, and as uncontrollable and nauseating as the female menstrual blood. A storyteller knows what she is doing; she "irrigates the dry field of both libertine and psychoanalytic science." The libertines cannot live without the nourishing fluid which they themselves cannot produce. But they are still immature and have much to learn, including the fact that mature libertines – like Juliette – are fully ambiguous as sexual beings.

Second, menstruation represents a uniquely female weakness that can be exploited in torture:

> The girl must be menstruating. She arrives at his home, a valet conducts her to a room in the cellar where the libertine stands awaiting her, but he is near a kind of reservoir of icy water.... She approaches the man, he topples her into it ... she is pulled back out at once, but as she is menstruating, severe disability is the very frequent result of her adventure.

This passion is indeed weird. The interesting part of it is the idea that menstruation can be used for a purpose, because it makes the woman weak and vulnerable to shock.

Third, menstrual blood is licked and drunk by a pervert: "A very young man, a young man with a very handsome face, used to find it vastly amusing to lick out my cunt once a month, and at a certain period.... He swallowed both fuck and blood." The friends disagree about this amusement, and especially its more perverse forms involving pregnancies and miscarriages. The friends at Silling agree that it is an unsympathetic amusement, though it is not totally condemned by them.[25]

The important fact is that Sade does not neglect the topic of menstruation. Since the storytellers know the feminine secret, periods can be mentioned and used. It provides an additional source of cruel pleasure, showing that the whores have more power than the libertine friends. Unlike the male rakes, the whores are subversive in their own perfect way. However, menstruation remains a problem both narratively and politically. The horror of menstrual blood reflects the fragility of male domination, phallocratic ideology, and anal practice. When the female storytellers go to work, female fluids cover the scene, flooding the whole field with their own liquid medium, in which the friends happily struggle. The males surrender their penetrative power in order to follow the logic of a free narrative, which has neither strict rules, tight arguments, dry lessons, nor truthfulness. The story welcomes listeners, changes its form as needed, flows hotly and freely, and produces all the pleasure there is. The turd is replaced by word. Without it, only the self-produced irritation of masturbation remains. Because of the female mouth, the hard power of the penis is transformed into something soft and flowing.

Gallop aims at establishing such a conclusion independently of Sade's text, but it seems that Sade has already said it. The Sodom of Silling is the true hell where an artificial social order succeeds in negating its own source of power, transforming anal practice into its fluid opposite. The anal scavenger is turned into a free predator. Waste is replaced by a prey. Sade turns male libertine power into that of a mere narrative mode. He is able to accommodate his undeniable hatred of vaginas and menstrual blood in this surprising move. The social contract at Silling is supremely subversive because it is self-negating.

## THE MATURE AND FREE PREDATOR

The ordeal the heroes at Silling must face is a terrifying one. They work hard at their project and achieve better and better results. They stage scenarios which reflect the principles of nature, ethics, and psychology in totally new and unexpected ways. Because the society is small and the theater resources are poor, all productions are just the abstract frames for what can be imagined. Perhaps this is all we can expect from life itself, Sade seems to say. Since there are not many grammars of human experience and gratification, the best we can achieve is a true understanding of such possibilities. The first step towards it is through the realization that the possibilities can be realized. In this sense we are free. Reality is only one possibility; an infinity of fictions can be acted out, if one knows how and has the power. In *120 Days of Sodom* Sade argues that it is possible to act out (almost) all the possibilities one is able to imagine. This is his catechism of personal freedom. One may also achieve something else, namely, an invulnerability to the exercise of power. Freedom has a double face: a person is free *to* realize whatever he may want to imagine, and he is free *from* anybody's power. Whatever happens to the heroes, it will be another stage production, and they will be prepared for it. The social contract entails freedom. In other words, what is artificial defies the truth.

Sade seems to claim that the normal ideology of liberty is wrong. It is not the case, as one tends to think, that one must be negatively free – free from constraints – in order to enjoy positive freedom. On the contrary, one need not be negatively free to be positively free. Life may be at its best a stage production, and at its worst only a rejected manuscript; in either case, it can be lived to the full whatever the external conditions happen to be. One can always stage a play, and perhaps this is enough to constitute all the positive freedom there is anywhere in the world. As Sade argues, fiction and theater are more concrete than what we call real social life. Therefore the social contract establishes a stage and produces a play. For Sade, of course, the home of discharge is on the stage, where full control is possible.

The same pattern evident in the *120 Days of Sodom* is repeated throughout Sade's mature work. The experimental scenarios are created so that theories of pleasure and pain can be tested again and again. Yet Sade's persons have the problem of never being able to consolidate their achievements. What they create disappears and leaves them in a state of uncertainty as to whether they understood it correctly. So they must try again, and this repetition includes philosophical discussion as well. Between furious sex scenes, the scenario is undone and the action postponed while the characters theorize about what they are doing. The result is always the same, as if they could not remember what they said earlier or could not believe that they got it right.

Philosophy is as repetitious as pleasure, and too incredible to be true. Repetition is the key to the Sadean style of the ecstatic life.

In Sade's own life in Paris, and in his later works, the society of Silling haunts him. The same characters reappear and follow the lines of the social contract made at Silling. Only one crucially important thing has changed. The characters are now mature enough to figure out what to do without anyone telling them. The high priestesses, the storytellers, are already gone; even the corrupt monks in the church where Justine is trapped manage without them. The Russian cannibal Minski has a unique life-style created all by himself. A mature person's imagination is enough to satisfy his or her thirst for variety. At this stage, the public domain of imaginary possibilities has changed into a private language. In other words, the new hero is able to write his own manuscripts and does not need the hand of a whorish storyteller whom he should worship as an untouchable mother goddess. The young Juliette, for instance, starts in a submissive role, but after reaching maturity she is ready to exploit her former friends and act out her own plans. In *Philosophy in the Bedroom* the novice Eugenie finally acquires her right to design a whole new scene. Her educator, Dolmance, says, "Allow your friend [Eugenie] and me to take charge; you others need merely obey the orders we give you."[26] In the same way, Silling is a place where people are educated.

If one reads, say, *Justine* and *Juliette* but forgets the lessons of *120 Days of Sodom*, one may wonder how those wicked ideas come to the libertine mind. To say that they just imagine the crimes which they go on to realize is true, but not illuminating. We should go back to the *120 Days of Sodom* to see where the imaginary monstrosities have their external source and their own type of intersubjective reality. The storytellers' stories need not be true, but they come from professional whores who have lived through many strange things. What they tell has value as a testimony to their own social conditions. In the later novels, a similar source is missing. Characters like the Minister of Justice, Saint-Fond, just happen to have a lively but cruel imagination. The theater they produce is private, and as such without interest to an audience who can neither relate to it nor see its origin.

However, once we understand that the heroes of the later novels are related to those in the *120 Days of Sodom*, our opinion of their theater may well change. Just as Silling is the model of the result of a social contract, so the private imagination of the later characters reflects the model of the four whorish storytellers. What the new heroes try to accomplish in their lives results from their imagination, which works as a private storyteller for that person. The master tells his own stories, which can be shared by his fellows, and which are translated into action through artificial scenarios. Such narratives reflect life as a whore or a slave in the society Sade describes. When the masters tell the stories of their own lives to themselves, the result is an enigma, which first invites interpretation and then is realized on the stage. The result is a discharge.

In this way, Sade's heroes proceed through a long learning process in order to become their own storytellers. Sade's *Philosophy in the Bedroom* and *Juliette* deal with education from the point of view of a good learner. Justine, on the contrary, never learns. Her life remains simple and one-dimensional; she is guided by what she calls virtue, which leads her from one disaster to another. She never enters the theater as an active interpreter of her own stories. Others can tell stories for her, but she is unable to decipher them. She is a hermeneutical invalid. One can defend Justine by saying that the fictions are as difficult as they are fantastic. The Sadean experience of social life is supposed to lead one to the gates of hell. What one experiences may look like an ultimate horror that no one can tolerate. Nevertheless, Sade himself maintains that human psychology is such that we are able to draw our greatest pleasures directly from despair. Once we understand social life, we need to find an answer to the problem of how to live with the experience of life which the whore-storyteller relates.

How can one handle the truth of the social contract? Sade says that the human mind is constituted in such a way that its greatest pleasures are excitement, rage, and other violent emotions, so that society must be built to serve those ends. They are fictions which a master loves because he knows, before Freud, that "virtuous continence is no longer rewarded with the assurance of love."[27] The master neither restricts his mind nor misses the social state of nature. He wants an artificial and cruel utopia. Only there can he learn to fulfill his desire to be a predator, free from all constraints and able to control his victims. After the learning process is over, he is his own predator and able to exploit his surroundings.

The social contract creates a social life which is both cruel and enjoyable, whereas the original state of nature (and France) was cruel but not enjoyable. After the social contract is finally transcended, the rake need not face terrifying and incomprehensible nature any more. The theater sets him free so that he can perfect his predatory plans; and because he lives a fictional life, natural laws are replaced by style. The person can do whatever he likes.

# 7

# STYLE AND THE AMBIGUITY OF VICE

Sade writes from his experience in prisons and mental asylums, and he writes about the value-changes he wishes to promote. But the worlds of facts and values are not the only playgrounds of the Divine Marquis. His works are also fictions, and their philosophical and pseudo-scientific aspects are embedded in the stories he wants to tell. Such fictions are as weird as the hard facts and objective values he talks about. A full account of Sade's narrative technique would show how he concentrates on small, repetitive vignettes, ambiguous descriptions, and opaque figures of speech which emulate stage rehearsals of subversive acts. In what follows I can only glance at his stylistic devices – his pragmatics of style. I shall focus instead on Sade's rhetoric, those literary techniques by means of which he creates impressions and changes the reader's reactions. I shall also consider the question of what these rhetorical tricks signify.

We must avoid the temptation to translate Sade's narratives into pictorial imagery. Actually, his language philosophizes rather than paints, although the casual reader gets the opposite impression. Sex and torture are themselves to be viewed by a Peeping Tom. The falsity of this attitude may not be easy to understand if one focuses on the events which are the subject matter of his tales. But as pictures these are devoid of interest, as can be verified by looking at the hundred engravings which illustrate the first edition of the *New Justine* and *Juliette*.[1] There is nothing to be seen beyond Sade's powerful language; the pictures themselves are uninformative. In explaining why this is so and how the language works, I shall concentrate on the repetitive structure of Sade's narrative as the structure of orgiastic pleasure itself; the ambiguous grammar of crime; the ontology of an opening (or a hole) taken as his key metaphor; and the reactions of the reader to the text as an instrument of torture.

The philosophical framework which is the background of Sade's style is summarized in the following table. It outlines the elements of development from a lower to a higher level (from left to right):

| | | | |
|---|---|---|---|
| *Education:* | Scavenger | Avenger | Predator |
| *Attitude:* | Shame | Fear | Apathy |
| *Method*: | Luck | Force | Control |
| *Pleasure*: | Sensual | Cerebral | Orgiastic |
| *Medium*: | Body | Experience | Language |
| *Structure*: | Work | Theory | Art |
| *Substance*: | Turd | Sperm and blood | Corpse |
| *Action*: | Gazing | Sex and torture | Death |
| *Ethics:* | Duty | Right | Virtue |

## REPETITION

When the focus is on the interrelation between sex and text, the repetitive structure of the text is identical to the structure of sexual pleasure. When one expands the view to include all kinds of satisfying acts – ultimately, all natural performances and their goals – there emerges a life consisting only of discharges. The irony of this is that what is originally supposed to be supremely stimulating reappears now as something so boring that one wonders why the Sadean heroes bother. They often struggle: some are so old that they are impotent and require an excess of stimulation before they achieve anything like a discharge. The human material is treated in a peculiar manner, of course, because what looks like a highly organized design – the body and the mind – is dissolved into a disorganized combination of flesh and blood, with the mind as the echo of a scream in an empty vault. Sade's workers are engaged in a counter-creation and try to undo what God created.

Some of the heroes realize that debauchery is a duty which must be performed whether they like it or not. They become aggressive and irritable. As it seems, their ultimate attitude towards their victims must be hatred, because what they do to them is so dull. The model for discharge is labor, and sex and torture are metaphorical expressions for the active life. Discharge alone is real. Even a corrupt and criminal life is a weak metaphor, to say nothing of a bourgeois career, which is a mere travesty of the good life.

Since Sade's people are a traveling theater group, his art is a stage production. It consists of three acts: philosophy, debauchery, and post-orgiastic peace. The victims are tortured, but they suffer no more than the audience does. Actually the victims *are* the audience. The double role – as victims and audience – creates problems, however. The dispensable people, who are not even fully formed persons, make up an indispensable audience. Just as Sade needs his readers, the heroes need the gaze of the audience. A demanding double responsibility is assigned to those who must suffer; they must experience a terror so deep that they will lose their self-consciousness and personal identity, while at the same time they alone may watch the emerging orgiastic pleasure. The audience is, therefore, needed because the heroes go out of their minds, reaching transcendence and the void beyond all understanding. Their best work exists only in the gaze of the audience.

In the case of simple passions, such an alienated arrangement works. The audience is afraid only to the degree that they become external to the situation and start looking at it from the outside. They are not part of the action, because they hate it. Their personalities are divided into two parts, one of which resists and one of which commands them to obey because of fear. Coerced choice presupposes a split personality. Yet the higher reaches of criminal and murderous passions are so demanding that there is no place for the gaze from outside. The victim is blind and paralyzed; the lights go out when the action reaches its climax. Since the audience does not see, it suffers, and hence it ceases to be what it used to be. The discharge has destroyed its own necessary condition – the wide-open gaze – and everything becomes nothingness. Sade's purpose is to describe discharge in its all-conquering, explosive might, where the irony of self-defeat is the final word, after which there is nothing. To discharge is to destroy.

As Sade argues, even if the Bible says that Sodom will burn eternally in hell, the fire has gone out a long time ago. The road to and from a holocaust can be mapped. Its geography proves to be both stimulating and dangerous:

> It is to be feared that the many volcanoes ringing Florence may someday cause it harm: these fears are amply justified by the signs of past upheavals one notices everywhere in the area. They suggested some comparative ideas to me: is it not very probable, said I [Juliette] to myself, that the fiery destruction of Sodom, Gomorrah, etc., made up into miracles for the purpose of instilling in us a terror of the vice which held universal sway among the inhabitants of those cities; is it not altogether likely that the

famous conflagrations were caused, not by supernatural agencies, but by natural forces?

Juliette then compares Florence and Naples to the Biblical cities of the plain, concluding that the sins are the same everywhere. She is finally motivated to engage in some suitable debauchery herself: "Wherewith I imagined myself transported to those happy Arabian towns, here I am in Sodom, I said, let us do here as the Sodomites do.... Augustine and I gazed dreamily into the pit and masturbated."[2]

Augustine and Juliette have an audience, as they realize when a giant figure emerges from the bushes and says he is the Hermit of the Apennines. As Sade's logic dictates, this person lures them into a trap by providing them with a tempting motive: "you deserve to see what I have to show you." Then he changes his identity into that of the powerful and cruel Minski. Finally, Minski himself becomes a victim of Juliette's magic; he is poisoned and robbed. He who watches must later suffer. Minski is unconscious when the entertainers leave his castle. Such incidents happen in Sade's texts all the time. Nothing is eternal; but all things rise from the ashes. The rhythm of the text reflects this by means of its circularity and repetition. The heroes go through the same routines; they come, they perform, they leave. The acts and scenes of the play reflect the same grammar of travel. First there is excitement and anticipation (with some keen philosophizing); then there is the actual love-play and torture; and finally, there are discharges over and over again. When the showtime arrives, the same play is staged again. Sex works in a similar way. A person is aroused, engages in the sex act, experiences a discharge, and feels drained. He tries a variety of tricks and experiments. Nevertheless, the natural rhythm of pleasure is always the same.

Like a traveling theater troupe, the heroes move to another place where their performance is once more a novelty and where their audience is already waiting. They even go to Siberia, where the only audience is animals. Nevertheless, the discussion and travel – the spiritual and physical journey – is repetitive. The result is an effect of meaningless chatter. But all this is different from the lives of the victims. The heroes rest and discuss things when they are exhausted. Their rest is a philosopher's rest, in the sense that their bodies recover and their minds work. The result of this intellectual work is a justification and a theory of what they are doing. But whatever they think during the period of recuperation, their actions always return in the same form. For instance, much of the talk is genuinely ethical. They repeat moral terms in their normal sense, analyze and lament the unjust state of society and the excessive power of its religious institutions, but without doing anything about it.

Orgiastic pleasure as repetition follows from Sade's basic idea that discharge is the transgression of all values and norms. Since it cannot be described, a special technique is required which utilizes the grammar of repetition – philosophical discussion, arousal, sex, torture, crime, discharge, exhaustion, and rest. This list can be reduced to the three elements of philosophy, discharge, and rest. Such a simple pattern is clear in the context of education, but it tends to become blurred when fully mature libertines are on the stage. Because they are able to perform longer, the structure of the text is also more varied, but it never quite loses its triangular pattern.

The simplest examples of repetition can be found in *Philosophy in the Bedroom*, which is a straightforwardly educational story. A more complicated case is found in *Justine*. It is a play in several acts, each of which has the same structure; together they form one narrative cycle. Justine (or Thérèse, as she is known during her travels) is hiding in the bushes when she happens to witness homosexual coitus between the Comte de Bressac and his valet Jasmine. They discover Thérèse, of course. The audience participates in the play, after which Thérèse is an observer, an actor, and a victim. Her role is complex and painful. The villains discuss the case, become aroused, and decide that "for once let us be just" – which means that after learning about the accusations against Thérèse for crimes she did not commit, they decide to punish her. She is tied to some trees in a very painful position so that "I [Thérèse] no longer existed save through the violence of pain."[3] She loses her identity, which means she can be safely untied. Her brief initiation is over, and the count takes her with him. Ultimately he wins her confidence, stupid as she is.

The next act takes place when the young count tells about his plan to poison his aunt, whom Thérèse has also learned to like. The entourage moves to Paris, where the count instructs Thérèse about his murderous plans and then teaches her his philosophy of vice. The narrative moves to its preparatory stage, philosophy. A long discussion on religion drives Thérèse to desperation because, although "I added a thousand other arguments ... they merely caused the count to laugh, and his captious principles, nourished by a more male eloquence, supported by readings and studies, I, happily, had never performed, daily attacked my principles, without shaking them."[4] The count gets so excited that he reveals his homosexual secrets to his aunt, receiving pleasure from her horror and confusion.

After four years have passed – suddenly, as always in Sade's narratives – the actual crime is exposed. First there is a theoretical discussion justifying the poisoning of the aunt. The justification is the familiar one that ties between family members are an indifferent matter when the pleasures of egoism are at stake. Thérèse decides to pretend obedience to her master and tell the whole story to the aunt: "The time had passed ... I saw in him nothing but a monster." The deceived count embraces and kisses Thérèse. From his point of view, this action is a direct result of the fact that he has fully established himself in his friend's eyes as a moral monster: "You are the first woman I have ever held in my arms," he declares in an ecstatic tone of voice. To him, Thérèse suddenly seems an ambiguous character, not a woman but a fellow criminal and a partner.

After Thérèse takes the poison to the lady, they test it on a dog, which dies in agony. The count, hearing these sounds, infers that they are the results of the poison. The aunt sends a message to the police, but it is intercepted. Thus Thérèse is left at the mercy of the count, who takes his revenge. Since the preliminaries have already been drawn out, not much verbal foreplay is needed before the action starts. The count only mentions the law of nature, and this minimal philosophy is sufficient to make him ready for his pleasure:

> What has your duplicity done for you, unworthy creature? You have risked your life without having saved my aunt's: the die is cast ... before you expire you must learn that the virtuous road is not always the safest, and that there are circumstances in this world when complicity in crime is preferable to informing.[5]

Thérèse is dragged out and thrown to the dogs, who bite her and molest her. After that she is given her clothes and let go. Her wounds heal quickly – she cannot die, because her education is not yet complete. The count has said that she must learn, and at the end of the book she completes her education and dies.

The Comte de Bressac episode is independent of the rest of the novel. More than half of it consists of philosophical discussion and the violent acts to which it leads. The violent acts are followed by descriptive material designed to introduce the next scene. The same pattern is repeated until the final climax, in which Thérèse confronts the animals whose images have haunted her, one of which she had tried to eliminate by poisoning. This does not succeed, because Thérèse can do nothing but talk and feel after having lost her personal identity when tied to the trees. As a member of the audience, she is unwillingly dragged into the play in the role of victim. When the curtain is drawn, she is back in her seat in front of the now empty stage: "Night was closing: it was almost beyond my power to move; I was scarcely able to stand erect; I cast my eyes upon the thicket where four years earlier I had slept a night when I had been in circumstances almost as unhappy!"[6] The whole episode ends in the bushes where it started.

Her journey is formed of four circles, each of which has the same structure, namely, discussion, crime, discharge, and a return to a new starting point. The themes of the discussion are already familiar, the characteristics of the people are predictable, the valet Jasmine duly disappears from the picture after the opening scene, and even the poison is the same as that used in other adventures. The sole novelty is the use of mastiffs in the final torture scene. The long drama gets its unique meaning from one word, "mastiff," and from one image – that of a young woman thrown to the dogs. Maybe Sade loves Nero, since that was the fate of the Christian martyrs in ancient Rome.

## THE GRAMMAR OF VIOLENCE

Travel leads to the formation of new groups. The two sisters Juliette and Justine meet new people, but they are either aggressively dominating or have the victim's lack of personality. The stage performance is therefore repeated. The heroes travel through a homogeneous medium of physical and social space–time. The episode concerning the fantastic Russian giant, Minski, is important because it is exceptional. Minski is a Gothic character, a monstrous cannibal. He is a symbol of the fear of the East and of its primal mysteries. When Sade writes about him, his style becomes clumsy, and the narrative feels as grotesque as Minski himself. Sade's style obeys the demands set by this character, so that everything is suddenly simply and naively powerful. We are dealing with a childlike character whose mind moves as follows:

> I have you in my power, he said once we had sat down. I can do with you whatever I please ... I am a Muscovite, born in a small town on the Volga bank. Minski is my name; upon my father's death I inherited his colossal riches and Nature had proportioned my physical faculties and my tastes to the favors wherewith fortune now gratified me.[7]

The monster refers to himself as if from outside. Because this is a stigma of a victim, Minski's style creates a corresponding expectation of defeat. But although his style is that of a loser, the description is that of a winner. The man is as ruthless as he is strong. But he cannot win because he got his grammar wrong.

Juliette and her entourage are now in trouble. Since the monster is rich and murderous, some must perish, and they do. As a cannibal, Minski is a second-order human being; his body is composed of other bodies. He even uses human beings as furniture. The table tops are the backs of his kneeling slaves; the result is that he can eat people from people:

> There is nothing mysterious about it . . . you notice that this table, these chandeliers, those chairs are each made up of a group of girls cunningly arranged; my meal will be served upon the backs of these creatures. . . . Twelve naked girls . . . brought the dishes; and as they were of massive silver and very hot, scorching the breasts and buttocks of the elements composing the table, there was a pleasant convulsive stir produced, it resembled the rippling of the waves at sea.

This is perhaps Sade's finest single image. The ambiguity which Sade exploits is easy to recognize. Minski loves and needs people like he loves food and tables. This does not make him one of them. He remains a fairy-tale giant who comes straight out of children's books.

Minski's passion is revealed to the reader thus: "I ate human flesh with my brave African comrade; I have preserved a taste for it; all this wreckage you see around you are relics of the creatures I devour; I eat no other sort of meat." Juliette relates, "My two men and I breakfasted heartily. As for Minski, he was served solider stuff: eight or ten virgins-blood sausages and two testicle pastries took the edge off hunger, eighteen magnums of Greek wine accompanied those victuals into his enormous belly." The worshippers of natural pleasures are now seen to be trapped by their own art. But Minski is a lonely monster in his mountain castle. He says simply, "I have few visitors" – meaning those he will not eat. His style of acting is too simple to be taken seriously. A bad philosopher, he has not much to say, although his manners are spectacular. People like Minski and Thérèse cannot win.[8]

## THE READER

Sade's text does not work either like literature or like a philosophical argument. In Sade's stories, the style, structure, rhetoric, and message are so closely connected that the text is intolerably dense, making it "a scandalous, scarcely approachable book, which no one can render public."[9] Yet it is a mistake to say that Sade is not readable. The text is quite accessible and enjoyable on its own terms. The real difficulty lies in the close connection between its message and its medium. The structure and style of the written text are so important that what is said becomes secondary. Even the length of the text and its repetitive nature are more important than what Sade actually says. One needs to unpack the structure of the text, its grammar, and its theatrical nature. Only then can one see how radical Sade is. Though the destructive nature promises pleasure to her followers, the pleasure appears to be an infinitely tedious performance, without variety, without creativity, promising nothing but ugliness in the end. Nature destroys. Work produces garbage. The dreams of pleasure are just illusions. The talk about pleasure is subordinated to the grammar of repetition, which is a mixed medium of boredom and terror. The same can be said of the use of the vocabulary of vice and virtue. The moral stuttering convinces the reader that something important may be happening behind that noise.

The structure of the subject matter, or grammar, dominates meaning, in the sense that the reference is not clear and the truth is a joke. To extract the message from the grammar becomes tedious and difficult. Sade's message does not come through via reading in the sense of a semantic interpretation. The viability of his ethics is questionable, since it is so inconsistent; he has no evidence for his theory of nature; and the reader gets sick of the sausages Minski enjoyed. Because he cannot understand it, the reader must either participate in the story or reject it. The former is Sade's last hope. If the reader does not participate, Sade has lost him as he has lost many. Yet he writes for somebody.

The text cannot be read as one reads novels or philosophy, but something else may happen. The reader must mobilize his introspection, look into his own motivation, and recall what he considers to be shameful. The reader notices that the text also is in pain. Sade writes from prisons and mental asylums where he is under threat of confiscation of his books, of censorship, and loss of privileges (paper and pen), so he transfers his hatred to the reader. To read hundreds of pages about eating excrement is nauseating, and depictions of torture soon become revolting. As a victim of the libertine Sade, the reader suffers.

The text can be enjoyed by adopting an ironical and alienated attitude and reading it in fragments. But then one misses the message. One must dare to get immersed in it, despite the fact that the experience is bound to be painful. The style has its pragmatic effects created by the repetitive plots and the characterization of the heroes. Yet Sade wants his text to work like an instrument of torture. The text is an act of violence against the reader, and if one enjoys it one is already a libertine, a twisted soul, a masochist.

Sade's ultimate parody is revealed by reading his books. One approaches them innocently, but that approach will prove to be nauseating. Why is one reading at all? Perhaps one is a pervert who wants to hurt oneself. If Sade is successful, the reader will realize and understand his own perverted tendencies. He may hate Minski's diet, but what can he do about it? The meal is already there on his own plate. If Sade is right, one should politely eat what is offered, and Sade has thus proved his point. People want to suffer, because their motivation is atavistic. Facing censorship, Sade achieves the truth in his own indirect way. What is boring, repetitive, unreadable, blasphemous, mad, and already forgotten is also dangerous.

The weapons which Sade hopes to use against the reader were also known by Plato. Plato's tone of voice is startling:

> But, I said, I once heard a story which I believe, that Leontius the son of Aglaion, on his way up from the Piraeus under the outer side of the northern wall, becoming aware of the dead bodies that lay at the place of public execution at the same time felt a desire to see them and a repugnance and aversion, and that for a time he resisted and veiled his head, but overpowered in despite of all by his desire, with wide staring eyes he rushed up to the corpses and cried, There, ye wretches, take your fill of the fine spectacle! – I too, he said, have heard the story.[10]

Sade repeats this riddle so many times that one confronts the truth and knows the ambiguous kind of person one is.

## AMBIGUITY

For Sade, crime is the subversion of the normal grammar of things. Though he never thematizes the issue, or gives an answer to many of the questions it entails, it seems that much of the interest of Sade's books rests on the ideas of a broken grammar and ambiguity. As a theory of vice, it may be too limited, but for better or worse this seems to be Sade's view. We need to make it less ambiguous somehow, and for this reason I shall offer some suggestions about how different rhetorical ideas apply to ethics. Of course, much evil originating from violent reactions, revenge, rage, and jealousy is outside ethics altogether. Yet insofar as we hope to systematize the moral core of life, we need to understand what ambiguity means. The following analysis will specify some narrow senses of the term, although I shall continue to use the simple umbrella sense. The following is only a tentative suggestion of some overlapping alternatives.

First, irony. Cowardice is an ironic condition in the sense that a heroic evaluation, which is immanent in the situation, is turned into the negative fact of cowardice. The libertine is supposed to be his own contrary: he enjoys punishing the weak much more than the strong. The story of such an action is riddled with ambiguity when courage turns into its opposite. Another irony: since all pleasure could have been stronger, its satisfaction entails disappointment. Therefore, the irony of pleasure is described as follows: "that has perhaps been too much for you, Thérèse, and certainly not enough for me; one never tires of this mania notwithstanding the fact that it is a very pale image of what one should really like to do."[11]

Second, an open question. No plausible interpretation can be given to a person's decision. In Sade's case blasphemy is such a decision. An atheist libertine talks against God, although he does not believe in God and despises other people's opinions. We can ask why he is doing so, but no answer follows. Blasphemy is a meaningless ritual whose performance is a riddle: "the *evil* I do others makes me happy, as God is rendered happy by the *evil* he does me."[12] Man is the image of God, who is vicious. To talk about such an analog is vacuous because it is mere blaspheming.

Third, vagueness. One cannot capture the meaning of what a person is doing, because the case is open to too many interpretations. For example: a drunk drinks too much to take care of his family, although he occasionally does it very well. Such a situation is vague, and we are not really sure what to say about it. We may struggle hard to classify the person as either a drunk or a fool, as either irresponsible or sick; but vagueness reduces the moral pressure, since the person cannot be classified and condemned. Sade calls this "capriciousness" and assigns it an important role in libertine life. Such a person may do good deeds, too, as long as he is not consistent about it.

Fourth, ambiguity in the narrow sense. An idea is ambiguous if it has two valid but contrary interpretations. Sade's typical example is that of a homosexual marriage in which a man is dressed as the bride; his assumption of the woman's role entails that he is she.

One may play with such examples of explanatory confusion forever. One might even feel tempted to present a classification of the types of crime along stylistic lines. Perhaps the result would not be interesting, since confusion entails conceptual instability, which is quite difficult to classify. However, rhetorical theory shows that the variety of evil is very large. An attempt to provide a simple typology is useless, because such things as murder and public nakedness do not resemble each other. But whatever the type of evil, it remains true that we are discussing a genuine problem. Some things are wicked, and as such cannot be recommended or even excused. Although there is much cultural relativity in these matters, we need not succumb to the relativist temptation to say there is nothing but subjectivity here. On the contrary, if one looks carefully enough at types of wickedness, it is easy to see that some aspects of the rhetoric of terror are such that we do not want to accept them. It is one thing to apply rhetorical theory, and another to accept its results as morally indifferent. Though the theory helps us understand the relativity of our own attitudes, the mechanisms of condemnation, and the uses of crime, it should not make us accept wickedness as what it is not. Though some agents are wicked, and some actions are evil, we do not want them. At the same time, their wholesale elimination may not be possible, because such negative things are part of social life.

In order to apply the ideas presented above, one needs to keep in mind that Sade is the author of stories and plays. The reader has no experience of anything like what Sade wants to talk about. His statements can neither be true nor even probable. Therefore, his narrative creates what there is. If his texts create a fictional world, then its criminal ideas do not denote things which are disconnected from the text. As I have said, the narrative itself is the crime. The key term here is subversion, or the ambiguous style whose elements are garbage, filth, bad taste, nausea, vertigo, contradiction, blasphemy, libel, crime, pornography, torture, kinky sex, and an unreadable book. Let us take a closer look at the fiction which is covered by the umbrella term of "subversion."

The Sadean idea of subversion, or what he calls a moral crime, entails first that the repetition of moral terms and violent actions alienates the reader from what is said. Second, it entails that an interpretation of the situation is never coherent. The story is, as we know, ambiguous both externally (through repetition) and internally. Though it may look innocent merely to break the rules of language, it is not. On the contrary, Sade captures an essential aspect of social control, the public manipulation of speech; it is at the core of ideas of retribution, censorship, and cultural hegemony. Through changing the rules of grammar, one changes things. When one changes things, something stops existing – something dies – without providing any understanding of what could replace it. Moreover, what exists is real because we can describe it by means of grammatical constructions. The losses are concrete. Sade redefines destruction by means of a novel method. Unlike those who think that losses are something which exist independently of our methods of grasping them, Sade's magic makes meanings and things disappear from language.

Of course, Sade's little stories are predictably repetitious, like primitive art or popular culture, cartoons and comics. Yet the topics cannot be defined so that their effect would not remain surrealistic. Two different possibilities exist: that vice is ambiguous, or that ambiguity is vicious. The first thesis says that it is not always clear whether we are dealing with a good or bad issue, as in the case of private revenge. The hero gets even with the villain in a way which cannot be unequivocally admired. The residual moral ambiguity is a sign of what we think is unacceptable. The second alternative refers to the case where we call an action or intention evil because it refuses to take any clear-cut form. Private revenge is wicked because it contains an element borrowed from the action it was supposed to correct. Revenge, as a justified intention, is similar to its cause, understood as something nasty. The explanatory moral structure cannot support revenge. However, the avenger has his private reasons for doing something that has consequences which are indistinguishable from those that brought about the need for revenge. According to Sade, wickedness is confusion in both senses.

For Sade, because ambiguity means freedom, evil has its own role to play. Social life is no paradise, and its mechanisms of disambiguation are often overpowering. The most ironical way to reduce the amount of evil in social life is to relax the control of language. What is not controlled cannot become a source of wicked plans, because there is nothing that could be ambiguated. However, this is really a metaphysical recommendation. Since social life is control, even over the most minute of things, the evil of confusion will always be with us. The ideally harmonious life is a myth.

The ideas of harm and loss entail a moment of surprise which is also inherent in regret. What a rational agent predicts cannot entail his regret; at most it constitutes a cost-related factor. What one knows, one tries to control. What one does not control brings about fear and terror. In that sense, the social system attempts to master fear and terror even more than it tries to control losses and harms. Because human life is imperfect, we have no hope of getting rid of the terror, except by designing anew its grammatical expressions and keeping these creations intact. It is against such stabilizing fictions that Sade directs his attack. Subversiveness implies surprise and instability.

Incest is one of Sade's favorite horror stories. A father marries his daughter and conceives a child by her. His moral crime is not violence, or even anything sexual. The child may be loving and consenting, like Eugenie de Franval. In the same way, the sexual relation may be a normal one. The moral crime is simply that the father becomes his own child's husband and the new child's father and grandfather. The family context becomes a mess in which social identities become tangled. Franval says: "Yes, Monsieur, I love my daughter, I love her passionately, she is my mistress, my wife, my daughter, my confidante, my friend, my only God on earth."[13] Franval piles up ambiguities when he deconstructs his daughter's identity. He creates a situation where no one knows who is who and what their social roles are. The following exchange occurs:

 – Valmont, have you ever taken the trouble to cast a careful eye on Eugenie from time to time?
 – Your daughter?
 – Or, if you prefer, my mistress.
 – Ah, you scoundrel! Now I understand.
 – This is the first time in my life I find you perceptive.
 – What? On your word of honor, you're in love with your daughter?

Franval's wife learns the incomprehensible truth from Valmont: "Franval in love with his daughter! Just Heaven! This creature whom I have borne in my womb, 'tis now she who breaks my heart so grievously!"[14] Eugenie's status has become fluid, as she is a daughter and wife at the same time.

Sigmund Freud writes about the universal horror of incest, and Hegel discusses the problem in his philosophy of law. Freud explains the phenomenon by means of the Oedipus complex, which in the primal society leads to the murder of the father by the sons who want the women of the family. The murder results in an inherited feeling of guilt in the next generations, which prevents them from arranging incestuous marriages.[15] The main problem here is that guilt need not arise in the original family in the state of nature. The sons get what they want, sexual freedom; since they do not yet have moral feelings, it is not at all clear why they should repent the act of parricide. For prudent reasons, they may find it necessary not to kill the leader of the pack, but that is all. The women could still be shared with the males who are in the right position, regardless of their family relations.

Hegel, on the contrary, provides a functional–logical explanation of why incest is universally forbidden. The purpose of marriage is to unite human beings so that something new will be created: "What is already united, I mean, cannot be united for the first time by marriage."[16] If the couple is a brother and a sister, or a father and daughter, nothing new is brought about. The parties are already united, so they cannot be brought together anew.

This explanation rests on Hegel's logic of the family and on the truth that social entities must be reproduced. The problem is that his account does not even hint at the "horror of incest." Hegel mentions shame, but does not elucidate it. His account points in the right direction, towards the ambiguity between the old and the new domestic elements which incest creates within the family structure. Yet he cannot reach beyond this and give an explanation why the act is such a serious moral wrong. Of course, for Hegel, morality is a matter of civil laws, and incest is simply unlawful. The aspect of horror, he might say, is merely a subjective thing and does not deserve our interest. The Sadean heroes disagree, because they appreciate horrors.

Another example is pain. When a person aims at pain, he aims at something which, through its accepted grammar, is to be avoided. Negative and positive goals get confused. Sexual perversions follow the same anti-logic. A normal sexual grammar distributes definite goals to the participants in the game. In Sade's world these roles vanish; at Silling genital intercourse is forbidden to the extent that some heroes abhor the sight of a woman's breasts and vagina.

Normal sex does not belong to advanced debauchery. Its role is restricted to the first levels of education and its rites of passage. As such, this is a simple and interesting truth. Sexuality as erotic behavior has an interest for the subversive life only insofar as its average forms are secret, private, intimate, and strongly motivating. All these are features of the ambiguity of its twisted grammar of action. Sexual intercourse in public or masturbation may serve as starting points.

These acts illuminate the nature of Sadean pornography, which defies description as something which is only sexual or even mainly sexual. On the contrary, since violence and sex come close to being transgressions of morality, Sade can utilize them as metaphors.

Masturbation violates the grammar of procreative sex because it is a solitary activity. Such examples may look relatively mild today, but they have been sources of guilt and shame in the past – even of persecution. Male homosexuality stops being a Sadean example once the gays organize, identify themselves, and tell a convincing story of their desires and love-life. Those who want to keep it a crime must censor such accounts. If they can prevent its grammar from emerging, they can also forbid homosexuality as something too shocking to be tolerable. Nevertheless, the censors still talk about it, and in so doing they keep alive the activity as vice.

In religion, Sade's blasphemy consists in his stubborn refusal to be afraid of eternal punishment or to worship an infinite power. This is incomprehensible. He would like to kill God, which is a meaningless suggestion. The case is related to the argument from invulnerability through one's willing acceptance of pain and harm. Enjoying one's own peril makes one immune to all exercise of power, including the Divine Will. One creates a situation where power in principle cannot be exercised.

Most of Sade's atrocities can be understood in this manner. Of course, Sade also describes torture and furious bisexual orgies. The results are shocking at first, but repetition causes the shock to wear off. Once the initial excitement is gone, the interpretative problems become visible. Why is torture interesting in the special context which Sade's works create? Supposedly it should give the reader the kind of pleasure that writers aim at. But we have trouble understanding how torture can be orgiastic and something desirable as a goal. It represents the opposite of those intentions that we normally have, and constitutes a travesty of human nature and virtues. In this sense a norm violation is not an action, but it utilizes an ironic account of the action; one sketches a situation whose meaning cannot be understood by using the background model provided for this purpose. One pretends to make a choice according to hedonistic principles, but one knows that pleasure cannot be understood in terms of pain without the loss of the meaning of the term "pleasure." Sade's viciousness is reflected in his attempt to tell a lie to his reader by claiming that he is a hedonist. His wickedness is an act of transcendence, which results in the experience of the semantic void. The only pleasure is that of fiction. Everything else is just pain.

According to Sade's reasoning, the state penal system, which has traditionally included torture and execution, is inferior to private forms of cruelty. However, this issue is not as simple as some interpreters of Sade have thought. Sade writes: "the atrocity of capital punishment... the law, cold and impersonal, is a total stranger to the passions which are able to justify in man the cruel act of murder."[17] It is often said that Sade claims that capital punishment is wrong because it is a cool decision. This cannot be accurate, because all libertine crimes should be committed in cold blood. The crime comes first, and because its performance is arousing it leads the rake to an orgiastic void. Only the uninitiated first get excited and then act. This is said to be both dangerous and not maximally pleasant. One must philosophize about the possible mischiefs, and then act according to perverse reason. Therefore, the best Sadean argument against capital punishment is to call it a well-defined act which is perfectly predictable and understandable. In this sense it may offer no discharge. Sade argues that executions are missed opportunities of enjoyment, and their disambiguated nature is the only reason why they are wrong.

An official executioner is no heroic figure. He may do horrible things, but Sade could not care less, because everything happens according to strict rules. Unlike official cruelty, Sade's cruelty is subversive. It expresses human freedom and creativity, while state violence expresses repression, control, and tyranny. Subversive action is uniquely individual, impossible to categorize, and indirectly creative. It is a fiction. State violence and church rituals are profoundly wrong because of their restricted nature. They are not fictions but hard facts. They bring about suffering without hope. From his own point of view, Sade's cruelty is indeed creative. A mechanism kills its victims with mad repetition and pure control. Because it is impersonal, it cannot be accepted by any person. Ironically, personal cruelty is preferable to such a form of cruelty.

Sade argues that vice is profitable, yet his own biography shows how false this thesis is. He tried to be wicked, but he never profited from it, except as a writer. Benevolence and the universal moral norms are what a reasonable decision-maker is supposedly to recognize. But Sade pays attention to their opposites because they defy description. To destroy youth and beauty is not grammatical, because the values that are not worth preserving are not values. Torture denies the nature of its object as a human being; twisted sex negates the laws of human interaction at its most moving and intimate level. Sex is no public performance, at least not in Christian Europe. According to the Sadean paradigm, this is why censors target sexual scenes.

The one type of cruelty I have not yet mentioned is that involved in murder, rape, and mutilation. Real crime and cruelty are both undesirable and immoral; there is nothing else one can say. Once we see that what is criminal and cruel is unclear, we should start resisting the counter-cruelty practiced by the state, and understand the subtle forms of fictionalized evil. One must reject the idea that wickedness is a transparent set of phenomena, though the reader may think at first that Sade has provided hundreds of pages of evidence in favor of such a thesis. Sade's narratives may look like descriptions of plain evil, but in actual fact the opposite is true: Sade's evil is an enigma.

## METAPHORS

The symbolism of the sacred openings of the human body is evidence for what I said about pleasure and vice. Here is one of the key sources of metaphor to be found in Sade's stories. The natural orifices of the body are all functionally similar; they can be forced open by penetration, and they can close up again. Liquids pour out when the body is cut, and the piercing of the body creates ruptures. Defloration is a process which actualizes a potential opening, but by so doing the orifice is closed by the thing which enters it. The same idea occurs in *Juliette* at the place at which the valley of Gehenna is mentioned. At the ancient site of execution, women strangle a criminal, force his mouth open, and pour molten lead into it. The opening closes for good through an act that can be performed only once. As Sade remarks, this is what the Bible means by eternal punishment: a drastic act of violence which can be done only once. The eternity of action is created by its future impossibility. Another example can be found in *Philosophy in the Bedroom* when the young female apprentice, Eugenie de Mistival, is given power over her mother. The daughter's Electra complex makes her let a syphilitic man rape her mother. Next she sews up the vagina so that the infected sperm can do its work. The hole is forced open; it is closed first by the penis, then by sewing, and then the whole scene is destroyed by the poison trapped in the womb.

This is one of Sade's most complex vignettes; it brings together psychology, myth, and metaphor. The laws of grammar become distorted during the process. Roland Barthes writes about this act:

Among the tortures Sade imagines (a monotonous, scarcely terrifying list, since it is most often based on the butcher shop, i.e., on abstraction), only one is disturbing: that which consists in sewing the victim's anus or vagina.... Why? Because at first sight sewing frustrates castration: how can sewing (which is always: mend, make, repair) be equivalent to: mutilate, amputate, cut, create an empty space?[18]

The ambiguity here is between opening and closing, along with all their complex associations. An empty space is created and destroyed. In the background we find a peaceful female craft – sewing – now used to destroy. The art associated with female submissiveness is turned into active violence.

Penetration may also be artificial – that is, not related to sex but to work: "Dolmance, who has finished his task, does nothing but increase his stabbing of the victim's buttocks as he discharges."[19] Holes can be created by daggers, needles, and guns, and they can be closed with blades, blood, bullets, and flesh. The hole is indeed a paradoxical entity, and therefore it arouses a number of emotions. It is the proper source of death as well as birth, and it is the source of climax. The mystical hole is something and nothing, while the blade which enters the body is a machine which creates nothing. One finds either an empty place, or one filled with something (like the blade). Something enters a medium to be replaced by the rush of another thing. Sade conceives of this flood which fills the empty place as discharge (and hence, the ultimate pleasure is transcendence). It is like blood which gushes into and out of a wound. But of course there must first be a hole – an abstract nothingness which can be found but not described. Once the rush takes place, the hole ceases to exist, and therefore the pleasure is also lost. The only possibility is to repeat the same little pattern: put the blade in (philosophy), create a hole (action), let blood fill it and pour out (discharge), and feel the disappearance of the void (exhaustion). The cycle can be multiplied. The repetitive boredom of life becomes visible through its empty spaces, at which one gazes.

A hole is nothing, and therefore a necessary condition of reaching orgiastic pleasure which is achieved by means of filling up the hole. Sade repeats the procedure when he writes the 1200 pages of *Juliette*. Another source of metaphors for Sade is the burning of the body. The act has deep Christian roots as a symbol for the final destruction or the denial of resurrection. Sade uses burning to stand for something of the same thing, but with an emphasis on how disappearance without a trace is a method of reaching the void and its pleasures: "then I'd put a match to those areas I'd rubbed with alcohol, and all the hair would go up in flames. He would discharge upon finding himself afire."[20] Self-destruction is at work here, too: nothingness is one's pleasure. Perhaps Sade's youthful passion for whipping can be classified together with burning rather than with piercing, since whipping produces a burning sensation and red skin.

One should not dismiss the symbolism of burning and the closing of holes as a mere atavistic perversion, for twentieth-century popular culture relives it all the time. The gun is a Sadean tool fit for stuffing the hole with a bullet and drawing out blood (instead of sperm) in an orgiastic manner. At the same time the situation is safely defined in terms of functional categories of work and tools. The feeling is almost transgressive. The grammar of shooting is deceptively defined entertainment. Because its symbolism is at once safely camouflaged and capable of arousing emotion, cruelty is fun. Sade is one of the precursors of modern popular culture.

Real murder is something else. Imagine a film showing the actual shooting of people for the entertainment of the movie audience. Why is this forbidden? Because the audience understands its grammar; real crime as entertainment is both ungrammatical and truly subversive. The audience enjoys a fictional death, but it abhors real killing as fiction. Reality and fiction do not mix, because the grammars are different. This is what public execution used to be all about, and it affected Sade's own life when he was sentenced to death. However, Sade writes fiction and does not sell real violence. Would he have done that, had it been possible? It is impossible to say, although Sade's biography provides a hint. Certainly, it is tempting to think that real violence in a theatrical setting constitutes the ultimate perversion; after all, one plays with a real human being, and not with some Juliette who does not come even close to being real. Sade himself, however, never killed for pleasure.

When one reads Sade, it is clear that real-life cruelty is not the point. Since fictional violence, bad manners, sex, and terror may be utilized equally well, no real violence is needed. Perhaps it does not even exist, in the sense that whatever happens in space and time first must be interpreted, then condemned as incomprehensible, before any crime may appear. Therefore, the key lies in a subversive plan, based on the ambiguous ideas of reaching for and filling up the void – the true sources of anxiety and horror. Sade seems to think that subversion as grammatical, textual, and cultural ambiguity alone presents a real threat to human existence. That is Sade's favorite aesthetic crime. He must have recognized how painful and inefficient any real-world perverse sex, sin, and crime are, since they trigger repressive legal action. Fiction cannot be locked up in cells or cured in mental hospitals in the same way as its writer can.

The symbolic story of the subversive life could be continued by looking at early Christian asceticism in some of its more appalling forms. As a catalog of horrors, Edward Westermarck's *Christianity and Morals* reads in places like Sade's *120 Days of Sodom*. Dirt, hunger, self-castration, and flagellations opened the gates of heaven to the holy man.[21] The Christian flagellant, in particular, is not far from the Sadean libertine. Both reach for personal transcendence through pain and blood. Both also deny the necessity of the mediating role of the church between themselves and their God. And they are equally puzzling; it is as difficult to understand why someone performs self-castration as it is to understand why someone risks the death sentence in Marseilles by engaging in the buggery of a male servant and prostitutes. In such cases one feels that orgiastic experience, whatever it is, can be reached by means of acts which are devoid of a normal semantic background model. They can be understood only at a rather far-fetched symbolic level by means of strange metaphors which justify us in calling the whole field of action subversive. Since the normal semantic understanding cannot work, a new background is needed. Whether one talks about saints or libertines, the fictional master plot must be equally grand and strange. Thus self-mutilation expresses the attempt to find a reality beyond physics and psychology from the killing fields of style.

# 8
# THE PRIMACY OF THE GOOD

Sade's favorite moral vice is the fictional ambiguation of values. Confusing reasons are generally private, although what we think of as good reasons must be public. Public reasons work according to an etiquette or conventional code of good conduct. After studying this issue, which touches on some details of Sade's philosophy, I shall take up again the problem of the moral limits that Sade's heroes are supposed to break. In this context I will connect the question to narcissism. As we recall, Sadean heroes need normative structures in order to create excitement by destroying them; but since such elements are absent from nature, they must invent barriers and pretend that they are real. If they are going to commit crimes they must find some valid laws first, and then break them. This is the ultimate task and problem for a true libertine. If it involves self-deception, perverse enjoyment can be stopped by teaching the libertines the plain truth. If they learn that all values and virtues are merely figments of their own imagination – a position to which they seem to be committed anyway – their enjoyment disappears. On the other hand, the moral rhetoric they use provides them with the moral pivot around which they can arrange their transgressive plans. They need truth, right, and good – but only to breach values. They desire the nothingness which waits beyond rationality.

## THE GOOD ON SURFACE

Let us look at an example which Sade offers. In Sade's *Ernestine*, which is not a black novel, the villain rapes the heroine after showing her the death of her lover:

> And taking Ernestine by the hand, he dragged her toward the

windows which looked out onto the public square, and hurriedly opened the blinds. "There, treacherous creature," he said to her, "see your Herman and his gallows." And indeed there on the square stood the bloody theater, and poor Herman, on the threshold of losing his life thereon, appeared with a confessor at the foot of the scaffold. Ernestine recognized him... she attempted to cry out, tried to throw herself out of the window, she felt her entire body growing weak ... all her senses began to fail her, and she collapsed.[1]

The features of the scene are familiar: a victim gazes at a theater, which entails both her passive role and the unlimited creative possibilities of the hero. But the present arrangement is also unique because of the window. It is a symbol of the good, or a well-defined peep hole into nothingness. Since she is unable to reject her values, the virtuous Ernestine cannot cross the empty space between the window and the stage on which her lover performs. Therefore she only watches; she cannot enjoy, so she suffers. Yet Sade's description of Ernestine's behavior indicates – ironically – orgiastic pleasure as well as pain. Next she is raped.

In the story, a certain judge is very eager to pass death sentences. He is a respected official and appears to be defending the law with force and conviction. Since he happens to have his house next to the scaffold, he watches every execution from his window, and only the upper part of his body can be seen from the outside. Unseen by anyone, he masturbates, timing his discharge so that he ejaculates simultaneously with the death of the criminal. His sperm and the criminal's soul leave their respective bodies at the same time. In the typical Sadean manner, the intended effect of the story is to create the illusion of harmony – some kind of social cooperation and justice – which happens after all to be deceptive.

In such a grand act, some points concerning ethics and the privacy of the perverse reason deserve careful consideration. The hero's dress, language, behavior, and even his voyeurism reflect the mastery of the fine art of being a judge. As a good judge, he serves the community through a demanding position. It requires deep learning (the study of law), personal integrity (deciding upon life and death), social trust (the citizens need him), and other valuable personal and social characteristics. He is an embodiment of retributive justice, and around him revolve social expectations, the authority of law, bureaucratic interests, and personal respect. These public aspects of the judge are subject to a convention and an etiquette, though Sade does not use these terms. But the audience and the criminal know how the procedure is conducted, and that once the judge deliberates on a case he retires into a private world beyond public convention. In this world the judge decides. Sade's claim is that privacy has nothing to do with the public aspect of reason and virtue. He seems to think that if something is private and cannot be observed, it is foolish to respect norms; norms are public by their nature.

However, such deep privacy and its associated idiosyncrasy is minimized by a set of special conventions. Here too is an etiquette, by which I mean a public code of conduct which does not include rules designed to change the rules. (This is to say that etiquette cannot be changed by applying etiquette itself.) The code may be complex in the sense that it takes into account a large number of exceptions to the norms. It may also have gaps and leave room for improvising. Both table manners and moral norms are like this. Law is not etiquette, nor are the rules of scientific evaluation of research. These two fields utilize their own self-correcting principles. Perhaps it can be argued that ethics is not an etiquette; certainly it should be argued morally that it is not. If we neglect this notion, etiquette, we cannot understand the Sadean solution to the question of how a pervert can transgress ethics. However, it is enough to maintain that the moral etiquette works in popular morality, although its rational correction may be a genuine, meta-level moral problem. Actually Sade deals with all morality as if it were etiquette in the sense of table manners.[2]

The judge must be able to justify what he decides; even if it is his decision, it is also something based on the law, and the decision is left open to an appeal. If this is so, the judge's private decision is part of the code which serves the public good in the best possible way. The moment of private deliberation has its own slot in the etiquette of proceedings, so that the concerned parties know how it is supposed to function, and how private thought can be criticized. The moment of privacy is minimized by making it a pseudo-public part of the code of manners. Publicity has its own place and function, which are needed because genuinely private thought cannot be criticized. Criticism and control entail knowledge which extends into the secrets of one's life. In this way the judge works at least under some pseudo-public conditions. Of course, how he decides is still his own knowledge, as Sade says.

The judge has his transgressive motives because of his position as an official who works in the public world of law. The simple fact that he has his own ideas of pleasure creates the tension whose utilization is vicious. He is able to pass the sentence in the name of law, while the execution is an act of murder. We can elucidate this subversive possibility by paying attention to the notion of etiquette. One cannot deny that the Sadean approach does have some value as criticism.

Sade's hero violates the legal code by making his reasons in favor of the death penalty private in a way that cannot accommodate the idea of critical deliberation. He decides because he wants to masturbate in his window. Whatever reasons he gives when passing sentence, the audience will never be able to discover his true motives, or the private grounds for his decision. This judge's thoughts are private in a deeper sense than an honest judge's should be. His reasoning is irrelevant both to the court proceedings and to the rules which govern them. In this way, whatever criticism is directed at him will miss the mark. The confusion between sex and retribution is the key to the privacy of motives here.

To break the etiquette is to take up a subjective argument which extends deeper than anything that is allowed by the etiquette. The rules can be understood as the barrier, or rather the normative structure, which the wicked person needs in order to be able to be wicked – that is, to be capable of violence. Etiquette is a code of norms which determines proper behavior and good manners, and it can only be violated by doing something that is not included in the etiquette. Such action may take either a covert or an overt form. The judge's action is covert, since he employs a subversive strategy. The second, overt strategy is that of a rebellion governed by its own etiquette.

Since etiquette does not allow for changes, according to the code itself, the covert change of the rules is a private affair. The audience cannot understand why a person burps at the table, even if he is punished for so doing. The reasons behind the pseudo-rebellious facade become private when the ideas are left outside the etiquette itself. As I see it, the wickedness of breaking the code of manners is simply inherent in the inexplicable nature of reasons. Since no one can follow the offender there, the situation becomes disturbing. Emerging anxiety demands punishment, which is a relief achieved by means of another etiquette.

A punishment is typically a highly ritualized act. Guests do not throw hot soup at the misbehaving friend. Instead they look sour, remain silent, and make small funny noises with their noses. The code of reactions is a sophisticated device. The person who fails to recognize it cannot be understood, and his behavior erodes the social life.

He is subversive or wicked, and must be ignored and ultimately avoided. The key to the Sadean type of the wickedness of will is in the escape to the privacy of reasons which lead to norm violations. In this sense wickedness resembles madness.

In *Juliette* Sade illustrates the idiosyncrasy of a mean person and the violation of a code of good manners. He does so in presenting a picture of Clairwil, a truly memorable person who is later murdered by Juliette:

> Clairwil, quite as eccentric in her comportment at table as in bed, quite as intemperate, no less curious in the article of eating than in the other of fucking, fed only on fowl and game, and they had to be boned and then served up disguised in all sorts of forms; her usual drink was sweetened water and it had to be iced regardless of the season, and to every pint of this liquid she added twenty drops of the essence of lemon and two spoonfuls of orange flower extract; she never touched wine but consumed large amounts of coffee and liqueurs; she ate in excessive quantity; furthermore, of the better than fifty dishes put before her she attacked every one. . . . That charming person, whose custom was whenever and wherever possible to secure the adoption of her private tastes, recommended them to me.[3]

She only eats camouflaged dishes which cannot be recognized for what they are.

Sade also provides an ironic description of the social conventions which regulate the grief felt by a wife. Juliette says,

> "Never was there a sublimer death than that of Monsieur de Lorsange; his acts and sayings were elevated, they were exemplary; his bedchamber turned into a chapel where sacraments of all sorts were celebrated continuously. He exhorted me, he preached to me, he bored me; recommended to me the little daughter he thought was his; and hemmed in by three or four confessors, breathed his last. Truly, had all that dragged on another two days, I believe I would have left him to die all by himself."[4]

Lorsange is a bore whose art of dying is reduced to its visible surface. The prescribed ritual is so predictable that Juliette wants to get rid of it. Since the daughter is not his own and his wife hates him, the ceremony is misplaced. Juliette could not care less for this show of proper public behavior.

Etiquette is approached by Sade through subversion, which means its symbolic destruction. The rules are respected only because they can be violated repeatedly. In this way the Sadean heroes are typically inconsistent. They need etiquette, yet they hate it. They destroy etiquette, but only symbolically, as if vice were mere fiction. They eat camouflaged dishes and they pretend to love. Be that as it may, perversity as the privacy of one's reasons undermines the logic of the code of manners. This topic can be placed in its context by recalling that Sade denies the Aristotelian point that virtue can be found between the excess and the lack of certain desirable character traits, such as courage or benevolence. Morality is an etiquette because the balance cannot be found; since the content of moral ideas is never correct, a fixed code of manners is all one can apply. To pretend otherwise is to substitute a dishonest ritual for the travesty of ethical life.

Because morality is fiction, Sade's wickedness is also the same as narrative ambiguity. The heroes do not want a change of norms; yet they do not follow them. They are not reformers in search of a better world. Secret violations change nothing. They want etiquette as it is, because they want to breach it. They are dishonest conservatives, in the sense of possessing ambiguous attitudes towards values. Moreover, these same attitudes are strictly irrelevant to the logic of things. One certainly can understand them, but only from outside of the good life and responsible social behavior. We need to adapt our imagination to a story which reflects the logic of perversity; but by means of his style, which no one can like or imitate, Sade fights against even this explanatory move. One can understand why the judge masturbates: because it feels so good. Yet the same explanation cannot work throughout the infamous *120 Days of Sodom* and its feasts of excrement. After 200 pages, the disgusted reader gives up inquiring why something like this is written, or why he is still reading it. Sade has shown his reader that the wickedness of his will is real – namely, that the man called the Marquis de Sade is wicked and his books are strongly subversive. Their logic is that of a private science outside the etiquette of good works of art.

To sum up, the source of pleasure is the breaching of values and norms, or the structural elements of the good life which stand between the agent and his nature. Since these normative elements are fictional and conventional, they are not real as they stand, but they are all there is, and the heroes must exploit them in full. Etiquette has its own social reality in the sense that people believe in it and follow it. Certainly nothing better is ever suggested by Sade. In fact, he is perverse and wicked because he has no integrated view on these matters. He is a social reformer who hates social reform. If he only hated reform, we could say that he is wrong, and we could change his mind. In the case of a mind without a trace of integrity, though, this would not make much sense. Sade does not err; he is simply wicked. He loves values because he can violate them, and that is why he does not want to change them. His language erects moral barriers and at the same time tears them down. His moral vocabulary suggests the surface of what must be subverted.

## THE DEPTH OF GOODNESS

What happens when one reacts negatively to the Sadean notion of ethics as a code of manners, an etiquette, which is there only to make the enjoyment of vice possible? Let me suggest the following two theses. First, ethics is unavoidable, so that one cannot get rid of it by means of any private decisions. Second, unlike vice, virtue is capable of giving content to a person's plan of life. Sade would agree with the first thesis. The second thesis is more difficult.

The problem is that the content of a life plan may be, like Sade's own pleasures, strictly private; but it can also be intersubjective. Unlike a person whose failures are mere variations on the great theme of virtue (or alternatively, of glamorous vice), Sade cannot be a narcissist. A narcissist must love himself for something; Sade, however, reaches for nothingness. A narcissist admires his own image, but one cannot see anything in the mirror of the void. As I shall suggest, the picture of glamorous vice is ultimately an error and an illusion.

But let us set aside the issue of narcissism so that the unavoidability of the good can be discussed first. Sade would (and should) admit that one can neither hope nor want to remove all normative structures from the social world. Since vice rests on the idea that the good can be transcended, this presupposes the existence of values. However, what is good does not rest on the recognition of what is wrong in the same way that wrong rests on the recognition of what is right. The good can be comprehended and exploited without recognition of its opposite. The wicked person must take the good and the normative social structure seriously, but only in order to leave it behind, or to move towards what is ambiguous and private.

Evil is the exploitation of what is private. In Sade's case it is fiction, and his crime is nothing less than the structure of his own censored novels. This does not deny the existence of virtue, the good, or the code of ethics. He cannot tell the story of evil things without specifying what is good. This follows, as I have said, from the fact that human action aims at the good. The problematic nature of evil results from our difficulty in refuting the stronger thesis to the effect that action aims at nothing but good; this makes evil look like an impossibility, or at least like an error or a failure. Yet as Sade shows, agents have their motives not to let the good ends dominate. The initially coherent account of human motives can become confused in many ways, as we have already learned from Sade. Moral confusion has its own function of generating pleasure, excitement, and would-be narcissistic self-presentation. Transgression is an unstable value notion. One oscillates between good and bad.

My argument, in a nutshell, is as follows. Evil means the absence of what is good, and this means that evil plans require the recognition of the good. Therefore, wicked intentions presuppose the knowledge of what is virtuous and right, at least in the sense that they present a better alternative than the one contemplated by the evil person. The next step is to argue that ascriptions of evil have no non-relational characteristics, or an essential description. To do this, Sade uses certain rhetorical strategies, as we have seen. These are supposed to reveal the evil things which instantiate the relational property of being without goodness. Evil lacks a content of its own, because the properties are merely relational and their descriptions are given by means of procedures like ambiguation which do not refer to any particular subject matter. The next step of the argument is to say that one cannot paint a picture of what is evil, except in the frame of the good. Therefore, a wicked life plan is also an impossibility. One's wicked intentions aim at no well-defined thought contents. In other words, if an agent attempts to be evil, we cannot say what he is aiming at without recognizing the good and the right which are excluded from the plan and which constitute the relational properties the plan needs. The wicked life is a negative one in the sense that it has no properties of its own. That the good life is the basic one will prove to be crucially important for the question of whether a wicked person may be a successful narcissist.

Let us call this view "the omnipresence of the good and the right." It has its negative and positive sides. We cannot get rid of values even if we tried, but there are no circumstances where we may try. The positive side of the thesis says that a Sadean wicked person cannot maintain that through his own deliberate planning he has created unstable circumstances in which the good does not dominate, and therefore whatever he does is wicked. If he achieved this, he could also paint a picture of what he is doing; the characteristics of his actions would be non-relational, or devoid of any reference to the good and the right. But this is impossible. One does not get rid of value without also robbing oneself of the pleasure of transgression.

Evil is often fictional, both in the sense that it is not real and in the sense that it is based on rhetoric. To provide indirect evidence for this thesis, I shall illustrate the characteristics of the moral code and its values: regardless of the circumstances, the elements of justice demand their realization. At the same time, those norms cannot be taken too seriously, in the sense that they should really govern events. This example helps us understand how Sade can recognize ethics and yet it means practically nothing to him. Now, instead of pleasure, simple survival is the point.

## ON A LIFE-BOAT

Both Thomas Hobbes and David Hume claim that in extreme social situations, law and morality lose their binding force and more primitive considerations take charge. Hobbes writes:

> If a man by the terrour of present death, be compelled to doe a fact against the Law, he is totally Excused; because no Law can oblige a man to abandon his own preservation.... When a man is destitute of food, or other thing necessary for his life, and cannot preserve himselfe any other way, but by some fact against the Law; as if in a great famine he take the food by force, or stealth, which he cannot obtaine for mony nor charity ... he is totally Excused, for the reason next before alledged.[5]

Regardless of what Hobbes says, however, one should not accept that survival cases collapse into the chaotic state of nature. Moral evaluation is not an optional approach to decision-making competing against some other motivational grounds. Yet in extreme circumstances moral reasoning does not apply in the standard manner. We can understand what happens if we think in terms of a moral etiquette and a rhetoric rather than in terms of valid practical reasoning.

Many recent treatises on ethics miss the Hobbesian point that safety is a person's primary motive and first consideration. Many writers do not consider safety an ethical concern at all, so it is not surprising that it does not figure in their conclusions when they write about ethics; at the same time, it cannot be denied that safety is an important human concern. In fact, it is a necessary precondition of well-being and of all social action. Safety need not be a moral notion only because a person takes care of his own life and tries to guarantee its continuity in a hazardous world. Of course, systematic safety measures should follow the laws of social justice and considerations of duty apply to them. If one looks at a case where one person considers killing another, it is easy to see that the case is a moral one. It is one's duty to refrain from harming one's fellow beings. Nevertheless, the victim may not want to consider other-regarding factors in the case where he fights for his own life. From the victim's point of view, the concern for safety is non-moral, as it may seem. I shall argue against this simplified notion.

When we say that safety is important, we mean that a person's survival is essential to all of his concerns. Such a basic safety interest is not moral, simply because it is egoistic in nature. In another sense security is a welfare measure, or a guarantee of one's future safety in the broad sense of happiness. Because welfare must be guaranteed to all in equal measure, security becomes an issue of social justice, and ultimately it becomes part of liberty. As I see it, it is a crucial mistake to refuse to detach ourselves from such a broad notion of security as a matter of welfare and liberty. Safety tends too easily to be an atavistic urge to survive at any cost when facing danger, fear, and panic. It becomes too narrow a notion.

The kind of criticism directed against egoism may apply to narrow safety interests, which are more emotional than rational and are certainly devoid of any universalization. If one is actually dying, to take the simplest case, one may not be expected to assume a generalized other-concerned point of view upon this issue. A person may want to do so, of course, but this is a supererogatory move. Nevertheless, the matters of survival are basically self-oriented cases. A possible reason why ethics does not apply to safety is that it is not a moral value in line with other values. Such a view is inherent in Stoic ethics. Diogenes Laertius describes Stoicism as follows:

> Self-preservation is the first drive in every living thing, the Stoics hold. . . . The Stoics demonstrate that the assertion made by some people that the first drive of animals is directed to pleasure is false; for, they maintain, pleasure, when experienced, is not an end but a by-product, produced only after nature has sought out and discovered those things that minister to the animal's exist-

ence and well-being according to its kind. It is a consequence, to be compared to animals' being in good condition or to plants' being in full bloom.[6]

Self-preservation and safety in this narrow sense are not values, because they are egocentric and not universalizable. They are personal goals. Values are what we maximize when we are safe, and as I have already argued, possessive values may become of secondary importance compared to other-regarding values, such as respect and love. The case is analogous to the Sadean idea of pleasure, which overrides ethics whenever it is aimed at. Yet the etiquette of ethics is needed all the time. It is a mistake to think that survival cases can be understood without a moral component, any more than Sadean pleasures can.

Before the end of the nineteenth-century, many well-documented cases of murder and cannibalism occurred when ships went down at sea and people tried to save themselves on life-boats. In a paradigmatic case, the master and the crew select those passengers who can occupy the limited space on one or two life-boats. The rest of the passengers are left to die. The boats get separated, and the survivors have little food and drink. They suffer from thirst and hunger, and they draw lots who should die first; since they may be too weak by the time someone dies naturally, they have to force the issue. Someone is then killed. The survivors see a ship, which may lawfully refuse to save them because of rough seas, because of lack of rations on board, or because of some comparable reason. If they are saved, their cannibalism does not usually lead to legal prosecution, though it did in the celebrated case of the crew of the yacht *Mignonette*. A. W. Brian Simpson has told the story of the legal proceedings against its cannibal crew, and how they were sentenced to death in England in 1884 and later pardoned.[7] No similar case was brought before the court, however, after this leading case was decided. The times had already changed.

The case of the *Mignonette* offers a wealth of relevant information about the peculiar etiquette that is involved in such situations. Simpson writes:

> Dudley and his companions knew the proper thing to do; someone must be killed that the others might live. They also knew that to obtain blood to drink, a living victim was preferable; to wait until death occurred was unwise. They knew too the appropriate preliminary course of action, which was to draw lots, a practice viewed as legitimating killing and cannibalism,

particularly if agreed upon by a council of sailors. Nor was the tradition of the sea as it applied to such critical situations confined to seamen, as a sort of professional secret.... The incidents I have described were all public knowledge. There was nothing whatever secret about the matter. What the sailors did when they ran out of food was to draw lots and eat someone.[8]

The normative frame in which the killing takes place is quite complicated. In addition to the lottery, it specifies how the victim behaves, how he is killed, and how nourishment affects the survivors. A full narrative is mobilized rather than a fragment which recognizes only the drawing of lots. One can predict how the decision will be made and put to work. In the case of the *Mignonette*, however, the crew did not report the use of a lottery. Although there is conflicting information, the most startling feature of the whole case is the inexplicable fact that they did not draw lots. And it would have been in their own interest to keep this failure secret.

If seamen can break the taboo on cannibalism, can they still keep the moral rules of fairness intact? The answer is apparently in the affirmative, because of the lots. An adequate interpretation is not that simple, though. The truth seems to be that the lots are drawn in a ritual manner so that the master and his officers survive but men belonging to racial minorities and young boys lose their bets. Such regularities show that the lottery is not a random one. Of course, in irregular circumstances and under extreme pressure we cannot expect anything else. The lottery is a ritual performed according to a traditional code of conduct. The form of the decision is perfectly just, although the content shows some bias. When the ritual lots are drawn, they are also rhetorically referred to during a later discourse. The person who suggests the lottery runs, *ex post*, a higher risk of dying than others. It is safer to put the responsibility on the dead man, since he can no longer be punished; accordingly, he is said to initiate the proceedings. Simpson writes: "one can never be quite sure where truth was sacrificed in an attempt to live up to the custom of the sea." The custom is more important than the truth, in the sense that the men have done all that is possible. Therefore, the survival motive need not surface as violence in the state of nature. Its alternatives are cases which include lots designed to work as a cover-up favoring the strongest parties. For instance, the master draws the lots privately and sends someone to tell the victim that he lost; the victim is then immediately killed. The master gives a strong message to his officers to the effect that, since they are safe, they can be trusted. A perfectly just procedure might not guarantee this to the officers.

The ritual and rhetoric of the lots give the state of nature its moral overtone. Not even in the most desperate of all situations, when all taboos are already broken, can the crew shake the moral norms. Yet we need not expect that the lottery is fair in any demanding sense. What is expected is some kind of expression of human deliberation and a concern for reason and fairness. It is a far cry from the ideal of morality in looking after people's entitlements and welfare, but the way in which power replaces morality in such social exchanges is well known to all the participants.

Why should we not say that morality, as a fair procedure, can also work in life-boats? The best answer I can think of is as follows. A moral continuum of consideration ranges from the chaotic state of nature, moral ritual and rhetoric, taboos, and fair procedures, to legal action. Legal action is out of place at sea in a small boat. Fair procedures cannot be put into effect even if the participants agree that everyone's life is important. The point is that because one person must be in charge, some others are in a vulnerable position because of their social and physical situation. The main purpose is survival, so that fairness considerations are secondary. Certain motives are not actually realizable. Since the only thing which is still realizable is moral etiquette, that aspect remains intact. This shows that a moral concern is indeed there, and that moral norms are followed as far as possible. Though the norms do not extend very far, it is still the norm, as a formal device, which organizes the exchange so that the best possible result can be achieved. Some utilitarians might argue that this is a moral solution to the dilemma. Other ethicists may claim, on the contrary, that the case is immoral but excusable. Therefore, survival overrides all other considerations in a sense which, however, makes the relevant act morally excusable.

My main purpose has been to show in what sense morality must be real to Sade's heroes. In the same way as the shipwrecked sailors believe in morality, so Sade must trust his own normative intuitions. In both cases, people need values, norms, virtues, and a tradition which they can follow. Otherwise they could not achieve even vice and the transgression of values. In other words, both extreme distress and freedom entail the application of moral considerations. Yet it is not easy to say exactly what the reality of ethics means. Certainly, there is no question of any overriding and universal application of moral norms. Both the unlucky sailors and the sovereign Sadean heroes know this much. They know they are dealing with an etiquette which is supposed to regulate and explain their behavior. At the same time they realize that it is a mere etiquette – the custom of the sea and of the bedroom, respectively – which cannot carry too much weight. The sailors know that tradition constitutes their sole shared piece of knowledge. Everything else is private. In the same way, the Sadean heroes know that the only stepping-stone to pleasure is ethics; accordingly, they need it, although they also know it is fictional.

Because the men of the yacht *Mignonette* failed to observe these fictions, their actions created an intolerable ambiguity which finally led them to a death sentence. Simpson writes:

> None of Dudley's written accounts of the story mentions any proposal being made to draw lots in order to select one to sacrifice to save the others. This is a most peculiar fact and not at all easy to explain, since it was in Dudley's favor to have recorded any attempts to have lots drawn.[9]

Dudley's reasons remain private and ambiguous. Sade calls this type of thing a moral crime, and claims it is pleasant to commit. No one who is familiar with Dudley's predicament, however, can agree. His unlucky fate was reserved for him by capricious nature. Only those who are able to control their environment can enjoy life. For Sade, this control is theater.

# 9

# SADE THROUGH THE LOOKING-GLASS

The control of what is assumed to be dirty and dangerous imagery may take two forms. First, the material is studied and duly banned because of the norms which apply to the case. Second, the whole issue is made taboo, or, as happens in the post-enlightenment world, the relevant issues are redefined so that the motive to examine the material becomes *prima facie* incomprehensible. The latter method takes us beyond the violence of legal censorship to the world of rational morality. However, such redefinitions create their own problems. The social world becomes so infused with moral terminology that a person's reactions to it are restricted. In other words, moral facts are presented in such a realistic manner that he must adjust his decisions to them. He can no longer insist that the world conform to his values. Though the moral reality changes him, he does not change the world.

How does a moral person become so thin, when the moral world is so thick with values? Sade struggles against such an anorexia by breaching all norms and creating his own unstable counter-values. His problem is the failure of narcissism; neither self-love nor libidinal solipsism makes sense when the meaning of one's actions is inexplicable. Since he is free from all moral confines, Sade cannot paint his own picture. But there is no narcissism without a person's self-image on a reflecting surface.

### DEALING WITH FILTHY THINGS

A pervert displays evil characteristics and he aims at a typical style of comment on his life plan. Socratic ethicists claim that the wicked life does not make sense, although this may be a mistake. A weaker thesis is available as well: that what has been condemned in ethics is the transition from a story of wickedness, like the Sadean narratives, to a wicked story, like the Divine Marquis's own life. According to this, it may be *prima facie* impossible for a story to be wicked in the same way that an action or a career is wicked. Therefore, to speak of a crime is not in itself a crime. Moreover, one can turn this point around and say that the narrative approach cannot capture the point of an evil life plan. In other words, the story of wickedness concerns something that does not exist; or, if evil exists, its story cannot be told without omitting its essence.

Nevertheless, it seems equally plausible that a story of wickedness may itself be something evil. A well-entrenched ideology of censorship rests on such a notion. If this view of censorship looks too unsophisticated, there are ways to enhance it. One could argue that the consequences of telling perverse stories are harmful to their audience; and because the author ought to know this causal connection, his actions are wrong. An indirect link is thereby forged between the act of narrating and the content of the narrative. Normally such a consequentialist view is accompanied by the hazy feeling that the narrative expresses bad taste and its content is somehow intrinsically undesirable. Pornography is an example. Since it is not art, the censors think that it is harmful as well as filthy, and therefore lacks even a minimal claim to greatness.

A more general utilitarian dilemma emerges in this context. If a murderer is executed, the social utility is maximized. Suppose the law is extremely cruel, and that the victim can be killed either by a machine or personally. If he is killed personally, this act can be enjoyed by the executioner. A utility calculus seems to rank the alternative so that mechanical execution is the worst option, and personal killing with enjoyment is the best option. The reason is that some extra enjoyment is at least possible in a personal killing. Notice that this extra enjoyment cannot be conditional on something which is likely to bring about social harm. The satisfaction should be created by one's service to law and justice. However, such a utilitarian conclusion is falsified by the intuition that the enjoyment derived from killing is without any value, or is a disvalue whose occurrence makes the totality worse. This notion of a wrong type of value resembles that of filth.

Certainly, without the ascription of filthiness, it is difficult to see why harmful causal consequences alone would justify the ban on pornography. If a choice is our right, we may make it, assuming that we are adults and that our choice does not result in objective harm to others. The victims must be protected, but that is all. The private use of dirty material is a different case.

An argument against the naively liberal view is that the censored items cannot be encompassed within one's rights because no reasonable person would claim such an entitlement. Yet the fact that something is filth does not itself negate its valued characteristics. What happens is rather that no nasty things are rights simply because no sensible and well-informed person would be interested in them. They are truly without value. However, this fact depends on the overall normative account which is given, or on the explanation of why they are filthy and as such incapable of carrying value. The metaphor of dirt must indeed be taken seriously. Such objects are not shiny or smooth. On the contrary, they are opaque; they stain and scratch. They leave their mark, which sticks like a stigma from which one cannot free oneself, and which hurts and infects. All these effects can be explained by referring to the objective world of facts.[1]

Not much weight can be put on the moral justification of censorship and moral paternalism. They are merely methods by which opinions are controlled in the social world. It is certain that they make sense in a minimal sort of way: one wants to get rid of evil stories, and if one has the power to do so, censorship is what practical reason dictates to the agent. In reality, of course, censorship and paternalism are indicators of some larger issues.

The study of Sade shows that the narrative content and the act of narrating cannot be taken apart in any neat way. They remain interconnected in the sense that to mention a perversion is at least bad taste, in the sense of participating in the bad life. Actually, moral discourse has its own ways of handling this problem of the style of participation. If the narrated contents are intrinsically undesirable, some precautions are taken. The writer adds to the narrative features which show both that one does not accept what is said and that one would not mention such ideas if something like an excuse did not apply to the case. Such a double rhetorical denial, or self-censorship, purifies the agent. Without it, he remains defenseless against accusations of involvement in the dirty contents of the story. Since guilt is contagious, the same argument applies to the reader as well.

The author's technique which overcomes his feelings of hesitation and guilt may be either a direct or an indirect factor. First, he may directly warn his audiences against accepting what he is saying as somehow commendable. He may argue that he is not using but barely mentioning facts, perhaps in order to criticize them later. A speaker may use facial expressions, tone of voice, and bodily gestures to convey a degree of alienation, pain, and disgust at what is being said.

His audience gets the idea that the agent has a special reason for being engaged in such subject matter, and that otherwise he would be doing something else. Because one must not go into the details, we have conventions of fiction. He may also provide a contrast to the good things in order to emphasize what is good. He may use irony. He may publicly repent of what he has done or thought. He may accuse someone else of the evil things to which he is alluding. He may suggest that perhaps the narrative is intended to be a joke. Mild social shocks are also entertaining (within the limits of good taste, of course). Many similar rhetorical strategies exist, and their use is a feature of decency and modesty, both important social virtues.

However, to speak of perversity, cruelty, and crime without a protective shield is to become guilty of profanity and of being a pornographer. The indirect control of filth takes place either by means of redefinition or by direct suppression. Given an embarrassing topic, one may tell a story which is different from the original one or suppress all related stories. For instance, a murderer may be seen as a victim of unhappy circumstances which, according to the scientific laws of psychology, have produced dysfunctional character changes in him. Alternatively, he may be put behind bars, as if to deny his existence. This makes the subject matter and its context definite. The second strategy is through annihilation, by means of which the person's existence is also denied. These strategies are different: redefinition is a success-notion because it destroys the object for good, making recovery impossible; plain rejection, like imprisonment, is a process-notion which refers to effects that can be reversed in case the subject is later rehabilitated.

It is not difficult to show how these methods of reasoned rejection can be criticized and made to look like an inadvisable type of censorship. The censored object may escape from its prison, just as Sade escaped both from Fort Miolans and (with the help of Guillaume Apollinaire) from the special collections of libraries. The real problem which works against indirect methods of banishment is a deep one: every censor becomes a pornographer, because the distinction between use and naming in the theory of language is no longer relevant. The linguistic shield the censor uses when he claims that he is only cataloging the horrors that society wants to be rid of is not effective. The fact that the censor is a pornographer does not follow only for the reason that he enjoys the material, consciously or unconsciously; such an explanation is *ad hoc*. The possible pleasure is not the point, although it is one of the myths of the impermissive society that pornography, violence, and filth are deceptive mechanisms of pleasure. On the contrary, it is difficult to see why one could not fight successfully against perverse pleasure as a psychological fact.

As I have argued in the case of Sade's black novels, the crucial fact is that they are not pleasant to read, and they do not describe pleasure in its Epicurean hedonist or psychological sense. They deal with pain and disgust. What Sade means by an discharge is only artificially related to pleasure, a relation which is hardly understood by the pornographer in his role as a censor. Discharge is the experience of the void achieved through the ambiguation of values. As such, Sade is dealing with the metaphysics of values, and not with psychology.

Moreover, Sade's heroes insist that a libertine should stay calm during his debauchery. A mature rake is profoundly apathetic. A censor mistakenly denies the existence of apathy, and thus reduces his own role to the passivity of a mere gaze. As an outsider, he becomes Sade's victim; the gaze is part of debauchery, because both victims and audience are needed. Since the censor is also a willing victim, he must be a pervert. His reluctance to escape, his self-deception visible in the self-confessed duty to protect other persons' innocence, turns into a vague decision which covers the nothingness in his being. Since he is a proto-Sadean whose innocence is already lost, his condition is ironic. My conclusion is that a censor who is afraid of psychological pleasure is a pornographer in a more straightforward sense than Sade is. Reasoned rejection of filth requires such direct contact with it that its motivation becomes at least questionable.[2]

The method of censorship entails an important point: if x is defined as evil, and if an agent does not reject x, he has created an ambiguous situation by refusing to reject something which is undesirable and as such already rejected. Evil facts logically entail their objectionable nature; one cannot claim that there should be an open choice in this matter. The wickedness of will is the rhetorical move away from such a fixed definition and toward narrative ambiguity. Since definition is control, and control is definition, ethics is primarily power in this sense.

A traditionalist concept of ethics exists that makes social facts like cowardice, lies, brutality, coercion, promises, gifts, and sympathy look "thick."[3] They are considered combinations of facts and values which are so intertwined that the elements cannot be taken apart. The well-established dogma of the Humean fact–value distinction disappears. A coward, for instance, is a person who does not act according to the virtue of courage. Here the term "person" is also a thick one, because its understanding presupposes the commitment to rationality. At the same time, courage is related to one's actions and personality.

A censor can achieve what he wants by controlling the definition of the concepts which characterize the cases he wants to see as pornography. He defines the concept of pornography so that it applies to the facts concerning Sade and entails their negative evaluation. Sadean pleasure becomes illegitimate. Nothing else need be done in order to guarantee a permanent control. In such a society, Sade cannot be recovered without a cultural upheaval. This is why his works lay buried for seventy years after his death. After the Great War, traditional moral concepts seemed no longer to apply, and before the new ones could be created, Sade was free. In the fragmented world of the twentieth century, the moralistic redefinition of Sade's vocabulary can no longer succeed.

Be this as it may, the key to successful moral paternalism and its subspecies, censorship, rests on the redefinition of facts so that they take on a negative moral connotation. This means that it is logically impossible to recommend them. Robbed of his free choice, the individual can recover his right only by escaping into another culture where either moral subjectivism reigns, or its thick value concepts are revolutionized.

## VIRTUE AND CONTROL

Let us look at the positive side of successful control in its ethical guise. I mean by personal autonomy an agent's characteristic and reasoned adjustment to his own values. Such an agent is responsible for what he does, and he exemplifies reliability among the personal features which are taken to be genuinely desirable. He is typically a temperate person, and if his values are acceptable he is virtuous. Certain features are not only good for the agent himself, but they are virtuous in a sense which comprises the ideal of a moral community and the valid plans of life. On the other hand, an aspect of privacy is involved, since the person is a unique creature who determines his own responsibility. The constellation of his values is like no one else's. Such a person is also the source of a potential danger, because the aspect of privacy is something to be controlled. It is as yet indefinite, since no control can be pure self-control.

Moral freedom can be said to consist in what is at once both public and defined. The agent's characterization of his private autonomy is translated into the public language of moral virtues and social goals.

Such a free person acts according to his own principles, but by so doing he observes the public virtues. These values are the same for all agents, but to a variable degree. Some vagueness remains embedded in the context of these psychological features, social roles, and changing social circumstances. Because many different facts are morally relevant, their contingent nature infects the otherwise well-defined free and virtuous life. This is the field of moral luck. However, in ethics one always aims at the highest virtues, which are also as distant as possible from the sources of indefinite understanding and factual contingencies.

The highest virtues and the greatest freedom are such that they concern all persons in similar situations in the same way. They are universal. The less perfect virtues apply only in some special situations. Ultimately, all virtue forms a unity, or one super-virtue, and freedom is the person's life lived according to it. Therefore, in its primary ethical sense virtue is public and well defined. In other words, the theory of virtue is a translation scheme by means of which we handle tricky cases of personal autonomy which otherwise threaten to remain intractable.

Moral norms and descriptions applied to particular agents make us recognize a person in a special way. Morality understood as control may be so thoroughgoing that a well-defined person becomes an instance of general rules. He is a social particular satisfying prescriptive features under a given description. As such, there is neither ambiguity nor individuality. The price one pays for being moral is that one's personality becomes so attenuated that it tends to disappear. Since all persons are exactly the same, their features cannot constitute a private threat; there is no ambiguity left in them. Only moral facts are thick.

For example, a perfect utilitarianism is a decision-making function which transforms some Cartesian products of values and facts into sets of utility numbers, which are defined as social averages. Initially, each person may represent a different function. The same logic, however, applies to every one. Such a second-level uniformity makes it possible to define all the particular functions under the general logic of collective utility maximizing. Moreover, this logic is normative; it specifies a model at which all the persons should aim, and all deviation from it is considered a lamentable failure. Since persons are merely instances of the general law, they are both perfectly known and open to adjustment. However, no person is only a moral agent. People also have feelings and dreams which make their inner life ill defined and typically private. The evil aspect of life emerges when one says that an ill-defined personality may have a role to play in ethics, too. But since ethics alone is the overriding concern, such a rebellious thesis may look inappropriate.

A personal style and life plan form the ground of the individuality of human beings. But because this consists of emotions and dreams and is uncontrollable, we may want to get rid of it. On the one hand we are threatened by wickedness, first as ambiguity and then as undefined nothingness; and on the other hand, we are threatened by strict definitions of freedom which entail a lack of individuality.

Only one way out of this paradoxical situation may exist: a kind of balancing act between what is evil and what is good. Of course, no well-defined rules control the interplay of the two extremes. The exact point of wickedness, its functional core, is that a person needs a source of ambiguity which defies all definitions and subsequent controls. Meta-level control concerning the balance between virtue and vice is a self-falsifying theory. In this way, evil and wickedness have their place in the world outside the great system of things. Wickedness is narcissism, but only in the sense that a person projects his private life upon reality while at the same time denying the etiquette of ethics. The person loves his own blurred image seen against the ruins of the good and the right. Wickedness entails private ideas in the public realm. It also means the opposite of the enlightenment concept of living according to general rules and formal reasoning. Other notions are possible, but Sade's rebellion must be seen in the context which is constituted in the Kantian way. He may have played with both Aristotelian and utilitarian ideas, but ultimately Sade lives in a world where virtue is universal and formal. It binds everyone alike and, like Kant's good will, must be understood without describing its contents.

Sade aims at the destruction of the tyranny of this ethics. In a sense he aims at the recovery of his own lost individuality – which of course he cannot find. The reason is that when formal virtues are transgressed, no such alternatives emerge which would have their own content-elements, or subjective life. Sade is subversive because he wants to destroy the ethics of personal autonomy based on general norms. In this respect he is prophetic. However, he is a prophet of nothingness, since he refuses to fill the void with romantic emotions and feelings. Sade rebels by adopting a baroque style, but all content remains alien to his grand design. He destroys the right thing, but he exaggerates by playing only with style.

Since an individual is defined as a factor in the narratives of social life and personal decisions, it follows that he has a double nature: he is an object of control and he is wicked. The manipulative interest in human existence is overpowering, both as self-control and as social control. People feel that their own denial of a definition is perverse – that is, they act against themselves. Their own individuality is felt to be perverted, in the sense that it is something from which they should be free; in fact, of course, they must resist such an impoverishment. People want to be autonomous, free, and well-defined persons; but then their desires are not mutually consistent.

Social control is a remarkable phenomenon which has not always been seen for what it is. In social life most aspects of public existence are controlled down to the smallest detail. Hardly anything remains outside etiquette and its associated sanctions. They range from linguistic idioms and dialects all the way to harsh army discipline. What is left outside is filth and evil. The result is a social life where private existence is almost absent. Therefore, we know practically nothing about our fellow humans. Private life disappears and becomes a matter of the person's hazy memories, dreamy rationalizations, and blessed repressions. As the private sector vanishes, the public alone remains as an object of control. Although its rules of regimentation may be broken, the price of guilt must be paid.

It is easy to give examples of social control. Language usage is a typical field. Women and men speak differently; style and dialect identify the speaker and indicate his or her status and values. Table manners, dress, gestures, and personal possessions also tell well-defined stories about ourselves. These fields carry their associated sanctions, too. An angry glance, a small silence, and giggles all indicate that others are entertaining thoughts of revenge ("I won't invite you again!") or pity ("I knew you were an idiot") or causal and reductive explanations ("he must have a stomach disorder"). Thoughts are standardized so that they are not really private at all but rather a perfectly appropriate part of the public story told about the event. The victim knows what the others think of him. He has created an ambiguity and broken the rules. If nothing happens, the case becomes strange in a new way. Why doesn't anyone react? What kind of people are these? Am I a hopeless case? I did not know that these people were so rude, what has happened to them? They have nerves of steel, that is it! Children do this: one burps and another tries to vomit in order to outdo the first kid. A vicious circle is formed that will lead to anarchy if their parents do not intervene.

My argument is that every aspect of human life is under the

controlling force of a good story. Ethics provides the most general features of such stories. Therefore, moral virtue cannot be a guide for personal life and individual feelings; and one constantly dismantles the definitions, including the moral ones, to avoid controls and to stay as one is. But it also follows that one is perverse and wicked if one has transgressed, however minor the transgression may be. The struggle towards a lost privacy and the safe ambiguity of a life plan may not lead towards more serious types of negativity, perversity, crime, or anarchy. Nevertheless, some actions display utter wickedness.

The Sadean goal is achieved by participating in life in such a manner that the narrative about life remains rhetorically open and vague. Such a fact is interpreted as privacy. Yet our own favored cases need not be as radical as Sade's. One may well say that the ambiguity of a person's life may be minimal, even negligible, and yet deserves to be called wicked. This is a psychological and sociological question. Some people in fact are more wicked than others. Some are intolerably nasty, so that we may hope to get rid of them in a perfectly well-defined manner. We use the ax, the rope, electricity, bullets, injections of poison; we take away their property, and we surrender them to the whims of other wicked people in prisons. We also ignore them and try to avoid them.

## THE FAILURE OF NARCISSISM

Narcissism is an understandable personal project. It is part of a person's attempt to retain his own individuality by refusing to receive a definition from the outside. Sade derives his enjoyment from this. Narcissism is one's self-admiration in the sense of seeing one's own image projected upon some homogeneous medium, so that one's libidinal energies are channeled through this single solipsistic outlet. In order to understand it, one needs a simplified psychological model consisting of a person, his self-image as the target of his gaze, and a background upon which the image is projected. Accordingly, the personal image must have some inherent contents which identify it as something which can be loved or admired. Of course this is not yet a theory of narcissism; it is only a picture which allows us to interpret some features which are typical of the human personality.

Consider four different characters: a temperate or fully virtuous person; an incontinent or akratic one; a continent one; and a wicked one. The first type need not fight against any tendency to do the wrong thing. His virtues are established character traits, and therefore they are realized in whatever he does. He may be a penurious customs officer who does not even consider a bribe offered to him, but refuses it as an impossibility.[4] A continent person, by contrast, knows he may do something wrong; he is not yet a fully integrated personality. He can, however, resist, unlike the incontinent character, who succumbs under the pressure from weakness of will, self-deception, and moral negligence. He may also fail to control his tendency towards one-sided virtue, so that he displays a Justine-type syndrome by being courageous without justice, or he may be honest without courage. His behavior may also exemplify glamorous vice – or make him a fool. The fourth type – the vicious personality – has already been described in connection with Sade.

Only the two middle types can express narcissism. The Sadean type of extreme vice cannot do so, and the temperate personality is also without narcissism. Since the temperate man only does what any other person in his position would do, he has no reason to be proud of himself, nor does he pay attention to his good decisions. To make an issue of them would mean that the principles at work in the situation are not fully integrated. There would have to be something – perhaps a special effort – which would entail an imperfection. Perfection means that one's emotional energies cannot be channeled through one's self-image, simply because the decision does not mobilize explanations or require one to assume an emotional stand. One does what is good and virtuous without resistance, temptation, or explanation. No individual moral person remains visible in the situation, although the agent is a well-defined moral character. As I explained above, this means that his action is predictable and not peculiar in any way. A temperate person disappears from the mirror.

Continent and incontinent people possess all the narcissistic potential. They struggle, sometimes successfully and sometimes not, against their idiosyncratic tendencies. They lose when their knowledge is challenged by desire and their long-range planning is made futile by the demands of instant gratification. But when they win, they can be proud of themselves, simply because they recognize something they first lacked and then achieved. They may even love their splendid vices, or incomplete virtues, because they are felt to be their own and something *prima facie* good. Let us suppose there is a robber who displays excessive courage but neither honesty nor benevolence. He may be proud of his lack of benevolence as well as of his courage, simply because he uses it as his identifying feature. His self-deception and negligence become sources of pride along with his genuine virtues.

Perhaps much of what is called evil in social life conforms to this pattern of self-deception. The wicked person is surrounded by admirers. His mental life looks rich and exciting, because it appears to be full of drive and creativity. Such features are used to explain the subversions, as if there were room for science even here.

The two main sources of narcissism are the limited virtue which is splendid vice and the minor source of strength which is continence. In both cases a person exemplifies individuality through his uncontrollability and the ambiguity of his reasoning; at the same time, he is virtuous. Unlike the case of the incontinent person, the continent man can be proud of himself without looking ridiculous. He may want to be a robber, but as a continent person he lets his sense of justice suppress this evil tendency. Nevertheless, he knows he is imperfect because he wants to rob, and this imperfection is also an individuating feature. It makes his character fuzzy in a way which does not fit any general model of virtue.

But how can one's evil characteristics serve as the individuating features, if evil is mere ambiguity? Perhaps we can say that the ambiguity of the plan of life and of neglected virtues and values serve as individuating factors. All perfect patterns are similar, unlike imperfect ones. Features which are not integrated remain visible – as if they were gaps on a smooth surface – and make their pattern discernible. Therefore, one need not refer to weaknesses as such. One may compare this to the case of Sade. His heroes try to transgress normative structures. Their goals are mere nothingness, whose nature Sade explains in terms of pure bliss and orgiastic pleasure. What those persons aim at cannot form an image in which they can recognize themselves. In terms of their pleasure, the heroes are all similar, and they cannot admire themselves on the grounds of what they are aiming at.

Moral values are the mirror in which one can see one's own image if one is not yet transparent to moral reason. A shadow on the surface indicates that the mirror is reflecting something which is real. In Sade's case, however, the person walks right through the looking-glass in order to find a new indescribable world. He cannot recognize himself. Everything becomes distorted to the extent that no personal identity survives. His orgiastic pleasure is nothing but the step through the medium which carries the pictures of others.

The case becomes different when the Sadean heroes philosophize about vice and plan to do something. In that context they behave like any incontinent and self-deceiving person would, except that they need not struggle against their vile tendencies. They entertain good ideas, they produce pictures of moral and religious alternatives; they want to be rich, respected, and happy; they describe themselves and their friends in a pleasing manner – only in order to act against their own selves. They manufacture not in order to sell, but to destroy. Such evil is always superimposed on what is good. Therefore, in this initial mood the heroes look like the supreme narcissists, even if their self-love is only transient. They would never agree, as normal continent people would do, that they are moral winners and fit to be loved. They hate the logical conclusions of their narcissist discourse.

Suppose a Sadean person thinks that he is extremely courageous but at the same time fully unjust. Would he love himself because of this? Sade's novels provide an answer – apathy – which is in the negative. The Sadean person abhors courage as a value, even in the sense of breaking it. The resulting void is his pleasure, and accordingly no room for self-admiration is left.

This is my criticism of Sade: the libertines do not receive love, because they are driven forward only by their own violence; but neither are they able to love themselves. They must be considered unhappy by any standards, at least outside their apathy and their orgiastic states. Moreover, during their moments of peak pleasure they are not recognizable as individuals at all. Their actions are equivalent to self-destruction. And again, such agents are mutually interchangeable.

Narcissism is a joy which characterizes poorly integrated people, who are typically continent or incontinent. Sade does not want to be one of them. His will is autonomous, and his intentions are rigid. Sade and temperate persons are equally beyond narcissism, but orgiastic possibilities remain open to Sade and not to the temperate character. Is it not true that Sade has chosen a fate preferable to the saint who receives no reward? Should we agree that it is better to be continent than temperate? This is alarming, because in that case Sade's destiny would be the best of all. Perhaps the ultimate criticism of Sade must be non-logical, and we would have to say that perverse and orgiastic experiences do not exist after all, and Sade has missed emotions and creativity. But this is an empirical question.

Sade himself as a novelist is not interested in hard facts. He cannot be understood as an anti-moral reformer who tries to convince his audience that they should change their life plans. On the contrary, he paints a landscape of the mind as it is beyond narcissism. The landscape has no color, or perhaps it is white, because

This elusive quality it is, which causes the thought of whiteness, when divorced from more kindly associations, and coupled with any object terrible in itself, to heighten that terror to the furthest bounds. Witness the white bear of the poles, and the white shark of the tropics; what but their smooth, flaky whiteness makes them the transcendent horrors they are?[5]

Sade offers a view to nowhere through the mirror, or everywhere beyond human thought and motivation. This translucent white is what we see when we read Sade, so that the reader can locate his own transcendental fears in it. Sade the Asylum Poet writes about his own distant enemies and longs for them. As such, his dreams are not his readers' dreams and need not interest them too much. However, his method captures something which seems to be a real feature of the human mind: pure perversity as the transgression of values. It drives one forward to do all the vicious things which often seem to inherit the world.

# NOTES

## INTRODUCTION

1. Airaksinen 1988a. Also, Airaksinen 1988b.
2. See Bloch 1931; Lennig 1971; Thomas 1976; Hayman 1978; Laborde 1989; and the invaluable biographical study, Lely 1961. We now have a major new biography, Lever 1993. Lynch 1984 reviews the contents of Sade's books. Two large bibliographies exist: Chanover 1973, and Michael 1986.
3. Hackel 1976.
4. De Beauvoir 1966; Barthes 1977; Carter 1979; Gallop 1981; and Hallie 1982.
5. Hobbes 1968, pp. 105–6.

## 1 SADE: PHILOSOPHY AND ITS BACKGROUND

1. Lely 1961, p. 279.
2. See "Chronology," in Grove Edition 1965, p. 115; and Bloch 1931, p. 88.
3. See Sade, "The Last Will," in Grove Edition 1965.
4. Chanover 1973, p. xii.
5. "Chronology," in Grove Edition 1965, p. 107.
6. Sade, "Reflections on the Novel," in Grove Edition 1966, p. 116.
7. See Sade, "A Note on My Detention," in Grove Edition 1965.
8. Sade, "Reflections on the Novel," in Grove Edition 1966, p. 110.
9. Lely 1961, p. 462.
10. Arendt 1965, p. 252. See also Golding 1988; Kekes 1988; but cf. Kraus 1987.
11. Sade, *120 Days of Sodom*, pp. 197–8.
12. Lynch 1984, Preface.
13. Berkeley 1949, § 153.
14. Ibid. § 152.
15. Rescher 1987, p. 90.
16. Chalker 1973, p. 66.
17. Hegel 1971, § 408 Addition.
18. Sade, *Juliette*, p. 255.
19. See Mandeville 1988; and Malthus 1970.
20. Poe 1975a, p. 281.

21 Erasmus 1983, pp. 276–7.

## 2 THE MEANING OF PERVERSION

1. Hobbes 1968, p. 137.
2. See Milo 1984, and also Stocker 1979.
3. Aristotle 1915, 1149b–1150a.
4. Freud 1977, pp. 61, 66–7. Cf. Solomon 1974 and Nagel 1979; see also Efron 1985.
5. Kramer and Sprenger 1971, p. 74.
6. Adorno and Horkheimer 1979, pp. 81ff. Cf. Korsgaard 1986.
7. Freud 1977, p. 73. For masochism and Leopold von Sacher-Masoch's views, see Deleuze and Sacher-Masoch 1989.
8. Hobbes 1968, p. 207.
9. La Mettrie 1912, pp. 120–1.
10. Sade, *Juliette*, p. 17.
11. Hobbes 1968, p. 190.
12. Hobbes 1978b, ch. XI, pp. 47–8.
13. See Hill 1986; Martin 1986; Dunn 1987; and Mele 1987.
14. Lee 1983, pp. 191–2.
15. Kamel 1983, p. 167. Cf. Paulhan 1965, pp. 31ff.

## 3 NATURE AND THE VOID

1. Adorno and Horkheimer 1979, p. 105.
2. See Klossowski 1966 and 1986.
3. Lawrence 1960, "Moony." See Doherty 1987, and also Moehle 1978, ch. 2.
4. Gallop 1981, p. 46.
5. See Adorno and Horkheimer 1979, p. 96.
6. Sade, *Juliette*, p. 396.
7. Ibid., pp. 747–98; the main discussion starts from p. 765. A comprehensive account of the theory of atheism presented by Clairwil can be found on pp. 370–400.
8. Hobbes 1968, p. 187.
9. Hobbes 1978a, pp. 116–17.
10. Bataille 1985, p. 5.
11. Sade, *Justine*, p. 664.
12. See Orwell 1961, p. 236.
13. Kafka 1988. See also the fiction by Strieber 1985.

## 4 HEDONISM IN PSYCHOLOGY

1. Hackel 1976, p. 91.
2. Sade, *Juliette*, pp. 1026–7.
3. Sade, *120 Days of Sodom*, p. 206.
4. Ibid., p. 212.
5. Sade, *Justine*, p. 704.
6. Sade, *120 Days of Sodom*, p. 233.

## NOTES

7. Lynch 1984, p. 57.
8. Kramer and Sprenger 1971, p. 42.
9. Sade, *Philosophy in the Bedroom*, p. 227.
10. Carter 1979, pp. 108–9.
11. Sade, *Philosophy in the Bedroom*, p. 202.
12. Carter 1979, p. 142.
13. Brillat-Savarin 1970, p. 52.
14. Ibid., p. 63.
15. Ibid., p. 53.
16. Ibid., p. 205.
17. Sade, *120 Days of Sodom*, p. 371.
18. Ibid., p. 330.
19. Carter 1979, p. 142.
20. Ibid., p. 149.
21. Naipaul 1987, p. 243.
22. Brillat-Savarin 1970, p. 60.

## 5 THE ETHIC OF VICE

1. Rawls 1971, p. 408.
2. Sade, *Juliette*, p. 216.
3. Hackel 1976, p. 2.
4. Sade, *120 Days of Sodom*, p. 652.
5. Hackel 1976, p. 98.
6. Brillat-Savarin 1970, p. 332.
7. Sade, *120 Days of Sodom*, p. 295.
8. Sade, *Philosophy in the Bedroom*, p. 222.
9. Ibid., pp. 342–3.
10. Herdt 1987, pp. 64–5.
11. See Gallop 1981, pp. 24–5.
12. Sade, *120 Days of Sodom*, p. 667.
13. Hobbes 1968, pp. 150–6.
14. Sade, *Juliette*, pp. 1027 and 1029–30.
15. Ibid., p. 369.
16. Ibid., p. 742.
17. Gallop 1981, p. 99.

## 6 THE PARODY OF THE CIVIL CONTRACT

1. Sade, *Juliette*, pp. 642 and 1192.
2. Hobbes 1968, p. 683; see also p. 187.
3. Sade, *Juliette*, p. 798; and *Philosophy in the Bedroom*, p. 324.
4. Mackie 1977, p. 36.
5. Sade, *Philosophy in the Bedroom*, p. 339.
6. Ibid., p. 313.
7. Ibid., p. 308. See also Graham 1985, pp. 175ff.
8. Sade, *Philosophy in the Bedroom*, p. 342.
9. Sade, *Justine*, p. 494.
10. Sade, *Juliette*, p. 889.

11 Ibid., p. 794.
12 Hobbes 1968, pp. 251–2.
13 Hallie 1982, pp. 82–3. For Sade and utopias, see Winter 1984.
14 Hobbes 1840, p. 156.
15 Sade, *Juliette*, pp. 418ff.
16 Sade, *Justine*, pp. 580–1.
17 Poe 1975b, p. 882; see also Melville 1972, ch. 42.
18 Sophocles 1982, p. 269.
19 Sade, *120 Days of Sodom*, p. 266.
20 Ibid., p. 237. Cf. the popular account given by Gonzalez-Crussi 1988, pp. 81ff.
21 Sade, *120 Days of Sodom*, p. 669.
22 Gallop 1982, p. 83.
23 Ibid., p. 84.
24 Ibid., p. 83.
25 Sade, *120 Days of Sodom*, pp. 327, 585, 607, and 347.
26 Sade, *Philosophy in the Bedroom*, p. 351.
27 Freud 1961, p. 75.

## 7 STYLE AND THE AMBIGUITY OF VICE

1 See *Illustrated Marquis de Sade*, 1984.
2 Sade, *Juliette*, pp. 576–7.
3 Ibid., p. 507.
4 Ibid., p. 517.
5 Ibid., p. 527.
6 Ibid., p. 530.
7 Ibid., p. 579.
8 Ibid., pp. 580ff., 584–5.
9 Blanchot 1965, p. 38.
10 Plato 1961, 439e-40a, p. 682.
11 Sade, *Justine*, p. 598.
12 Sade, *Juliette*, p. 396.
13 Sade, *Eugenie de Franval*, pp. 411–12.
14 Ibid., pp. 394 and 398.
15 Freud 1950, pp. 141–5.
16 Hegel 1967, § 168 Addition.
17 Sade, *Philosophy in the Bedroom*, p. 310.
18 Barthes 1977, pp. 168–9.
19 Sade, *Philosophy in the Bedroom*, p. 366.
20 Sade, *120 Days of Sodom*, p. 506.
21 Westermarck 1939, ch. IX.

## 8 THE PRIMACY OF THE GOOD

1 Sade, *Ernestine, The Swedish Tale*, in Grove Edition 1966, p. 775.
2 For Bataille on Sade, see Bataille 1985, pp. 91–102. See also Bataille 1986, part II, chs II and III.
3 Sade, *Juliette*, p. 295.

4 Ibid., p. 562.
5 Hobbes 1968, pp. 345–6.
6 Diogenes Laertius 1969, p. 237.
7 Simpson 1984.
8 Ibid., p. 140.
9 Ibid., p. 60.

## 9 SADE THROUGH THE LOOKING-GLASS

1 See also Foucault 1988, esp. pp. 282–9.
2 Cf. Stewart 1988.
3 See Williams 1985, p. 143.
4 For an account of weakness and virtuous life, see Trianosky 1988.
5 Melville 1972, p. 288.

# BIBLIOGRAPHY

### SADE'S WRITINGS

#### Collected Works

D. A. F. Sade, *Oeuvres complètes*. Definitive edition, 16 vols. Cercle du livre précieux, Paris, 1966–7.

#### Translations

In the notes I refer to the following editions and translations published by Grove Press:

*The Marquis de Sade: Three Complete Novels – Justine, Philosophy in the Bedroom, Eugenie de Franval, and Other Writings*. Ed. and tr. Austryn Wainhouse and Richard Seaver, Grove Press, New York, 1965.

*The Marquis de Sade: The 120 Days of Sodom and Other Writings*. Ed. and tr. Austryn Wainhouse and Richard Seaver, Grove Press, New York, 1966.

*The Marquis de Sade: Juliette – Six Volumes in One*. Tr. Austryn Wainhouse, Grove Press, New York, 1968.

#### Republication of Engravings

*Illustrated Marquis de Sade: Justine and Juliette – All the Prints*. Ed. David Mountfield and Robert Short, Liber SA, Fribourg and Geneva, 1984.

### OTHER WORKS

Theodor W. Adorno and Max Horkheimer 1979, *Dialectic of Enlightenment*. Tr. John Cumming, Verso, London. See "Excursus II: Juliette or Enlightenment and Morality."

Timo Airaksinen 1988a, *Ethics of Coercion and Authority*. University of Pittsburgh Press, Pittsburgh.

Timo Airaksinen 1988b, "An Analysis of Coercion," *Journal of Peace Research* 25.

# BIBLIOGRAPHY

Hannah Arendt 1965, *Eichmann in Jerusalem*. Penguin Books, Harmondsworth.

Aristotle 1915, *Ethica Nicomachea*. Tr. Sir David Ross, in *The Works of Aristotle*, Vol. IX. Clarendon Press, Oxford.

Roland Barthes 1977, *Sade, Fourier, Loyola*. Tr. Richard Miller, Jonathan Cape, London.

Georges Bataille 1985, *Visions of Excess: Selected Writings 1927–1939*. Tr. A. Stoekl, C. R. Lovitt, and D. M. Leslie, Jr, University of Minnesota Press, Minneapolis. See esp. "The Use Value of D. A. F. Sade."

Georges Bataille 1986, *Erotism: Death and Sensuality*. Tr. Mary Dalwood, City Lights Books, San Francisco.

Simone de Beauvoir 1966 (1952), "Must We Burn Sade?," in Austryn Wainhouse and Richard Seaver (eds), *The Marquis de Sade: The 120 Days of Sodom and Other Writings*. Grove Press, New York.

George Berkeley 1949 (1710), *The Principles of Human Knowledge*. Ed. A. A. Luce and T. E. Jessop, in *The Works of George Berkeley*, Vol. II. Thomas Nelson, London.

Maurice Blanchot 1965 (1949), "Sade," in Austryn Wainhouse and Richard Seaver (eds), *The Marquis de Sade: Three Complete Novels*. Grove Press, New York.

Iwan Bloch 1931, *Marquis de Sade: His Life and Works*. Tr. James Bruce, Castle Books, New York.

Jean-Anthelme Brillat-Savarin 1970 (1825), *The Philosopher in the Kitchen* (La Physiologie du goût). Tr. Anne Drayton, Penguin Books, Harmondsworth.

Angela Carter 1979, *The Sadeian Woman*. Virago, London.

P. Chalker (ed.) 1973, *Trinity College, Dublin: History and Guide to Campus*. Murphy Chalker Associates, Dublin.

E. Pierre Chanover 1973, *The Marquis de Sade: A Bibliography*. Scarecrow Press, Metuchen, NJ.

G. Deleuze and L. von Sacher-Masoch 1989, *Masochism: Coldness and Cruelty and Venus in Furs*. Tr. J. McNeil, Zone Books, Cambridge, Mass.

Diogenes Laertius 1969, *Lives of the Philosophers*. Ed. and tr. A. Robert Caponigri, Henry Regnery, Chicago.

Gerald Doherty 1987, "White Mythologies: D. H. Lawrence and the Deconstructive Turn," *Criticism* 29.

Robert Dunn 1987, *The Possibility of Weakness of Will*. Hackett, Indianapolis.

Arthur Efron 1985, "The Sexual Body: An Interdisciplinary Perspective," *The Journal of Mind and Behavior* 6.

Erasmus 1983 (1526), *Concerning the Eating of Fish*. Ed. and tr. John P. Dolan, in *The Essential Erasmus*. New American Library, New York.

Michel Foucault 1988, *Madness and Civilization*. Tr. R. Howard, Vintage Books, New York. See Conclusion.

Sigmund Freud 1950, *Totem and Taboo*. Tr. James Strachey, Norton, New York.

Sigmund Freud 1961, *Civilization and Its Discontents*. Tr. James Strachey, Norton, New York.

Sigmund Freud 1977, *On Sexuality*. Tr. James Strachey, *The Pelican Freud Library*, Vol. 7, Penguin Books, Harmondsworth.
Jane Gallop 1981, *Intersections: A Reading of Sade with Bataille, Blanchot, and Klossowski*. University of Nebraska Press, Lincoln.
Jane Gallop 1982, *Feminism and Psychoanalysis*. Macmillan, London.
Martin P. Golding 1988, "On the Idea of Moral Pathology," in A. Rosenberg and G. Myers (eds), *Echoes from the Holocaust: Philosophical Reflections on a Dark Time*. Temple University Press, Philadelphia.
F. Gonzalez-Crussi 1988, *On the Nature of Things Erotic*. Harcourt Brace Jovanovich, San Diego. Ch. 4 deals with Sade.
A. C. Graham 1985, *Reason and Spontaneity*. Curzon Press, New York. See pp. 171–84 on Sade.
Roberta J. Hackel 1976, *De Sade's Quantitative Moral Universe: Of Irony, Rhetoric and Boredom*. Mouton, The Hague.
Philip P. Hallie 1982, *Cruelty*. Wesleyan University Press, Middletown. See ch. "Sade and the Music of Pain."
Ronald Hayman 1978, *De Sade: A Critical Biography*. Constable, London.
G. W. F. Hegel 1967 (1821), *Philosophy of Right*. Tr. T. M. Knox, Oxford University Press, New York.
G. W. F. Hegel 1971 (1830), *Encyclopedia Philosophy of Mind*. Trs. William Wallace and A. V. Miller, Clarendon Press, Oxford.
Gilbert H. Herdt 1987, *Guardians of the Flutes*. Columbia University Press, New York.
Thomas E. Hill, Jr 1986, "Weakness of Will and Character," *Philosophical Topics* 14.
Thomas Hobbes 1840 (1640), *De Corpore Politico*. Ed. Sir William Molesworth, in *The English Works of Thomas Hobbes*, Vol. IV. John Bohm, London.
Thomas Hobbes 1968 (1651), *Leviathan*. Ed. C. B. Macpherson, Penguin Books, Harmondsworth.
Thomas Hobbes 1978a (1642 [1651], *De Cive*. Ed. Bernard Gert, in *Man and Citizen*. Peter Smith, Gloucester, Mass.
Thomas Hobbes 1978b (1658), *De Homine*. Tr. Charles T. Wood, T. S. K. Scott-Craig, and B. Gert, ed. Bernard Gert, in *Man and Citizen*. Peter Smith, Gloucester, Mass.
Franz Kafka 1988, "In the Penal Colony," tr. Willa and Edwin Muir, in *The Collected Short Stories of Franz Kafka*. Penguin Books, Harmondsworth.
G. W. Levi Kamel 1983, "Leathersex: Meaningful Aspects of Gay Sadomasochism," in Thomas Weinberg and G. W. Levi Kamel (eds), *S and M: Studies in Sadomasochism*. Prometheus Books, Buffalo.
John Kekes 1988, "Understanding Evil," *American Philosophical Quarterly* 25.
Pierre Klossowski 1966 (1947), "Nature as Destructive Principle," in Austryn Wainhouse and Richard Seaver (eds), *The Marquis de Sade: The 120 Days of Sodom and Other Writings*. Grove Press, New York.
Pierre Klossowski 1986, "Sade, or the Philosopher-Villain," *Substance* 15.
Christine M. Korsgaard 1986, "The Right to Lie: Kant on Dealing with Evil," *Philosophy and Public Affairs* 15.

## BIBLIOGRAPHY

Heinrich Kramer and James Sprenger 1971 (1486), *Malleus Maleficarum*. Tr. Montague Summers, Dover, New York.
Elizabeth M. Kraus 1987, "God the Savior," in Robert C. Neville (ed.), *New Essays in Metaphysics*. State University of New York Press, Albany.
Alice Laborde 1989, "The Marquis de Sade's Biography Revisited," in Colette Verger Michael (ed.), *Sade: His Ethic and Rhetoric*. Peter Lang, New York.
Julien Offray de La Mettrie 1912 (1748), *Man a Machine*. Tr. M. W. Calkins, Open Court, La Salle, Ill.
D. H. Lawrence 1960, *Women in Love*. Penguin Books, Harmondsworth.
John Alan Lee 1983, "The Social Organization of Sexual Risk," in Thomas Weinberg and G. W. Levi Kamel (eds), *S and M: Studies in Sadomasochism*. Prometheus Books, Buffalo.
Gilbert Lely 1961, *The Marquis de Sade: A Biography*. Tr. Alec Brown, Elek Books, London.
Walter Lennig 1971, *Portrait of de Sade: An Illustrated Biography*. Tr. Sarah Twohig, Herder and Herder, New York.
Maurice Lever 1993, *Sade, A Biography*. Tr. A. Goldhammer, Farrar, Strauss and Giroux, New York.
Lawrence W. Lynch 1984, *The Marquis de Sade*. Twayne Publishers, Boston.
J. L. Mackie 1977, *Ethics: Inventing Right and Wrong*. Penguin Books, Harmondsworth.
Thomas Robert Malthus 1970 (1798), *An Essay on the Principle of Population*. Penguin Books, Harmondsworth.
B. Mandeville 1988 (1732), *The Fable of the Bees*. Ed. F. B. Kaye, Liberty Classics, Indianapolis.
Mike W. Martin 1986, *Self-Deception and Morality*. University Press of Kansas, Lawrence.
Alfred R. Mele 1987, *Irrationality: An Essay on Akrasia, Self-Deception and Self-Control*. Oxford University Press, New York.
Herman Melville 1972 (1851), *Moby-Dick; or, The Whale*. Penguin Books, Harmondsworth.
Colette Verger Michael 1986, *The Marquis de Sade: The Man, His Works and His Critics: An Annotated Bibliography*. Garland Publishing, New York and London.
Ronald D. Milo 1984, *Immorality*. Princeton University Press, Princeton.
Natalia R. Moehle 1978, *The Dimensions of Evil and of Transcendence*. University Press of America, Washington, DC.
Thomas Nagel 1979, "Sexual Perversion," in *Mortal Questions*. Cambridge University Press, Cambridge.
V. S. Naipaul 1987, *Guerillas*. Penguin Books, Harmondsworth.
George Orwell 1961, *1984*. New American Library, New York.
Jean Paulhan 1965 (1946), "Marquis de Sade and His Accomplice," in Austryn Wainhouse and Richard Seaver (eds), *The Marquis de Sade: Three Complete Novels*. Grove Press, New York.
Plato 1961, *Republic*. Tr. Paul Shorey, in *Plato: The Collected Dialogues*. Bollingen Series LXXI, Princeton University Press, Princeton.
Edgar Allan Poe 1975a, "The Imp of the Perverse," in *The Complete Tales and Poems of Edgar Allan Poe*. Vintage Books, New York.

Edgar Allan Poe 1975b, "Narrative of A. Gordon Pym," in *The Complete Tales and Poems of Edgar Allan Poe*. Vintage Books, New York.

John Rawls 1971, *A Theory of Justice*. Harvard University Press, Cambridge, Mass.

Nicholas Rescher 1987, *Ethical Idealism*. University of California Press, Berkeley.

A. W. Brian Simpson 1984, *Cannibalism and the Common Law*. University of Chicago Press, Chicago.

Robert Solomon 1974, "Sex and Perversion," *Journal of Philosophy* 71.

Sophocles 1982, *Oedipus at Colonus*. Tr. Robert Fagles, in *The Three Theban Plays*. Viking Press, New York.

Susan Stewart 1988, "The Marquis de Meese," *Critical Inquiry* 15.

Michael Stocker 1979, "Desiring the Bad: An Essay in Moral Psychology," *Journal of Philosophy* 76.

Whitley Strieber 1985, "Perverts," in F. D. McSherry Jr, C.G. Waugh, and M. H. Greenberg (eds), *A Treasury of American Horror Stories*. Bonanza Books, New York.

Donald Thomas 1976, *The Marquis de Sade*. Weidenfeld and Nicolson, London.

Gregory W. Trianosky 1988, "Rightly Ordered Appetites: How to Live Morally and Live Well," *American Philosophical Quarterly* 25.

Edward Westermarck 1939, *Christianity and Morals*. Kegan Paul, Trench, Trubner.

Bernard Williams 1985, *Ethics and the Limits of Philosophy*. Harvard University Press, Cambridge, Mass.

Michael Winter 1984, "The Explosion of the Circle: Science and Negative Utopia," in E. Mendelsohn and H. Nowotny (eds), *Nineteen Eighty-Four: Science between Utopia and Dystopia*. D. Reidel, Dordrecht.

# INDEX

Adorno, Theodor W. 190
Airaksinen, Timo 189
Apollinaire, Guillaume 178
Aquinas, Thomas 46
Arendt, Hannah 13, 189
Aristotle 12, 21, 22, 23, 28, 33, 36, 166, 190

Barthes, Roland 3, 157, 189, 192
Bataille, Georges 108, 190, 193
Beauvoir, Simone de 3, 189
Bentham, Jeremy 84
Berkeley, George 17, 18, 19, 20, 189
Blanchot, Maurice 192
Bloc, Iwan 189
Brillat-Savarin, Jean-Anthelme 81, 82, 83, 84, 85, 86, 91, 191

Carter, Angela 3, 78, 87, 189, 191
Chalker, Peter 189
Chanover, E. Pierre 189
Collard, Royer 6
Contarini, Thomas 19, 20

Deleuze, Gilles 190
Diogenes Laertius 170, 193
Doherty, Gerald 190
Dudley, Tom 174
Dunn, Robert 190

Efron, Arthur 190
Epicurus 80, 81, 84, 85

Erasmus 23, 24, 190

Foucault, Michel 193
Freud, Sigmund 28, 29, 31, 32, 107, 153, 190, 192

Gallop, Jane 3, 52, 115, 133, 134, 135, 189, 190, 191
Golding, Martin 189
Goldsmith, Oliver 19
Gonzalez-Crussi, Frank 192
Graham, A.C. 191

Hackel, Roberta J. 3, 69, 102, 104, 189, 190, 191
Hallie, Philip P. 3, 124, 125, 189, 192
Hayman, Ronald 189
Hegel, G.W.F. 17, 20, 153, 154, 189, 192
Herdt, Gilbert H. 106, 191
Hill, Thomas E., Jr. 190
Hobbes, Thomas 4, 20, 21, 26, 33, 35, 36, 56, 57, 60, 103, 109, 110, 117, 118, 120, 121, 125, 169, 189, 190, 191, 192, 193
Horkheimer, Max 190
Hume, David 169

Irigaray, Luce 133, 134

Kafka, Franz 64, 65, 190

# INDEX

Kamel, G.W. Levi 190
Kant, Immanuel 30, 31, 33, 182
Kekes, John 189
Klossowski, Pierre 190
Korskaard, Christine M. 190
Kramer, Heinrich 190, 191
Kraus, Elizabeth N. 189

Laborde, Alice 189
Lacan, Jacques 133
La Mettrie, Julien Offray de 33, 190
Lawrence, D.H. 48, 49, 190
Lee, John Alan 190
Lely, Gilbert 6, 78, 189
Lennig, Walter 189
Lever, Maurice 189
Lynch, Lawrence W. 16, 74, 75, 189, 191

Machiavelli, Niccolò 20, 21, 97, 117
Mackie, John 119, 191
Malthus, Thomas Robert 21, 189
Mandeville, Robert 21, 189, 193
Martin, Mike W. 190
Mele, Alfred R. 190
Melville, Herman 192
Michael, Colette V. 189
Mill, John Stuart 84
Milo, Ronald D. 190
Moehle, Natalia R. 190
Montalivet, Count de 6
Montreuil, Lady de 7, 8

Nagel, Thomas 190
Naipaul, V.S. 89, 191
Napoleon 6, 7

Nero 146
Nietzsche, Friedrich 100

Orwell, George 64, 190

Paulhan, Jean 190
Plato 106, 149, 192
Poe, Edgar Allan 21, 22, 23, 24, 27, 28, 31, 32, 34, 39, 40, 41, 42, 43, 79, 120, 129, 190, 192

Rawls, John 95, 191
Rescher, Nicholas 17, 189
Rousseau, Jean-Jacques 107
Royce, Josiah 95

Sacher-Masoch, Leopold von 190
Simpson, A.W. Brian 171, 193
Smith, Adam 17
Sokrates 103
Solomon, Robert 190
Sophocles 129, 192
Sprenger, James 190, 191
Stewart, Susan 193
Stocker, Michael, 190
Strieber, Whitley 190
Szasz, Thomas 7

Thomas, Donald 189
Trianosky, Gregory W. 193

Westermarck, Edward 119, 160, 192
Williams, Bernard 193
Winter, Michael 192
Wittgenstein, Ludwig 4